MEMOIRS

MEMOIRS

Pierre Elliott Trudeau

M&S

Canadian Cataloguing in Publication Data

Trudeau, Pierre Elliott, 1919-
  Memoirs

Issued also in French under title: Mémoires politiques.
Includes index.
ISBN 0-7710-8588-5 (McClelland & Stewart)
ISBN 0-7710-0036-7 (St. Martin's Press)

1. Trudeau, Pierre Elliott, 1919- . 2. Canada – Politics and government
– 1963-1984* 3. Prime ministers – Canada – Biography. I. Title.

FC626.T7A3 1993   971.064'4'092   C93-095020-8
F1034.3.T7A3 1993

Reference Numbers for National Archives of Canada Photos (NAC-TC)
p. xv PA189567; p. 29 PA187047; p. 57 PA187112, PA187114, PA187113; p.62 P257,703; p.63 P257,699; p.72 PA185290; p.75 PA185,299; p.78 PA180805; p.79 PA187048; p.80 PA187049; p.86 PA189551, PA189558, PA189566; p.87 PA189557; p.93 PA189556; p.101 PA175935, PA180807, PA187060; p.109 PA189550; p.111 acc.1989-014 file 73-6; p.116 PA189555; p.120 acc.1977-050; p.121 acc.1977-050; p.122 PA180804; p.153 PA187058; p.154 PA187059, acc.1977-050; p.155 PA187102, PA187111, PA187107; p.162 acc.1977-050; p.163 acc.1989-014; p.166 acc.1989-014 b.5605-1; p.171 acc.1977-050; p.187 PA187116, PA187115, PA187108, PA187073; p.195 PA175947; p.197 acc.1989-014 item75-7; p.201 PA187070, PA187069, PA187068, PA187071, acc.1987-014 b.5607; p.204 acc.1977-050 b.4941; p.207 PA187110; p.211 PA187076, acc.1977-050; p.213 acc.1977-050, acc.1977-050; p.215 acc.1989-014 b.5607; p.217 acc.1989-014 b.5607; p.221 PA184104, PA187105, PA187103; p.225 acc.1977-050; p.226 acc.1977-050; p.227 acc.1977-050; p.237 acc.1981-181; p.249 acc.1981-181; p.278 acc.1989-014 item80-03A; p.279 acc.1989-014 item80-03b.; p.285 acc.1989-014 item80-08; p.289 acc.1989-014 env.83.05, acc.1989-014 env.83.05; p.304 acc.1984-099; p.307 acc.1989-014 item80-13; p.314 acc.1984-099; p.315 acc.1984-099; p.328 acc.1977-050; p.337 acc.1989-014, acc.1989-014; p.339 acc.1989-014 b.5607; p.347 acc.1989-014 b.5607.1; p.356 acc.1989-014

Text Design: Kong
Design Assistant: Trish Lyon

The publishers acknowledge the support of the Canada Council and the Ontario Arts Council for their publishing program.

McClelland & Stewart Inc.
The Canadian Publishers
481 University Avenue
Toronto, Ontario
M5G 2E9

To my father and mother

Contents

Preface · *ix*

Part One · *1*
1919 – 1968 The Road to 24 Sussex Drive

Part Two · *89*
1968 – 1974 Power and Responsibility

Part Three · *173*
1974 – 1979 Victory and Defeat

Part Four · *259*
1979 – 1984 "Welcome to the 1980s"

Part Five · *343*
Life After Politics

The Photographs: A Publisher's Note · *369*

Index · *373*

Preface

Every book has a history, and this one is no exception. Perhaps to begin at the beginning would take me back to my earliest days as prime minister. Even in those years, friends who were aware of my background as a writer and an editor would express the hope that I was keeping a journal or at least making notes so that at the end I would, in their words, "write a book about all this."

To that my response was always a definite no. I was not in politics to acquire material to write a book. I was too busy doing my job and living my life to spend time keeping notes for some future volume of memoirs. And although out of courtesy I might perhaps be willing in due course to spend some time with historians who were writing serious books about my time in politics, I was unwilling to appoint an official Boswell to whom I would feed a self-serving version of events.

In fact, I must confess that the genre of autobiographies has always seemed to me slightly suspect. There is something self-aggrandizing about the political leader who surrounds himself (or herself) with teams of researchers and literary assistants, who then produces many volumes, rife with footnotes and references to Cabinet papers and internal memoranda, that treat almost every single day in office as worthy of attention in detail. Almost inevitably, the times covered in this way come to seem the most important in the history of civilization, and the decisions taken by the leader seem to be positively heroic. Certainly, "were there world enough and time" I could fill a few volumes in such a way, and they might be of keen interest to a small, very academic audience who would revel in the footnotes. But they would not, I feel, be of general interest.

As a result, for many years after my departure from politics in 1984 I continued to resist arguments made by publishers and others that I should relent and agree to write about my times. Some of the arguments, I should say, were very strong. I think especially of those put forward by my old friend Ramsay Cook who argues, like the good historian that he is, that I owed it to myself – he had too much finesse to invoke posterity – to put on the record my version of the events in which I was involved and of which, necessarily, I had a unique view. The CBC was even more persistent. Pierre Juneau and Cameron Graham kept urging me over the years to tell my story on camera, as Mike Pearson had done. The bulk of the film would go to the National Archives, but a few hours of CBC Television would also come out of it. I would always end up by refusing, invoking other priorities.

No doubt over time, like water dripping on rock, these often-repeated arguments must have had their effect. Then in 1989, a group of friends and colleagues who met regularly over lunch began to feel the need to get our version of our times in government on the public record. A book ensued: *Towards a Just Society: The Trudeau Years*, edited by Tom Axworthy and myself and published in 1990.

The spell of silence having been broken, I was more amenable to considering the next "easy" step: televised memoirs. The same friends and I discussed the possibility of making a documentary about my life for French and English television. Finally, after months of thinking about it, I decided to go along with the proposal made by Rock Demers and Kevin Tierney of the Montreal-based film company Les Productions La Fête, with whom the CBC and Radio-Canada would work according to their usual guidelines.

In preparation for the film series, a rough canvas was prepared in a succession of meetings attended by the producers, who were assisted by an able research director, Thomas Cadieux; at these meetings and at other times I was greatly assisted by two friends, Gérard Pelletier (whose impact on my life will be obvious from what follows) and my former principal secretary in the Prime Minister's Office, Tom Axworthy, both of whom were able to jog my memory on many occasions.

That canvas was then turned into a story line by Brian McKenna, the director, and I was invited to spend endless hours in a studio, responding to questions asked by two skilled interviewers, Jean-François Lépine and Ron Graham, both distinguished journalists and writers. To assist us on the French production side, Pierre Castonguay became involved; and further interviews were conducted by Terence McKenna.

I had to answer all the questions asked of me on camera

without prior notice or briefing, the director having decided that it would make better television. For me, this meant much less work; but human memory being what it is, it is fair to say that spontaneity was obtained at the price of a fair amount of imprecision, particularly when I am quoting the words of others.

As soon as it became clear that the material needed for a television series was considerably different than that which one would normally find in a written memoir, I decided to go ahead with this book, as one complemented the other. Arrangements were made with Avie Bennett and Doug Gibson at McClelland & Stewart, and with Pierre L'Espérance and James de Gaspé Bonar at Éditions de l'Homme, and from then on, the book project very much took on its own direction.

Over the past months the book has taken shape. The account of my life that I gave over countless hours of interviews was put into chronological shape by Gérard Pelletier, who dealt with the first two sections, and by George Radwanski, a former editor of the *Toronto Star* and the author of a 1976 biography entitled *Trudeau*, who organized my description of events in the second half of this book. I am extremely indebted to these two friends.

These versions of my recollections then came to me, with the editorial comments of Doug Gibson attached, and I worked to revise them in cases where my spoken words did not read as well as they should, or to expand on those areas that had been treated too lightly. But these are, of course, reminiscences rather than a detailed scholarly day-by-day account; such books are being written by others, and I wish them well.

This, then, is a personal and informal account of my political life as I remembered it when prompted by questions from the interviewers. If any inaccuracies have crept in, they are not the fault of Barbara Czarnecki, the painstaking copy editor, nor of my invariably helpful assistant Michèle Sansoucy, nor of those friends such as Ramsay Cook who have so kindly read the final manuscript. Those mistakes of emphasis or interpretation that may be found are my own. I must also apologize for a certain looseness of style throughout: the reader must remember that this is essentially an oral memoir, and that the spoken phrase is rarely as precise as the written.

Since the project was bilingual from the outset, I am grateful to George Radwanski, Wayne Grady, and Gérard Pelletier for their assistance in translations from our other official language. Rob Ferguson was also of great assistance in his research for the captions of the photographs.

To those many people – perhaps numbering in the hundreds of thousands – whose paths have crossed mine and who might expect with some justice to find their contributions recorded here, I apologize. You may not be named in the following pages; but whether you were a Liberal Cabinet colleague, a Canadian voter whose support we sought, or a young Canadian whose future we tried to improve, you are a part of this book.

Pierre Trudeau
Montreal, August 1993

At the federal-provincial conference, February 1969.

MEMOIRS

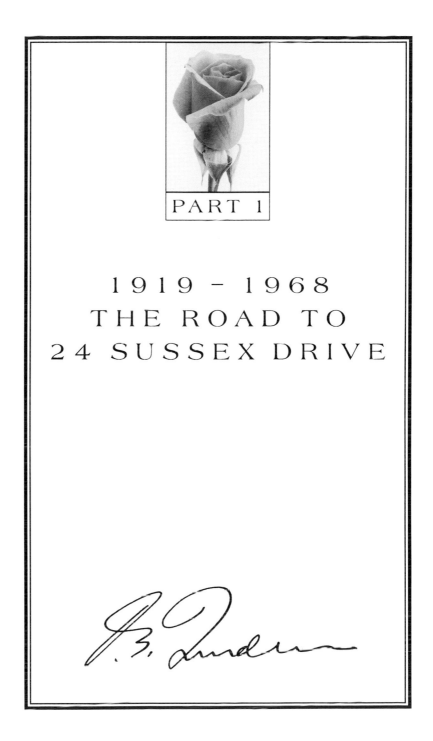

PART 1

1919 – 1968
THE ROAD TO
24 SUSSEX DRIVE

I was born into a family, a home, and a neighbourhood of modest means. At that time, the north end of Rue Durocher was part of Outremont, but it really had little to do with that Montreal suburb's snobbish reputation. Our house was a few steps from the Montreal city limits, and it was no different from the ordinary homes on other streets of the city.

In 1919, when I was born, my father was not at all rich; he had not yet made his fortune. In those days, he worked almost around the clock. He had been born on a farm, in Saint-Michel-de-Napierville, south of Montreal, while my mother's roots were urban. Their respective families were a striking contrast. My Trudeau grandparents were typical Quebec farmers who had spent their lives on the land they had inherited from their parents. My Elliott grandfather, on the other hand, was at various times a tavern operator, a real estate agent, a merchant – in short, an enterprising Scot. He had married a French Canadian, Sarah Sauvé, and built his career in Montreal. Both my father and my mother had received a good education, and they were determined to have their children follow in their footsteps in this regard. And so I started very early in the "baby class" – the nursery school of that era – at École Bonsecours, which was run by nuns. I have only happy memories of those early days.

I have a sense that life really began for me when I came into contact with "my street," as we used to say in those days, and got to know the other boys in the neighbourhood. The place lacked neither colour nor variety. I found myself among Catholics, Protestants, and Jews, French Canadians, Irish, Scots, francophones, anglophones. The neighbourhood was a microcosm in which all of Quebec's main cultural groups were represented, with the sole exception of aboriginal people.

The school environment in which I spent my early years reflected this diversity, but not to the same extent, because children who did not belong to the Church were excluded from Catholic schools. Académie Querbes, in the parish of Saint-Viateur-d'Outremont, offered a choice of French or English instruction in the first three grades, so it was attended by a number of English-speaking children of mainly Irish origin. My parents enrolled me on the English side, for reasons I do not know.

The English-speaking classes at Querbes were quite unusual. They were, in fact, similar to the one-room schoolhouses that existed by the thousands in those days in rural Quebec. All three grades were taught in the same room by the same teacher, which led to an incident very early in my first year at school.

My grandparents

*1 and 2.
My Trudeau
grandparents.*

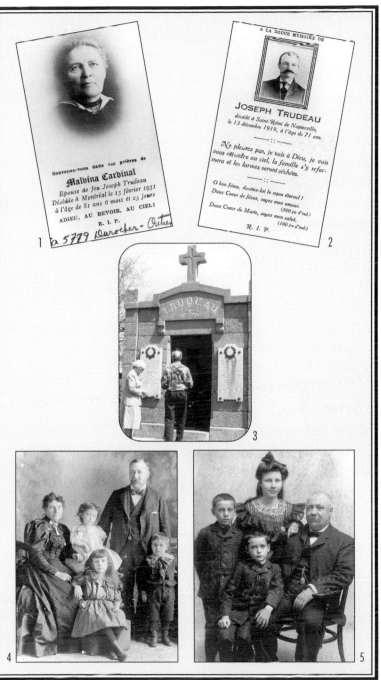

*3. My sister,
Suzette,
and I visit
the old
family
tomb in
Napierville .
(Les Productions La
Fête/Jean Demers)*

*4. My Elliott
grandparents.*

*5. My mother
is shown with
her brothers
and with my
grandfather,
whose watch-chain
always fascinated
me as a child.*

(Trudeau Family)

My friend Gerald O'Connor, one of my very first pals on my street, was starting school on the same day. O'Connor stood out from the rest of us because of his height and his Irish gift of the gab. He and I had looked forward to the beginning of school as an adventure we would share together. But as soon as I arrived in class on the first day, I saw that his desk and mine weren't even in the same part of the room. I was very upset. We had been separated. He was in the second grade while I had been put in the first, for reasons I couldn't understand since we were both the same age and had been on the same path until then.

Being split up like that bothered me a great deal, and I complained to my father as soon as I got home.

"It's not fair," I told him. "I should be in the second grade, too."

"Then it's simple. Go see the principal and ask him to put you in the second grade."

"Couldn't *you* ask him, Daddy?"

"No! It's your problem. Knock on his door and ask him yourself."

My father always insisted that his children be self-reliant. Even when we were very young, if he believed we could do something by ourselves, he refused to do it for us. So I summoned up my courage and knocked on the principal's door. He was sitting behind his desk, and his black cassock completely filled his armchair. I still remember that I found him huge and intimidating. My voice must have been trembling when I explained what I wanted. And yet my request almost immediately produced the desired result. I don't recall whether the principal made me take any kind of test or whether he consulted the teacher, but I was promptly promoted to the second grade, in the same row of desks as Gerald O'Connor.

If I remember that episode to this day, it is no doubt partly because of the outcome. But it is also because I overcame my shyness. Like all children, and maybe more than most, I was shy. I was reluctant to stand out. I had to be pushed into doing so – but then there was no holding me back.

That is how in my early years I acquired a reputation as a fighter. I only half deserved it. I was pretty puny, and certainly didn't look fearsome. But my father, who loved sports, enjoyed giving me boxing lessons from time to time. He also taught me some fighting tricks, such as using a bear hug to overcome an opponent. Once, he even brought a famous boxer from Montreal – Léo "Kid" Roy, the featherweight champion of the day – to our summer place in the country. And Roy, who was immensely popular in those days, showed us dazzled kids his golden championship belt.

Did I, then, brag to my friends on the street about my boxing expertise? I may have. And I'm sure I didn't keep it a secret from them when my father bought me a pair of boxing gloves as a present. In any event, they didn't hesitate to press me into service whenever there was a confrontation. If some rascal from another street came to ours and challenged us, my friends would push me forward, egging me on: "Go on, Pierre! You can do it! Go on!"

And I wouldn't dare to refuse, for fear of losing face.

Going to the country was an important part of my childhood and my adolescence, and it took two quite different forms.

On the one hand, there was the Trudeau house in Napierville. It was always full of uncles, aunts, and cousins, and it was surrounded by everything that is fascinating to children on a farm – a chicken coop, a pigpen, a big

My parents standing in the snow outside 577 Rue Durocher, the modest house that was home for the first twelve years of my life.
(Trudeau Family)

vegetable garden, and, further on, fields that stretched far-ther than the eye could see, dotted with haystacks and crops. I especially remember visiting there for a few days every year for New Year's. I can still see my grandmother, always dressed in black, with her hair tied back in a bun. Our cousins were tough, and were better than us at hockey.

For summer holidays, by contrast, my parents had a spartan little wooden house at Lac Tremblant. We had to fetch water from a well and use lanterns for light. There were very few cottagers in that area in those days; in fact, it was still pretty much a wilderness. We spent whole sum-mers there, and my mother would invite some cousins – the Leblonds from Lac des Pins – so we would have company for games, swimming, and hikes through the woods. I am sure it was those summers that kindled my great love for the outdoors and canoeing. On weekdays, the house was

My family

1. My sister, Suzette, my brother, Charles (Tip), and me, in what looks suspiciously like a photographer's studio.

2. With my mother.

3. At Lac Tremblant, with my mother. As you can see, there were very few cottagers in those days.

4. Above the lake, going for a walk – after a fashion – with my father and Suzette.

5. My father some years later, at one of our family holidays at Old Orchard Beach in Maine.

(Trudeau Family)

*At Lac Tremblant,
with me at the oars.
(Trudeau Family)*

relatively quiet, despite the presence of so many children. My mother's serenity established an atmosphere of calm in which we would sit around reading, between swims in the cool Laurentian waters. But on Friday nights, when my father came up with his friends to join us, things would start to get boisterous.

He came up by car, which at the time was somewhat risky. On the way to our place, you had to drive up the side of Mont Sauvage, hoping that the car wouldn't stall. But for my father, being the owner of a garage, driving a car was both profession and sport. He loved to drive, and we would listen for the faraway sound of tires on the bridge across the outlet of the lake; that would mean he was arriving.

All weekend, the cottage would resound with discussions, laughter, exclamations, and shouts. My father was very extroverted. He spoke loudly and expressed himself vigorously. His friends were the same. Their political arguments never lacked liveliness. Charles-Émile Trudeau was

At our spartan little wooden house at the lake. I am in the feathered head-dress, and the photographer appears to be in imminent danger.
(*Trudeau Family*)

a Conservative, but several of his friends belonged to the Liberal Party. And so, very early in my childhood, I heard about the political rivalries that typified Quebec society in that era. I didn't understand any of it, of course, but some words intrigued me, such as the term "political machine," which kept coming up in the conversation. I tried in vain to imagine what such a machine would look like. Was it a machine that manufactured laws?

Our weekend guests didn't spend all their time having debates and discussions. They liked to get involved in our games, they liked to play cards, and they liked to drink and feast. At mealtimes, there were sometimes as many as twenty people sitting around the rustic wooden table, and my mother had to cook for all of them. And then, on Sunday evenings, my father and his friends would leave as they had come, and the house would become quiet again.

In the fall we would go back to school, and family life would settle into its normal routines. Nearly every day, my father came home for dinner, took a quick look at our schoolwork, then went back to the garage where he had his office. That was the only time in the whole day that we got to enjoy his company. My mother's constant and attentive presence helped to make up for my father's relative absence. In my childhood memories, I see her leaning over my sickbed (nobody could avoid childhood sicknesses in those days, since there were very few vaccines); I find her always ready to help me with my work; I wait eagerly for her to sit down at the piano to lead us in a sing-along or to introduce us to a new piece of music; I accompany her to the concerts or ballets that for us were special treats or rewards. I marvel, too, at her skills as a teacher. She knew better than anyone else how to strike the right balance between discipline and freedom. As we became better able to fend for ourselves, she showed increasing respect for our initiatives and decisions. She exercised her authority with a light hand; I don't recall having felt it pressing down on me – except after a few inexcusable escapades that she punished quite energetically!

As he did when we were in the country, but less often, my father invited a lot of his friends to our home. I remember, for instance, a big oyster party in the basement of our house. That time, the mayor of Montreal, Camillien Houde, put in an appearance. All I remember of him is how incredibly portly he was, which made a big impression on such a little guy as I was then. They certainly talked politics that night. Houde was a Conservative like my father, and the names of Louis-Alexandre Taschereau, the Liberal premier, and Maurice Duplessis, who was then a Conservative member, figured prominently in the conversation. I guess I had very little interest in the political matters they

We all stand very still for our class photograph at Académie Querbes. I am in the front row, wearing a white sweater. (Trudeau Family)

used to discuss, because I never asked my father any questions on the subject, and he for his part made no attempt to arouse my interest.

At the beginning of the 1930s, a successful business deal significantly changed our lives. At the very moment when what was to become the Great Depression was starting to spread across North America, the Trudeau family became very well off. By selling the garage and the chain of service stations that he had built up by his relentless hard work, my father made a lot of money and became an investor in businesses such as Sullivan Mines, Belmont Park amusement park, and the Montreal Royals baseball team. He wasn't fabulously rich, but he had a fortune that was quite respectable for the time.

That is no doubt why I have only vague memories of the worst economic crisis of the twentieth century. While the Depression was ruining a great many families and making life almost impossible for the poor, for us it was the time when we bought a bigger and fancier house on a more upper-class street, McCulloch Avenue, at the foot of Mount Royal. For me, in the summer of my thirteenth year, it was even more memorably the time of the first big adventure of my life: a two-month trip to Europe.

My father had already crossed the Atlantic to visit Europe several times. But in the summer of 1933, he decided to take the whole family – my grandfather Elliott, my mother, Grace Elliott Trudeau, my fifteen-year-old sister, Suzette, me, then aged thirteen, and my eleven-year-old brother, Charles, nicknamed Tip – on a pleasure trip. Thus began my career as a globetrotter, a career I have pursued throughout my life. It has been sixty years since that trip, and yet I still have a thousand vivid images of it in my mind. Of course, the political significance of the things I may have seen escaped me completely. I admit that the gleaming motorcycles of Hitler's soldiers on the highways made a bigger impression on me than the rearmament they signified. In Italy, the colour of the sea, the shape of the towering pines, and the splendours of the Vatican were more important to me than the draining of the Pontine marshes for which Mussolini was being praised. But I do recall the balcony from which Il Duce harangued the Roman crowd assembled in the square.

What I remember most are the weeks we spent in France. Not only did my father show us some of the historic monuments that abound in the country but we also visited family in Normandy. A brother of my mother's, Gordon Elliott, had been living there a long time, since after the

First World War, in which he had served as a pilot. He lived in Varengeville, a small town near Dieppe where we spent several days. We stayed at the beach hotel in nearby Pourville, a place-name I've never forgotten, and visited my uncle's house several times. He introduced us to his neighbours and friends, who included the great painters Miró and Braque. They were already famous at the time, but we children were struck less by their celebrity than by the strangeness of their names.

Life in a French village was a memorable experience for us. There was a dramatic contrast between Varengeville and the English countryside where we had recently travelled, and an even sharper contrast between life here and life in Montreal or Napierville. For the first time, we experienced the remarkable feeling of being almost totally out of our element.

Throughout this trip, I also began to learn the art of handling transactions in foreign countries. True to his views on bringing up children, my father assigned us tasks

Two beach snap-shots. The kid making faces at the camera (left, with my father in the fore-ground) shows encouraging signs of growing up just a few years later (facing page). With me are Tip and Suzette.
(Trudeau Family)

that tested our boldness and our initiative. In Paris, he sent my brother Charles and me out to buy all the *Oeuvres libres* – which were famous editions, at the time, of literary works – that we could find in second-hand bookstores. (This memory came back to me, in the 1950s, when a team made up of Claude Hurtubise, Jean-Louis Gagnon, Gilles Marcotte, Gérard Pelletier, and myself founded our own *Oeuvres libres*, which we called *Writings of French Canada.*) In Italy, he let us deal by ourselves with the Italian employ-ees of the place where we were staying. In Germany, when we stopped our car in front of the hotel where we hoped to stay the night, he would send me in to make the arrange-ments. With my few words of German, I had to manage to find out whether there were rooms available and then to complete the transaction of renting them. It wasn't always easy.

On my return to Montreal at the end of this trip, a dif-ferent kind of challenge awaited me: returning to high school, which I had started the previous year.

My parents had chosen Brébeuf, more formally known as Collège Jean-de-Brébeuf, which was a French-speaking institution. I mention this because, although it was natural for upper-class Outremont residents to enrol their sons in this school, which was closest to their homes, quite a few French-Canadian families chose a different Jesuit high school, which was much farther away: Loyola, where classes were conducted in English.

Over the years, I have often been asked how, in a bilingual family like mine, we handled the problem of what language to speak at home. My answer is: it was the most natural thing in the world. I never felt that there *was* any problem. My father spoke to us in French, and my mother spoke in either language, depending on the subject and on how she felt at the time. My Trudeau grandmother, uncles, aunts, and cousins always spoke French; my Elliott grandfather spoke English with my mother, but switched to French to talk with my father. Did that create any difficulties for us children? Very few and very minor ones. In elementary school at Académie Querbes, for example, I was transferred to the French side in fourth grade after having studied in English for the first three years. Was it a difficult transition? Hardly. I remember only that there were certain words in French of whose gender or spelling I was unsure. But these uncertainties didn't last long. You might say that, long before it was formally invented, I benefited from "total immersion."

The move from Querbes to Collège Jean-de-Brébeuf was a much more important transition for us. It was no longer just a matter of moving up a grade within the same familiar elementary school. We were stepping into a new world, entering an unknown environment that from the outside looked both fearsome and appealing. It was fearsome because for us it was still *terra incognita*. We knew little about it. And what we did know, such as that we would have to study Latin and Greek, remained shrouded in mystery. But high school was also appealing, because it brought us closer to the adult world. At the age of twelve we saw it as a rite of passage that would open the doors first to university and then to the great outside world.

My father told me about his first day at Collège Sainte-Marie and how my grandfather Trudeau had warned him: "High school is serious business. You have to work hard. If you don't pass your classes, you'll come back to Saint-Michel and I'll send you straight out to work in the fields." (This approach seemed to work: of my grandfather's sons, three left the farm to attend the classical course in high school, and two went on to become lawyers, the third a dentist.)

In the autumn of 1932, Pierre Vadeboncoeur and I began together the classical course of studies for which Querbes had prepared us. So I didn't enter this unknown world all alone, and right from the first year, I made new friendships at Brébeuf that have lasted my whole life.

But in those days, when you started high school, you weren't greeted only by new schoolmates who made you welcome. Some "upperclassmen" made a point of perse-cuting the "freshmen," to amuse themselves and to make their higher status obvious to everyone. I did not escape their attention. One noontime, during lunch, one of these older students decided to provoke me by throwing a banana in my soup. I immediately fished it out and flung it into *his* soup. I hadn't anticipated the effect this would have, because I didn't know that I was violating an unwrit-ten law: freshmen were not allowed to retaliate when an upperclassman provoked them.

"Right," said my persecutor, in a rage, "if that's the way you want it, we'll settle this outside as soon as we leave the lunchroom."

"Okay – if you want," I said.

I was acting confident; there was no question in my mind of backing down. But deep down I didn't have the slightest wish to fight it out with this older guy, because I wasn't at all sure I would have the upper hand. He too had done some boxing. So I didn't push it any further while waiting for dessert.

At the end of the meal, we both stood up. We stared each other in the eye for a long moment.

"Okay," he said. "Just this time, I'll give you a break."

And he walked away, to my great relief. But I had learned that you can win some confrontations just by acting confident.

My first contact with the teachers was no less intimidating. The first teacher I encountered at Brébeuf, Father Richard, was from France. He walked into class armed with a long pointer and an extraordinary volubility of speech – and volume, for he made a great deal of noise. But he was a good teacher and I adjusted quickly to his approach. So did my friends. Pierre Vadeboncoeur and I soon became the nucleus of a group that included, if I recall correctly, two or three other graduates of Querbes. I also made some new friends very early on, among them Guy Viau, who was better than me at hockey, even though I was captain of the team. So the transition to Brébeuf was not very difficult, and I promptly got down to work.

My new teachers quickly got me really interested in knowledge and learning. As far as I can recall, I had never been much of a workhorse in elementary school. In high school, it was an entirely different matter. Although I was very unruly in the classroom, I gradually became a hardworking and diligent student. I took everything new I had to learn as a challenge, whether it was Latin or later Greek.

But it isn't only teachers and books that make up an education; schoolmates can contribute a great deal to it as well. Thus, to the extent that I have such talents, it is to Roger Vigneau that I owe my knowledge of Stravinsky and my pursuit of excellence in sports; to Guy Viau, my appreciation of art; to Denis Noiseux, the sharpening of my thinking and my critical faculties. And finally, it was Pierre Vadeboncoeur who, towards the end of high school, truly introduced me to the art of writing well in French.

When I returned from our trip to Europe, I began classes in syntax, which was a landmark of the second year at

Brébeuf. I was now an upperclassman, already well accustomed to the institution where I would be spending the
next seven years. It must already be obvious that I have very
fond memories of Collège Jean-de-Brébeuf. The Jesuits
were good educators, exceptional teachers. In an era and in
a society where freedom of speech was not held in high
regard, they encouraged their students to speak out. They
insisted, of course, that the discourse be focused on what
they were teaching, but we were able to go beyond this
framework without incurring too great a risk.

For someone like me, who for a long time had always
wanted to have the last word, it was a joy to constantly test
how far I could go without going too far. I had already
begun this sort of exercise with my father at the beginnings
of my adolescence, and I continued to indulge in it with
my teachers at Brébeuf. I quickly began to develop some
effective techniques. For instance, I soon realized that I
must never interrupt a teacher to make an impertinent
remark, because that would be certain to infuriate him. But
if I waited until he paused and then I slipped in a wisecrack
that went against the current of his magisterial discourse,
the class would burst out laughing before he had a chance
to get angry. I got a big kick out of doing that, a childish one
no doubt, but one strong enough to make me want to do
it again at the first opportunity. In this way, opposing
conventional wisdoms and challenging prevailing opinions, with my friends as much as with my teachers, became
a habit that has remained with me all my life.

From there, it was only a short step to developing a certain form of artful provocation; I hastened to take that step.
Like several of my friends, I was in fact encouraged in this
by a non-conformist Jesuit, Rodolphe Dubé, better known

as François Hertel, the pen-name under which he wrote his books. This unusual man, who later left the priesthood and lived out the rest of his life in France, influenced a whole generation of students outside as well as within Brébeuf, where he taught literature and philosophy. What drew us to him? No doubt it was his originality, his offhand way of defying social conventions and saying out loud what other people would only think to themselves. Young people always like the unusual, and his students were no exception to this rule.

But something more was at work. To an extraordinary extent, Hertel was our guide into a number of new fields. In literature, our program of studies concentrated above all on the classics. It was Hertel who introduced me to authors who were less commonly read in our circles at the time – French writers at first, but also English, American, Scandinavian. I remember the hours I spent reading, thanks to him, Ibsen and Dostoyevski, Thomas Hardy and Léon Bloy. In music, it was the same thing. He introduced me to the works of composers who were not appreciated, at the time, in Quebec. And it was he who took us to see the painters who were pioneering modern art in Montreal. Alfred Pellan, Paul-Émile Borduas, and their disciples were still on the fringes of the art world, but Hertel preferred their works to those of already renowned painters. He naturally gravitated towards every-thing that was new or contrary to the tastes of the day.

Hertel's sense of humour was yet another magnet for us. We could easily involve him in the weirdest pranks and mischief we could dream up. For instance, I devel-oped a trick that involved going rigid and toppling forward, putting out my hands to break the fall only a

A lively reunion of the Club of the Dying some years later, in Paris in 1947. I am on the left, then aged twenty-six, beside Andrée Desautels. On the far right is the "Mayor of Montmartre"; seated in the centre is François Hertel (Father Rodolphe Dubé); and, perched beside a long-forgotten chanteuse, my old schoolmate Roger Rolland. (Canapress)

split second before hitting the floor. Being a bit of a ham, I used to do this to astound onlookers. Hertel wanted to learn how, and Roger Rolland too. Once we were a trio, Hertel said: "Let's form a club, and surprise people."

Thus was born the Club of the Dying. Right in the middle of a reception or an even more serious gathering, we would keel over one after another, to the great consternation of everyone around us. A somewhat silly way to get attention? No doubt. But fun nonetheless.

Not all our initiatives were so bizarre. I remember a summer project I undertook around the same time with a classmate, Jean-Baptiste Boulanger, who is now a psychiatrist. In school, this precocious boy amazed me. At the age of ten, he had written a biography of Napoleon that had earned him a medal from the Académie française. A native of Edmonton, he was fluent in three languages: French, English, and Ukrainian. We decided together to read over one summer the great works of political writing – Aristotle, Plato, Rousseau's *Social Contract*, Montesquieu, and others – and to exchange letters giving each other our impressions and our comments on each of the works we read. Boulanger knew more than me in this field, and that was why I hung around with him. In sports, too, I would seek out the company of boys who excelled at a particular activity, in order to learn to excel at it myself.

As I have already said, the teachers at Brébeuf wakened in me a passion for knowledge to which I have remained captive ever since. For instance, if a teacher told us to skip the tenth and twelfth chapters of a book on physics or biology because they weren't part of the program, I studied those chapters just as diligently as if they were going to be on the exam. Why would I deprive myself of knowledge that I had right there in front of me, at my disposal? I was equally keen to see how far my mind could reach and how much I could achieve physically. I had some friends who avoided intellectual life like the plague. But their accomplishments as divers, skiers, or pole vaulters drew me to their company.

I think that the intellectual atmosphere in those days encouraged this personal quest for self-development. For instance, thanks to my younger brother, Tip, who was more focused on the arts than I was, I learned about music with a group of his friends. He would invite them to our house Sunday evenings to listen to records he had obtained. I soon started bringing my own friends to these gatherings. There were a good twenty of us, boys and girls, listening religiously for hours. And then we would usually comment on, analyze, and debate about what we had heard. Sometimes a member of the group brought a new recording he had discovered and we compared two versions of the same work. Do young people today still have groups of this sort? I know that now there are educational radio and sometimes television programs that have the same goals. But in those days the thrill of discovery shared among friends was an integral part of our lives. And our group was by no means the only one of its kind.

On the other hand, throughout my high school and even university years, I had not the slightest interest in either the news in general or political developments in particular. Reading newspapers or listening to the news on the radio struck me as a waste of time, an unjustifiable squandering of energy, when there were so many books to read, so many great writers to get to know, so many poets and philosophers to enjoy, so many sports to be active in, so many countries to discover! Compared with such exhilarating activities, current events appeared to me to be insignificant.

One day – I think it was in literature class with Father Robert Bernier, a Franco-Manitoban who had a great influence on me – we were asked to write an essay on what we wanted to do with our lives. There must still be a copy of my piece somewhere in my files. I remember that I expressed extravagant ambitions. I wanted to be first a sea captain, then an explorer, then an astronaut – a term that had not yet been invented, except to denote a character out of Jules Verne. In short, I wanted to know everything and experience everything, in every realm. Maybe the essay even envisaged that some day, at the end of my life, I might

*During my years at
Brébeuf I developed a love
of skiing that has stayed
with me all my life. Here
Tip and I demonstrate
very traditional ski
clothes, poles, and skis.*
(*Trudeau Family*)

become an important figure such as a governor general or a
prime minister. But first, I would have explored the world.

This love of travel that I showed even then has never
left me. It was accompanied by a great enthusiasm for
the wilderness that I learned to visit first at Lac Tremblant,
then in Boy Scouts, and finally at Camp Ahmek, the Taylor
Statten camp in Algonquin Park, where I spent two summer vacations. There, with English-speaking colleagues
from Ontario, in most cases, I learned the techniques
of camping, canoeing, sailing, and survival in the bush. I
learned them so well that by the time I was around twenty,
I was ready for the major expeditions for which I recruited
a few of my friends.

The first of these was the trip to Hudson Bay that I had
long dreamed of undertaking. In the summer of 1941, I
suggested to Guy Viau that we head for this destination by

canoe. If Radisson and Desgroseillers were able to do it in the seventeenth century, I told him, why wouldn't it still be possible to do it today? So we recruited two other friends, the Desrosiers cousins, we got together the necessary equipment, and we hit the road — in this case a watery road, the Ottawa River. Leaving Montreal across Lac des Deux Montagnes, we followed the old *voyageur* route west along the Ottawa for several hundred miles; after Mattawa we angled north and crossed Lake Timiskaming, then, after many lakes and rivers, reached the Harricana River and followed it all the way to James Bay. Then, after a canoe trip of at least 500 miles, we had to cross part of the bay to reach Moosonee on the western side. From there we were able to get to the Canadian National Railway's station in Cochrane in northern Ontario, where we freighted our canoes back to Montreal. As for us, we hit the road and hitchhiked back.

The success of this first expedition made me eager to undertake other ones. Again with Guy Viau, plus Jean Gélinas this time, we toured the Gaspé on foot, declining offers of rides from passing cars, and sleeping in barns, in empty classrooms, or under the stars. Another summer, Guy Viau and I travelled through the three Maritime provinces by motorcycle, taking a particular interest in the cooperative movement that had sprung up in answer to the hard times in Antigonish and Sydney in Nova Scotia. Yet another summer, with Carl Dubuc and Gaby Filion, I retraced the route taken by François Paradis, the hero of *Maria Chapdelaine*, who left La Tuque and headed north through the forest in the hopes of rejoining Maria for Christmas in Péribonka, on the opposite shore of Lac Saint-Jean. Alas, he had frozen to death; we were more fortunate.

What prompted me to undertake these adventures? No doubt it was the pleasure of living on the water and in the forest, and the joys of good fellowship. It was also a certain sense of history that gave me the urge to connect with the exploits of our great *coureurs de bois* ancestors. And certainly another reason was that I liked to set myself challenges so that I could test myself in meeting them. Rightly or wrongly, in my childhood I was considered a rather frail child, endowed with neither strong health nor strong muscles. No doubt I was determined to overcome these weaknesses.

I also wanted to have as many different experiences as possible, a preoccupation that caused me to devote one entire summer vacation to working in the Louvicourt and Sullivan gold mines way up north in Abitibi. And, to add yet another reason, I was also eager to learn first-hand the geography of my country, which I wanted to know from east to west and from north to south.

I had already travelled by car with my family through the western provinces, including British Columbia. So I knew Canada from coast to coast very early in my life. All that remained was to travel around the Far North, which I did much later, sometimes by airplane but also several times by canoe on expeditions down the rivers that flow into the Arctic Ocean.

In 1944, I widened my horizons to the south when I left for Mexico by train with a group of Montrealers that included my sister, Suzette, Father Robert Llewellyn, Monsignor Olivier Maurault, who was rector of the Université de Montréal, Dostaler O'Leary, Gaston Pouliot, the Breecher brothers, and several other students like ourselves. Because this was during the war, it wasn't easy to travel abroad, but Mexico was one foreign destination it

In 1944, I and a group from Montreal visited the University of Mexico in Mexico City, where we were supposed to study Spanish. Here, at the back of the group, I seem to be striking what might be called a statuesque pose.
(NAC-TC)

was still possible to visit. According to the itinerary, we were supposed to spend most of the trip studying Spanish at the Escuela de Verano in Mexico City. But once we got there, I and a few other characters soon took off to learn Spanish on our own while hitchhiking across the country. Thanks to Father Llewellyn, we also got to know some French industrialists who were friends of his, and took part in discussions that opened our eyes to yet another part of the world, Latin America.

But all this talk of travel is taking me too far into a digression. Before this trip to Mexico ever took place, two great bombshells had exploded – one in my personal life, the other in history.

In the middle of the year I was fifteen, a winter night was interrupted by the terrible blow that left its mark on my adolescence and my life: the death of my father. He had fallen gravely ill on a trip to Florida with his baseball team, the Montreal Royals, and my mother and Suzette had rushed to travel to his bedside. We were very worried. An aunt had moved in to take care of my brother and me in the absence of our parents, and it was she who received the news of his death in the middle of the night. Aroused by the ringing of the telephone, I came out of my room to go downstairs and find out what was happening. But I froze on the landing when I heard the awful words: "Your father is dead, Pierre."

How can I describe what I felt at that moment? In a split second, I felt the whole world go empty. His death truly felt like the end of the world. That's the only way I can put it. My father had been a loving presence in my life, a reassuring force but also a stimulus, a constant challenge. He was the focal point of my life, and his death created an enormous void. All of a sudden, I was more or less the head of a family; with him gone, it seemed to me that I had to take over.

Of course, it was my mother who took on most of the responsibilities at first. But she made a point, very early on, of involving us young adolescents in the decision-making process. Thus I gradually became accustomed to handling certain family business matters, which were by no means the most important ones but which nevertheless gave me the sense that I was succeeding my father in managing his assets.

My mother, Grace Elliott Trudeau, after my father's death.
(Trudeau Family)

The other great bombshell that marked my teenage years was, of course, the outbreak of the Second World War in September 1939. I must admit that it affected me far less than my father's death, first of all because it had no comparable impact on my own life. The war was an undeniably important reality, but a very distant one. Moreover, it was part of current events, and as I have explained, they did not interest me very much. At that point in my life, I intellectualized everything with all my might. Was the war in Europe important? Sure, I told myself, but ancient campaigns like the Trojan Wars also deserved to be learned about. They too were important and had had a considerable impact on our civilization.

Obviously, I could not let myself seem to be unaware of something everyone else was discussing. In 1940, after graduating from Brébeuf, I began to study law at the Université de Montréal. In the months after the fall of France, as the Battle of Britain raged and London was blitzed, the war was a prime topic of conversation among the students. But the instinct that has always made me go against prevailing opinion caused me to affect a certain air of indifference. So there was a war? Tough. It wouldn't stop me from concentrating on my studies so long as that was possible.

But one cannot indefinitely remain aloof from a phenomenon of such proportions. I am sure I was vaguely aware, at the start of the war, that it might constitute the most dramatic adventure the men of my generation would ever confront. But if you were a French Canadian in Montreal in the early 1940s, you did not automatically believe that this was a just war. We still knew nothing of the Holocaust and we tended to think of this war as a settling of scores among the superpowers. And then, of course, there was the conscription issue.

I remember that at the beginning of the war a Mr. Gourd, a family friend, took me to the Forum to hear a speech by Ernest Lapointe, who was Prime Minister Mackenzie King's right-hand man and Quebec lieutenant.

*My graduation
photograph,
when I
finished
high school.
(Trudeau Family)*

And so I heard this politician solemnly promise this huge crowd that his government would "never" impose compulsory military service on Canadians. French Canadians still remembered the 1917 conscription crisis, with its riots and its deaths. Lapointe's promise was therefore seen as enormously important, and it led Quebecers to feel certain that re-electing the Liberal Party would ensure that the next government would never introduce conscription.

Yet that was exactly what it did do, after having been "freed from its commitment" in 1942 by the English-speaking population of Canada in a referendum. But a huge majority of French Canadians (72.9 per cent) were opposed to this measure. When the Liberals subsequently decided to get Major-General Léo LaFlèche elected in a by-election in Outremont, a young lawyer named Jean Drapeau ran against him as the "candidate of the conscripted." Drapeau mounted a vigorous campaign, and I participated in it by speaking at one of his rallies. That was, I believe, my only participation in the politics of that era.

Abstaining from any form of participation in the military was more difficult, however. You were either conscripted into the army, or if you were a student you had to join the Canadian Officers Training Corps. This required us to go to an armoury in the city twice a week to do drills and learn how to handle weapons. Each summer, in addition, the COTC sent us to Camp Farnham for a few weeks of additional training. Nearly all former students who are my age remember the COTC, whether fondly or otherwise. For my part, I recall a run-in with an officer who was giving us orders in English. Since he was addressing French-speaking recruits, I wanted to know why he wasn't commanding us in our own language. But as you might expect, my request had little effect. Neither the times nor the army favoured bilingualism in federal institutions.

But apart from these military duties, which I fulfilled like everyone else, the war really did not command my attention. For instance, everyone listened faithfully nearly every night to the CBC Radio reports of Louis Francoeur, who detailed every twist and turn of the battles. As for me, I don't recall *ever* having heard him. But sometimes the war caught up with us in unexpected ways. During our hiking trip through the Gaspé, for instance, Guy Viau, Jean Gélinas, and I were harassed several times by soldiers guarding the coast. At the time, Canada was in the grip of a real war hysteria. Is it true that the Gulf of St. Lawrence was swarming with enemy submarines? I have no idea (although I know that one Canadian ferry, the *Caribou*, was torpedoed, with heavy loss of life), but a lot of people were absolutely convinced of it at the time. There were even all sorts of myths built up around this notion. German sailors were said to have come out of their submarines at night to drink beer in the villages and dance with Gaspésienne girls!

The authorities were sufficiently convinced of an enemy presence that they imposed a curfew on the river banks and a general blackout on the villages after sunset. And the soldiers stationed on the peninsula were so concerned with the so-called "fifth column" that they went hunting for spies – who happened to be us three harmless guys. No doubt what made us look suspicious was that we were acting like vagabonds – we were walking with packs on our backs, we declined the rides we were offered, and we slept anywhere we could. Several times, military vehicles pulled up alongside us and we were asked: "What are you doing on foot on the highway?" They seemed to find what we were doing highly abnormal.

One night, just as we were falling asleep stretched out on the porch of an abandoned house, we saw flashlights moving towards us in the distance, through the tall grass between the road and our makeshift dormitory. We quickly figured it out: "People from the village must have reported us, and here come members of the coast guard who think we're Germans." We waited silently for them to come near. And when they finally rushed at us, weapons at the ready, we sprang from our sleeping bags naked as jaybirds, yelling: "Don't shoot, gentlemen, don't shoot!" They realized their error then and withdrew, leaving us to sleep in peace.

We also dreamed up some pranks with a military flavour. One day, when I was staying at Roger Rolland's house in the Laurentians, he showed me an attic where his parents had over the years amassed a huge jumble of ill-assorted objects. There we found some German uniforms from the Franco-Prussian War of 1870, including pointed steel helmets, and some Austrian or German coins. We decided on the spot to put on the uniforms and helmets, get on our motorcycles, and go visit our friends, the Compagnons de Saint-Laurent, who were staying that summer on the mountain behind Saint-Adolphe. We wanted to surprise Jean Gascon, Jean-Louis Roux, and some other buddies with a costumed visit worthy of the actors they all were. But, alas, they had already left, and we surprised only the young caretaker left on the property.

Once we were back on the road, we had the bright idea of scaring a few acquaintances along the way. In Sainte-Agathe, for instance, we stopped at the house of an English-speaking family whose daughters we knew. Unfortunately the girls weren't home, but that didn't stop us from asking for a drink once we were in the kitchen. Nor did it stop us from toppling forward, in the best tradition of the Club of the Dying, which startled the wits out of a servant who thought we were indeed dead. Further on, at the intersection of two roads, a local thought I was chasing my companion and he pointed dramatically and yelled, "He went that way!" I'm not sure if we were trying more to astound the passers-by or each other, but we had a lot of fun.

$$\approx$$

I graduated from the Université de Montréal with a law degree in 1943, articled for a year, then enrolled in a master's program at Harvard, in Cambridge, Massachusetts. It was only at Harvard, in the autumn of 1944, that I came to appreciate fully the historic importance of the war that was ending. In that super-informed environment, it was impossible for me not to grasp the true dimensions of the war, despite my continued indifference towards the news media. We had among our professors several Europeans who had fled Nazi persecution, including Heinrich Brüning, Hitler's immediate predecessor as chancellor of the Reich. I realized then that I had, as it were, missed one of the major events of the century in which I was living. Did I feel any regret? No. I have always regarded regret as a useless emotion. And I have never looked back at my mistakes, except to make sure I would not repeat them. In any event, immersed as I was in the super-charged intellectual climate at Harvard, I had no time to indulge in moods.

How did I come to be at the most famous of American universities? It was quite simple. Once one decided to study "political economy," as it was called in those days, Harvard was the obvious choice. But choosing that field of study in the first place was less obvious. I was torn for a long time between law, psychology, sociology, and political science. I had a vague intention of spending my life teaching, but I didn't yet know what subject. Before deciding, I consulted a lot of people. I remember that Pierre Vadeboncoeur and

I even requested and obtained a meeting with Henri Bourassa. Do people of his stature still take the time nowadays to meet with young people in search of advice?

I also went to see André Laurendeau, a man whose knowledge and shrewdness impressed me. I had found some of his articles in *L'Action nationale*, a magazine he had headed for several years, to be outstanding. In response to my questions, he said that our society was terribly lacking in economic expertise. Only Édouard Montpetit and Esdras Minville represented that field of knowledge in our province. There was an urgent need, said Laurendeau, for young people to follow in their footsteps.

That's why I took the joint degree in economics and political science. And in that field, the internationally recognized centre of excellence was in North America, practically on our doorstep: Harvard. Since I had always had top marks at Brébeuf and in university, my application to Harvard was accepted, and I have never regretted it.

What an extraordinary experience I had on that famous campus! And what discoveries I made! As soon as I arrived, I realized that in intellectual terms I was barely coming out of childhood. Classmates and professors alike were at an astounding level of culture and erudition. Students of my age or younger had a knowledge of Roman law far superior to mine – and yet it wasn't even their specialty, while I, a twenty-five-year-old lawyer, had just spent a year studying it. And among the professors were the world's leading lights in various areas. Driven out of Europe by the Nazis or by the war, they were recruited by Harvard.

I also realized that the Quebec of the time was away from the action, that it was living outside modern times. I was struck by the contrast between my home province and the United States, this frenetic country brimming with energy and vitality. Harvard was an extraordinary window on the world. I found myself surrounded by intellectuals who throughout their lives had been eyewitnesses to change in the four corners of the world. It felt like being in symbiosis with the five continents. It goes without saying that this was a complete change from the rather parochial climate I had known in Montreal. And the level of studies, the quality of teaching, and the physical plant at our disposal (libraries, lecture halls, museums, etc.) were all at the leading edge.

We all have developments in our lives that take on a critical importance in determining our future course; I regard my stay at Harvard, followed by the École libre des sciences politiques in Paris and the London School of Economics, as among those decisive moments. At these three institutions, I completed a search that I had begun at Brébeuf in my adolescent years. On what values would I base my life? The issue of freedom had obsessed me since high school and my first year of philosophy. I was interested in the religious aspect of this subject as well. Reconciling predestination, the infinite power of God, with human freedom intrigued me much more than the notion of original sin. Certain Jesuits suspected me of being a closet Protestant, not only because I insisted on closely questioning the most established truths but even more because I regarded my conscience as the ultimate court of appeal. It was my conscience I wanted to obey, taking precedence over even the commandments of the Church or the rules of the college.

My studies at Harvard quickly confirmed my beliefs about individual freedom. The view that every human must remain free to shape his own destiny became for me a certainty and one of the pillars of the political thought I was working to develop. But thanks to two French thinkers, Jacques Maritain and Emmanuel Mounier, I never came to believe in the doctrine of absolute liberalism. I was already familiar with Maritain's books and Mounier's magazine *Esprit* before I left Canada for Paris in 1946 to enrol at the École libre des sciences politiques. But I deepened my knowledge of their thought during my stay in France. It was there that I became a follower of personalism, a philosophy that reconciles the individual and society. The person, according to these two teachers, is the individual enriched with a social conscience, integrated into the life of the communities around him and the economic context of his time, both of which must in turn give persons the means to exercise their freedom of choice. It was thus that the fundamental notion of justice came to stand alongside that of freedom in my political thought.

I never met Jacques Maritain. As for Mounier, a happy coincidence had us standing at the same bar in a Latin Quarter bistro after a lecture by Georges Bernanos. But my adherence to personalism was not the result of a sudden flash of insight. Quite the contrary, it was the outcome of long reflection.

I don't want to give the impression that my student days in Paris were nothing more than a long and austere intellectual and spiritual exercise. Though the immediate after-effects of the war were still being felt in Europe in 1946, there was a *joie de vivre* that certainly affected young people like myself.

On the one hand, yes, postwar rigours complicated life: everything was rationed, from food to gasoline, and including clothing and medicines. (I had some personal

Revisiting my old student haunts

1. In 1992 I took a stroll through the largely unchanged Harvard campus.

2. Gérard Pelletier and I enjoyed reminiscing about our days together in Paris when I was a student and he was a frequent visitor.

3. We showed my son Sacha the view from my old room in an unfashionable hotel in the shadow of Notre-Dame . . .

4. . . . and talked over old times outside a favourite bookstore.

5. Amid unusually comfortable surroundings at the London School of Economics I chatted with Michael Ignatieff, son of the distinguished Canadian diplomat George Ignatieff.

(Les Productions La Fête/Jean Demers)

Scenes from La Bohème? In this shot taken during our student days in Paris, Roger Rolland seems to be experiencing a rude awakening. (Canapress)

experience of this, having to undergo an appendectomy in a hospital that was short of anaesthetics and used them in painfully insufficient quantities.) Travel of any sort, even within the city, presented serious problems. Cars were scarce, taxis almost non-existent. There were a lot of bicycle-taxis that transported passengers in wooden boxes on wheels that the owners towed, by pedalling very hard. And so the streets were almost deserted; only military vehicles travelled in any numbers. But what a dream those great empty avenues were for someone like myself who had a motorcycle. I roared across Paris at speeds that under other circumstances would have cost me my life – or at least my

freedom! And since this means of transportation used little fuel, gas rationing tickets allowed me to take jaunts through the countryside and even quick trips to neighbouring countries.

My friend Roger Rolland, who was also a motorcyclist, arrived in Paris at the same time as me to continue his studies. The two of us stayed at first at the Canadian students' house on the university campus. Then, wanting to get closer to the life of the Latin Quarter where we were studying, Roger soon found an antiquated little hotel, in the shadow of Notre-Dame and very near the church of Saint-Julien-le-Pauvre. The rooms were modest and the comforts limited, but the bells of the cathedral served as our alarm clock and paced our days. We couldn't study very late into the evening because at a certain hour the owner of the hotel would plunge us all into darkness by shutting off the power. But we would talk long into the night about our futures, the future of Canada, and that of the entire world.

Everything around us encouraged us to ponder such weighty matters. We were witnesses on an almost daily basis to the spread of communism in Europe. Young people, in particular, were truly fascinated by the Soviet model. Because the Red Army had just cleared away the Brown Plague (as Nazism was called) in Eastern Europe, because the savage capitalism of the pre-war Depression period had shown itself in many respects to be a deplorable failure, and because Moscow's propaganda was very effectively manipulating public opinion, Marxism-Leninism was gaining ground in the West as spectacularly as it is collapsing today. And the beauty of the intellectual climate in Paris was that all the tendencies of contemporary political thought were articulated by worthy spokesmen – the Christian left, the worker priests, and proponents of orthodox Marxism as much as Catholic *intégrisme*, the existentialism of Jean-Paul Sartre, and pure liberalism.

Of course, we could not remain indifferent to developments back at home. We were living abroad for a while, but we knew that in a few years we would have to go back to Quebec. What kind of situation would we find there on our return? Incidents like the one sparked by the French film *Les Enfants du paradis* did not augur well. I'm sure many people remember this supposed scandal that was based solely on ignorance and narrow-mindedness. We had just seen this masterpiece of French cinema in Paris, and enjoyed it immensely, when we learned that the premier of Quebec had banned its showing in the theatres of his province. Having found out that the film had been shown at the Université de Montréal without prior screening by Quebec's censors (because the French embassy in Ottawa had provided the students with a copy), Duplessis had

flown into such a rage that the censors immediately understood his wishes and banned the film completely.

We Montreal students studying in Paris – a group that
included among others Jean Gascon, Jean-Louis Roux, and
Roger Rolland – were outraged by this blow to freedom of
expression. We wrote a letter of protest – only to see every
Quebec newspaper with the exception of the daily *Le
Canada* refuse to publish it. Thus we began, more or less
consciously, our long battle against the spirit of a political
regime that was to endure for more than another decade. At
the same time, along with Gérard Pelletier, who was often
in Paris while travelling through Europe on behalf of a fund
aiding student victims of the war, we were already talking
vaguely of starting a magazine. It was, in fact, launched in
Montreal four years later, and was called *Cité libre*.

But before going back to Canada, I had two more adventures – one intellectual, the other socio-geographic – that
were to influence the whole rest of my life. The first was
attending the London School of Economics and the other
was backpacking through Eastern Europe, the Middle East,
and the Orient.

My stay in London involved the exceptional good fortune of being at the London School of Economics during
one of the most illustrious periods in its history. The intellectual climate was extraordinary. I had known beforehand
that this was a school unlike any other. Before I left for
England, my aunt in Varengeville had said to me: "So you're
enrolling at this famous school filled with black men and
red women?" An odd description, with its mix of ethnicity

and politics, but it turned out to be an accurate one. The LSE was exactly that: a remarkable ferment of diverse nationalities and political opinions, among professors as much as among students. The intellectual climate was most stimulating. Among my classmates were male and female militants of every political stripe: out-and-out Marxists, doctrinaire communists, social democrats, committed liberals, and even a few conservatives.

The remarkable fervour that characterized the postwar period in Europe reigned supreme at LSE. The Labour Party was in power. Political life was teeming with colourful personalities whom my main teacher, Harold Laski, would invite to the school. I remember a brilliant speech by Aneurin (Nye) Bevan, the great Welsh orator who was a minister in the government. Laski himself moved in both academic and political circles. An eminent professor, he was at the same time the chairman of the Labour Party. He had an absolutely outstanding mind. When I arrived in London I was already familiar with his many writings, most notably his *Grammar of Politics*, an encyclopaedic work that for some unknown reason no longer gets any attention.

I also recall the name of another exceptional professor, Glanville Williams, a specialist in public law who steered me to the Swedish author Knut Olivecrona and his book *Law as Fact*. What is wonderful about a university like LSE is that you not only receive teaching of a very high quality, you also learn where to find the knowledge you are seeking. And you make unexpected discoveries: it was a Marxist professor who introduced me to the work of Cardinal Newman, a great master of English prose as well as theology.

At the time, I was particularly interested in authors who developed a general theory of the state. I wanted to know the roots of power, I wanted to know how governments work and why people obey. Does the ultimate authority lie in the state or in the human individual? Whom should one choose: Antigone or Creon? I learned the philosophy of T.H. Green, whose liberalism preceded the personalism of Maritain and Mounier in saying that the focal point was not the state but the individual – the individual seen as a person integrated into society, which is to say endowed with fundamental rights and essential liberties, but also with responsibilities. This position is very close to that of the Fabian Society, the ancestor of the British Labour Party. I found myself in London while this party was putting into place what was later to become the welfare state.

No doubt because the last months of my life that were dedicated entirely to studying were spent at the London School of Economics, it was there that everything I had learned until then of law, economics, political science, and political philosophy came together for me. My reflections as a student, undertaken at Harvard, Paris, and London, reached their conclusion at LSE. When I left this institution, my fundamental choices had been made. I was to acquire more knowledge and to encounter countless options throughout my life. But my basic philosophy was established from that time on, and it was on those premises that I based all my future political decisions; it was that philosophy that underlay all my writings.

As for my formal studies, I had completed my exams and orals for a doctorate when I was at Harvard. What still remained was to write my thesis. This requirement provided me with a pretext to travel around the world. I had already chosen my subject: the interplay between two doctrines, Christianity and Marxism, which were competing for the loyalty of people in Asia. I chose India as my area of study. That country had plenty of Canadian missionaries who would be willing to help me, and it was swarming with Marxists as well.

But the real purpose of my trip was to confirm that the earth was round – in other words, to complete the process of discovering the world that I had begun in Mexico and continued at Harvard, Paris, and London. This time, the trip would not be first and foremost an intellectual odyssey. I intended to range more widely, to mix with local populations, to experience their lifestyles, and to learn their habits, their troubles, and their reactions. To accomplish this, I decided to use the modes of travel of Everyman: on foot with a backpack, in third-class coaches on trains, on buses in China and elsewhere, and aboard cargo boats on rivers and seas. This trip was basically a challenge I set myself, as I had done with sports, with canoeing expeditions, and with intellectual explorations. I wanted to know, for instance, whether I could survive in a Chinese province without knowing a word of Chinese, or would be able to travel across a war-torn country (there was no shortage of regional conflicts at the time) without ever succumbing to panic.

And so one fine spring day in 1948, I left England. By moving constantly eastward, I was sure to end up eventually back in Canada. But I didn't have any firm itinerary. I devoted the first two months, into the summer, to exploring Eastern Europe, the countries that had recently fallen under communism as a result of the victories of the Red Army. It wasn't a restful journey. To use Churchill's metaphor, the Iron Curtain had descended, isolating this region and making access from the West more difficult with every passing day. Guns and soldiers and border guards were everywhere. This provided me with a very harsh initiation into the globetrotter's craft. To cross certain borders, I had to make myself false documents. I was deported from one country after a day of detention. In short, I was learning the art of roaming the world at a very turbulent time; I was also learning the tricks of the trade. By the time I reached Turkey at the end of the summer, I had already visited Poland, Czechoslovakia, Austria, Hungary, Yugoslavia, and Bulgaria. Visas filled every page of my passport. Since there was not yet a Canadian embassy in Ankara, I had to go to that of the United Kingdom, where they attached a British passport to my Canadian passport. I note this detail because it was to spare me from some serious problems, as we shall see.

Turkey was my gateway to the entire Middle East, where I had promised myself to visit a number of places. The Holy Land was, of course, prominent among them. That year, Palestine was convulsed in war over the State of Israel, whose independence had just been proclaimed, on May 14, 1948, by the Jewish national council. This, too, was not a place you could just walk into, surrounded as it was by warring armies. So I stopped in Amman, the capital of what was then known as Transjordan. I stayed in student lodgings, and went to an establishment with the very un-Arabic name of the Philadelphia Hotel (Philadelphia being the old Western name for Amman) to get the latest news on the situation. There I encountered a solemn group of journalists gathered from the four corners of the world to cover the Israeli-Arab conflict. They had turned the hotel into a newsroom from which they sent their respective newspapers flurries of dispatches based on whatever in-formation drifted in from across the River Jordan.

"Why are you staying here?" I asked one of them. "Are you covering this war without ever setting foot in Jerusalem?"

"We'd love to go there, but it's impossible."

"How do you mean, impossible?"

"We don't have the necessary travel documents. And in any event, the road between Jericho and Jerusalem has just been blocked by Palestinian forces. It's too risky."

Having decided, for my part, to run that risk, I soon spotted trucks in the main square of Amman loaded with Arab volunteer soldiers who were leaving to do battle in Jerusalem. I jumped aboard one of these vehicles, already loaded with some twenty armed soldiers, and a few minutes later we were on our way. Amman was barely sixty kilometres from Jerusalem. We crossed the Jordan over the Allenby Bridge, followed the highway through Jericho, and got to the walls of Jerusalem without a hitch. I had been determined to see this city; it was with immense pleasure that I walked through it, a pleasure mixed with other strong emotions since I had had to cross a street on the outskirts of the Old City under Israeli-Arab crossfire. I was on my way to visit a Canadian Dominican priest whose address a priest in Beirut had given me. Crossing this street, running the gauntlet of the bullets, was the only way to reach his monastery. On the way back my troubles really began. Since I was in violation of a curfew, two Arab soldiers grabbed me by the collar and, without any further formalities, threw me in jail. It was only mildly interesting to learn that my prison was the Antonina Tower, where Pontius Pilate had judged Christ, for I was informed that I would be charged with

The clothes I wore (and the long beard I had grown) got me into serious trouble in the Middle East in 1948. The area was at war and I was imprisoned as a suspected Jewish spy. It was not the only time during my somewhat eventful world tour that I saw the inside of a foreign jail. (Canapress)

espionage and that the death penalty awaited me if I was convicted.

My imprisonment could have been dangerously long, had it not been for the intervention of the Dominican I had just visited. At my request, he persuaded my jailers that I was a Canadian student and not a spy for the Haganah. No sooner was I hauled from my cell after a not very pleasant day and a night, than I was ordered into another truck loaded with rifle-bearing soldiers, just like the first, that was heading in the opposite direction down the same road I had travelled the day before yesterday, back to Amman.

Unfortunately for me, the Arab soldiers who surrounded me had not heard the Dominican's testimony. As far as they were concerned, I was indeed a Jewish spy; they had seen me come out of the prison, the long beard I had at the time made me look even more suspect in their eyes, and they had been ordered to bring me back to Transjordan to stand trial. They didn't feel very kindly towards me, to say the least. The trip this time was very uncomfortable and punctuated by several threats of death. They let me know by vivid and easily understandable gestures that there was nothing to stop them from killing me and dumping my corpse into the ravine that bordered the highway. But I did my best to act confident, and they did nothing beyond turning me over to the authorities in Amman, still under arrest.

I knew nobody in this city, of course. But since I was bearing the British passport I had received in Turkey, I contacted Her Majesty's embassy and sought its protection. That protection turned out to be very effective. My identity was established to the satisfaction of the Jordanians, and I regained my freedom.

After this first contact with soldiers in action, I was to experience several others. I didn't seek them out, but as luck would have it the travel route I had chosen was strewn with obstacles created by armed conflicts of that time. It was incredible – everywhere I went seemed to be at war. In Pakistan, I arrived very shortly after India had been carved up, and the border between Lahore and Amritsar was overrun by masses of refugees. In Afghanistan, the Pathans were already fighting among themselves. I travelled there by jeep; an armed scout accompanied us to warn us of ambushes and to give us a chance to return fire if we were fired upon. It was the same in Burma, where civil war was raging.

And likewise in Indochina. The French were still there; we had to travel by convoy. To reach Angkor Wat, I took advantage of the presence of a famous French archaeologist to whom the authorities wanted to show the famous temple. They had even cleared the jungle all around the temple in anticipation of his visit. It was there that I saw Khmer Rouges (known at the time as Isaraqs) for the first time; soldiers chased, caught, and beat them before our eyes. Another day, on the way to Saigon, we were attacked by a

Viet Cong patrol, almost twenty years before their forces became known around the world. And, of course, when I arrived in China, there was war there, too: the armies of Mao Zedong and Chiang Kai-shek were doing battle. In short, even though my intentions were always peaceful, I was caught up despite myself in a number of armed conflicts.

I will not recount here all the episodes – some terrifying, some comical, others tragic, and many others edifying, demonstrating the courage and kindness of ordinary people – that I experienced in the course of this trip. I will tell about one of them, though, perhaps the funniest of all and one that proves that poetry is a *useful* art.

It happened in Iraq, between Baghdad and Basra, more specifically at Ur, the birthplace of Abraham, where I wanted to go. I had read somewhere that the English archaeologist Sir Leonard Woolley had made some important discoveries there. So I took the train from Baghdad to Basra. I first broke my journey at Babylon. Reboarding the train, I travelled for several hours through the night until finally, at dawn, they announced the station where I wanted to get off. A miserable shack passed for a station-house, and around it were a few people, several camels, and desert as far as the eye could see. I asked the first man I came to: "Where is Ur?" He pointed his index finger towards the horizon, and in the distance I saw the Ziggurat, an enormous stone structure. I left my backpack with the station-master and set off across the desert towards the pyramid.

Since the sun was still low in the sky, the air was cool and walking was pleasant. I soon found myself all alone in the ruins of the ancient city, where I wandered for hours. I picked up a few tile fragments, inscribed with Sumerian characters, that date back to the days of Abraham. (I still have them.) Around midday, I decided to climb the very narrow, very long, and very steep stairs that led to the top of the Ziggurat, to get a panoramic view of the whole site. After a while, I realized I was not alone. A couple of desert tramps had spotted me and were moving towards me threateningly. They made it clear that they wanted money. One of them indicated by gesture: "Let's see your watch." Since I wasn't wearing one, I replied, "Let's see your knife" and snatched it from his belt. They persisted: "We want whatever you've got. Hand it all over." But now it was I who was holding the knife. I suggested to them that we should go down from the pyramid and discuss things at ground level. We headed towards the stairs. Ever polite, I let them get onto the stairs ahead of me, while I stayed at the top and shouted down: "Now come and get me."

They didn't move. Then, to get them good and frightened, I began screaming to the skies all the poems I have memorized, beginning with Cocteau's verse about antiquity. I spewed octosyllables and alexandrines by the dozens. I accompanied them with dramatic gestures. I did this so well that they believed me to be dangerously deranged. They probably thought I had lost my mind from being too long in the sun. After a long while of wild-eyed reciting, I started down the stairs myself, still yelling; to my great relief, I saw them take off. I was never more grateful for the long-ago obsessiveness that had made me memorize the works of my favourite poets!

Over the course of my long journey, there were also some pauses that I welcomed as a respite from travel. In

Lucknow, in northern India, I met a colleague from the London School of Economics who had become a professor, so I stopped there to deliver a few political science lectures to his students. For a few days, I ceased to be the impoverished vagabond who would be left to cool his heels at the counters of YMCA hostels while clean-shaven and properly dressed clients were taken care of first. But after each such stop, I resumed my travels with renewed enthusiasm, ready for another round of adventures.

Going up the Brahmaputra River was one such adventure that is worth mentioning. This waterway, whose source is in the Tibetan plateau, runs through the gorges of Yunan, Assam, and Bengal before flowing into the same marshy delta as the Ganges. The Sundarbans, the coastal lands that make up the southern part of this delta, are covered with a jungle I had been dreaming about since I was a child, having seen it in a book I received as a gift. The book praised the lushness of this jungle; what had stayed with me, above all, was the vivid description of the tigers that lived on the banks of the Brahmaputra in this area.

In a harbour on the outskirts of Calcutta, I saw a flat-bottomed boat that I was told carried tea and was, in fact, leaving for the Sundarbans en route to pick up a cargo in Assam. I immediately concluded that I had found the way to get to this jungle. I walked over, introduced myself to the captain, and asked him to take me aboard. He hesitated, wanting to bargain, then finally agreed, warning me: "We can't feed you, bring your own food." No problem! I went to get supplies at the nearby marketplace, where I saw a remarkable confrontation. Two good-sized bulls decided to violently settle some score between them and, in the process, they were busily knocking over merchants' stalls before our eyes, and trampling fruits and vegetables with-out anyone lifting a finger to stop them. I was astonished by this passiveness until I remembered the notion of "sacred cows." In India, you don't get rough with cattle; they are protected by the faith of the Hindus. After this unexpected diversion, I returned to board the barge and begin a mar-vellous journey.

The jungle was a wonder, and the boat proved to be an excellent means of exploring it. We chugged for hours on end through extraordinarily lush vegetation that was inter-rupted only by a few fishing villages. We encountered croc-odiles, we saw brilliantly coloured birds. It was a dazzling spectacle. But I never would have thought the trip would be so long. On a map, it looked like a modest distance to travel. But maps don't tell you about the shallows that are all over the delta at the mouth of the Ganges. Time and again, the bottom of the vessel would scrape on sand. We would have to back up and manoeuvre slowly in search of water deep enough to travel through. But that wasn't easy, because the navigable channel zigzags through the riverbed, sometimes on the left, sometimes on the right. The days passed, and my food supplies finally ran out. So much so, that for my Christmas dinner that year, I devoured a tiny tin of Iranian caviar I had bought in Baghdad and now found at the bottom of my backpack. Nothing else!

And so I ended this cruise on an empty stomach. When the boat arrived at Dacca I received a warm welcome from some Canadian missionaries, members of the Order of the Holy Cross who were from Montreal and had a house here. They took me to a small rural village named Padrishippur, where I celebrated New Year's with them. But there I was to have yet another adventure.

One evening, the Fathers said to me: "Tomorrow we're

In India with a backpack

1. I adopted the head-dress of the subcontinent.
(Trudeau Family)

2. Posing with the famous backpack and the well-worn walking boots.
(Trudeau Family)

3. Here the backpack has turned temporarily into a hat, under the hot Indian sun.
(NAC-TC)

4. At Padrishippur, near Dacca, I received a very warm welcome from Canadian missionaries, although this photograph casts doubt on it.
(NAC-TC)

5. A more staid shot taken before my departure eastward through Indochina and then by train and bus through the civil war between Mao Zedong and Chiang Kai-shek in China. (NAC-TC)

going to buy our supplies of rice at the floating markets, as we do every year on this date. Do you want to come with us?" Naturally I accepted the invitation and we left in the middle of the night, aboard two small covered boats, planning to reach the market at daybreak. But a thick fog came up with the dawn and we lost our way. We were very lucky to have got lost, because the other skiff was attacked by pirates who stripped the passengers and fled with their belongings, their money – even their clothes. That's how you escape from pirates: by not being on the boat that they're robbing.

Pushing ever eastward, I eventually reached China. As you might well expect, this immense country held some big surprises and discoveries for a traveller like myself.

For the purposes of the Harvard thesis I still intended to write, the China of that time was the most interesting field of observation one could imagine. On the one hand, missionaries of every Christian faith were still there in great numbers. In the name of the Church, whose message they had been preaching in the Orient since the sixteenth century, the Jesuits affirmed an eminently lively Catholic presence in China. The name of Teilhard de Chardin, to mention only one, was closely associated with China, where he had led archaeological excavations since 1928. Other churches were heavily involved in Chinese missions, and the universities had great numbers of Chinese students who pursued their studies under the direction of priests and of lay professors recruited by them both within the country and in Europe and America.

As for Marxism, that was the ferment that would, in a

few years, transform all of China. The Communist Party was soon to put in place a regime that to this day governs more than a billion human beings. But for the time being, there was war. The capital, Nanking, had just fallen to the Red Army, and the main forces of Chiang Kai-shek and Mao were facing each other across the Yangtze River.

I arrived in China on the Hong Kong–Canton train. At the Chinese embassy in Ankara, I had had the foresight to obtain a merchant visa to visit the annual trade fair in Canton. From there, it was an easy matter to travel without documents across this country whose authorities were in disarray. Easy, but hardly reassuring. The train on which I was riding to Hengyang was stopped en route by starving troops in search of food. I reached Changsha aboard a Chinese bus. Then, still by bus, I reached Nanchang and from there Hangchow, the city of a thousand marvels, and finally Shanghai, where I saw the spectacle of a people in retreat.

Staying at a YMCA hostel, I had full scope to observe this extraordinary and tragic phenomenon. The city was full of wounded soldiers dragging themselves from place to place in search of I know not what. In the morning, the sidewalks were strewn with the bodies of people who had died during the night. The whole city was a bizarre flea market where everyone, from the poorest to the richest, was trying to peddle his or her possessions for money to flee south or abroad. In the middle of all this torment, it was a joy for me to discover, at Zikawei, the Jesuit parish and university, an oasis of serenity. Here I met up with my former classmate Paul Deslierres, now a missionary and teacher, with whom I had gone all through high school before he went into the priesthood.

Shanghai was the last stop on my travels in China. From there, I boarded a homeward-bound ship that took me first to experience a forty-eight-hour stop in Yokohama, Japan's largest seaport. I couldn't leave the harbour area here, because the Canadian government representative refused to give me the necessary authorization. But I nevertheless had time to see the devastation, the disorder, and the misery that were reigning in the Empire of the Rising Sun. Mistaking me, because of my long beard, for a sailor on shore leave, Japanese black marketeers stopped me in the street to offer anything from a girl to a precious piece of art, in exchange for a handful of cigarettes.

I made the voyage from Japan to Hawaii in the memorable company of families of diverse nationality who were fleeing, for the second time, from the Red tide. At the time of the October Revolution, some of these passengers had fled Russia and settled in China, where they had rebuilt their lives. Now, thirty years later, the same upheaval, inspired by the same ideology, was driving out of China both the victims of October who had made their fortunes there and refugees of more recent vintage, Hungarians, Poles, and Roumanians who had fled east after Yalta. Now Mao's People's Army was closing its pincers on the forces of Chiang Kai-shek, who would soon retreat to Formosa-Taiwan. Before the end of 1949, the People's Republic of China would be proclaimed in Beijing. For my travelling companions, it was time to flee yet again, and this time they were determined to go all the way to America. There was no question of stopping anywhere en route. These men and women, enlightened by experience, had made their choice; they saw our continent as the only haven where they would feel safe from communism. For them, I discovered in our conversations, America was the promised land, a dream. What emotions and what sobs of gratitude there were as we arrived under the Golden Gate Bridge in San Francisco!

For me, on the contrary, it was a return to reality – my own reality, into which I would have to step for good upon returning to Canada. After years of study abroad, capped by the twelve months I had spent roaming around the world, that threatened to be a nasty shock. It was. Homecoming is first of all the joy of reuniting with relatives and friends, of feasting with the people who welcome you back, of revisiting familiar places. But it is also the disappointment of finding that nothing has changed. From afar, one cannot help but idealize the place one has left behind, erasing from memory the negative aspects of the familiar landscape. In one's mind, without fully realizing it, one reshapes according to personal hopes and experiences the situation to which one will return. But the situation itself doesn't actually change.

And so I found myself back in the Quebec of the 1940s with all its weaknesses and its many problems. Duplessis had been governing the province when I left, in 1944; he was still governing it when I got back. His government was profoundly conservative and resisted change with all its might. And Quebec had stayed provincial in every sense of the word, that is to say marginal, isolated, out of step with the evolution of the world. That was the time when our *chansonnier* Jacques Normand mockingly predicted: "When the Soviets invade, they'll rename Montreal; they'll call it Retrograd." There was a striking contrast with the

The strike at Asbestos was, in my words, "a turning point in the entire religious, political, social, and economic history of the province of Quebec." It certainly attracted widespread support as people in Montreal raised funds for the striking miners. (Archives du Québec)

countries I had just visited, which had been thrown into turmoil by war but which their leaders were seeking to rebuild "for the new man." Nothing like that was happening yet in Quebec, but there was nevertheless a bubbling of ideas that already, in a very timid way, presaged the changes to come.

A few days after coming home, I got back in touch with Gérard Pelletier. He was spending his time in the Eastern Townships covering the strike of the asbestos miners for the daily *Le Devoir* and seldom left Asbestos. But I happened to catch him during one of his trips to Montreal. The labour conflict at Asbestos had been dragging on for nearly four months. "I'm going back there this afternoon. Do you want to come with me?" Two hours later, we were heading east to the small town, and for several days I joined the miners in their battle; I made a speech at a strike meeting. What I

found there was a Quebec I did not really know, that of workers exploited by management, denounced by government, clubbed by police, and yet burning with fervent militancy. I was later to describe the strike – and the ferocious response it provoked – as "a turning point in the entire religious, political, social, and economic history of the province of Quebec."

When I got back to Montreal, I completed my discouraging overview of the situation. I found that the same outdated élites were still in power in virtually every field, and that the intellectual climate they maintained was stifling. My search for a job ran up against the pettiness and the prejudices of the political establishment. I wanted to teach, to "share my newly acquired knowledge," as Édouard Montpetit had said on returning from his studies abroad. I applied to the Université de Montréal, which was much in need of qualified political science professors. But on three occasions over the next decade, I was stonewalled, and I learned that Premier Duplessis himself had intervened to block me, the first time with the rector, the second time with Dean Minville, and finally, when I tried for a third time, with the secretary general of the institution. Le Chef didn't want any professors "who had studied in a communist environment, in London and in Paris."

What to do in such a situation? One either tries to change it, or gets the hell out and forgets about it. I had an offer from Professor J.A. Corry, an eminent Canadian political scientist, who was teaching at Queen's. But I had absolutely no intention of getting the hell out. I wanted to teach in Quebec. I wanted to stay in my city, Montreal. But since you can't always get what you want, it was in Ottawa that I soon found myself, in the summer of 1949, as a civil servant in the Privy Council Office.

How did I come to be there? By visiting some friends, including several schoolmates from Brébeuf, and acquaintances such as Jules Léger, Pierre Dumas, and D'Iberville Fortier, who had all opted for the public service. And why the Privy Council Office? Because as the secretariat to the Cabinet, it was the key decision-making centre, and because I wanted to observe in practice what I had just finished studying in theory. Gordon Robertson, one of the great public servants of the time, was well disposed to having me there. I have never had cause to regret this choice. The two years that I spent there were an apprenticeship that was later to prove very useful.

But I didn't have the temperament of a bureaucrat and I eventually decided to shift my focus. In Montreal, most of my friends were already involved in action. In 1950, Jean Marchand, Pierre Vadeboncoeur, and Gérard Pelletier were working with labour unions, Roger Rolland was creating programs for Radio-Canada, and Charles Lussier was practising labour law with Guy Desaulniers and later with Jacques Perrault. My younger brother, Charles, was already a brilliant architect with the firm of Rother, Bland, Trudeau. What's more, the vague idea conceived in Paris was taking shape; the *Cité libre* team had come together. The first issue of the magazine was due to appear in July of that year. I was associated with the project from the beginning. It interested me a great deal. I saw it as a means of influencing social and political thought, but my status as a civil servant prevented me from putting my name on certain articles I wanted to write. It also didn't take me long to grow weary of commuting between Ottawa and Montreal for each of the many meetings of our editorial team. To clinch matters, Jean Marchand and Jean-Paul Geoffroy persuaded me that in Montreal I could be useful to the labour movement that was in the forefront of the fight for social change in Quebec.

What stands out in my memory about my departure from Ottawa in the fall of 1951 is a conversation I had with Gordon Robertson. He had brought me into the public service and the Privy Council Office; now he couldn't understand why I wanted to leave both.

"Why?" he asked me. "You are useful here and we need men like you. You have a good future if you stay here. Why leave?"

"Because I want to return to Quebec. In Ottawa, everything is going pretty smoothly. French Canadians are beginning to make gains here well enough. Right now Quebec is where the important battles are being fought. That's where I can be most useful, even if my influence is only marginal. The labour movement is offering me work and..."

"Wait a minute! It was in the 1930s that the unions needed support. Now they are strong and powerful; they don't need help any more."

This view was apparently accurate in the case of the anglophone provinces, particularly Ontario. It illustrates how badly Quebec was out of step with its neighbouring province, because in Quebec the labour movement was in urgent need not only of well-trained leaders like Gérard Picard and Jean Marchand, but also of economists and sociologists. Robertson didn't go overboard in trying to keep me in Ottawa, but I sensed in his attitude a kind of pity for the fate of the poor boy who was going back to the land of Duplessis in the belief that he could have some influence there.

It was the beginning of a new phase in my life, very different from what I had just been doing. No more sitting around! Instead of the same East Block office every day, shared with the same co-worker, there were constant trips all over Quebec. Several times a month, I jumped on my motorcycle to go to Sherbrooke, Chicoutimi, Arvida, Shawinigan, Quebec, Joliette, or Rimouski, where I gave classes at the labour action schools. In each of these towns by turn, the CTCC (the Confédération des travailleurs catholiques du Canada, which was to become the CSN, the Confédération des syndicats nationaux) brought together several dozen militants, the elected leaders of their local unions. I taught them some basic economics, enough accounting to be able to make sense of a company's balance sheet, and a bit of political science. In some areas, I was also asked to explain what was wrong with Social Credit theories. At the same time, I got to know the union leaders all across the province.

Labour arbitration hearings were also a travelling road show. These short-lived tribunals, established to rule on a labour contract in a particular enterprise, were made up of three persons. The unions and the employers each named one arbitrator. If they could agree on a chairman, they

Family
snapshots
from the
1950s and
1960s

(Trudeau Family)

appointed him themselves; if they couldn't agree, the Ministry of Labour appointed its own choice, usually a judge of the provincial court. I thus made the acquaintance of many judges appointed by the ministry. But with a few fortunate exceptions, neither the choices of Premier Duplessis, who had made these men judges, nor of Minister of Labour Antonio Barrette, who inflicted them on us as chairmen, struck me as very enlightened. The quality of these people, under the Union Nationale, was not impressive.

Some unions also asked me to help negotiate their collective agreements. I particularly recall one such negotiation that kept us all summer in Arvida. My counterpart was Antoine Geoffrion, son of the great civil lawyer Aimé Geoffrion and himself considered one of the bright lights of the Montreal bar. I was more than a little proud to find myself, who had practised hardly any law, dealing face to face with a lawyer of his stature. Our exchanges were fascinating.

That being said, I learned a lot of labour law through my participation in these arbitrations. I also learned how to argue a case. I got to know all aspects of the labour milieu. And the arbitration tribunals introduced me to all the corners of our province I didn't get to visit for the labour action schools. That's because the tribunals conducted their hearings on site, in the towns where the factories in question were located, be it Lac Saint-Jean or Abitibi, the Eastern Townships or Trois-Rivières. A little later, some so-called international unions affiliated with the FUIQ (Fédération des unions internationales du Québec) asked for my services in writing briefs, and I helped with several of their cases.

This work, demanding as it was, still left me the time to

In China again in 1960 with my old friend Jacques Hébert, the distinguished publisher. We wrote a book about our trip, appropriately entitled Two Innocents in China. *(Canapress)*

take a few trips to Africa, Europe, the Soviet Union, and China to attend various political science conferences. And it also left me the time to take on, as a lawyer, certain cases that appealed to me because they involved civil liberties. That is how I came to free my friend Jacques Hébert in the Court of Appeal after he was charged with contempt of court in the Wilbert Coffin affair.

People have often asked me whether, in the 1950s, I already had political ambitions. I have always answered in the negative, which was the truth. Leaving Quebec was out of the question, as far as I was concerned; it was here that I wanted to be active. But how could I ever have considered belonging to a party like the Union Nationale? I profoundly loathed its reactionary conservatism, and its leaders, in their turn, hated the ideas I represented. Any coming together was impossible. As for the Liberal Party of the day, it had begun to democratize its provincial structures under the influence of Georges-Émile Lapalme and Jean-Louis

Gagnon, but the process was turning out to be very slow. Let's just say that the Quebec Liberal Party took a long time to shed the bad habits it had developed during its lengthy tenure in power.

There was also the CCF party, which was to become the New Democratic Party in 1961. I had a great many friends in that party, from McGill University professors Frank Scott and Michael Oliver to Eugene Forsey, Jacques Perrault, and Thérèse Casgrain, the *grande dame* of French-Canadian feminism. The party's program, similar to that of the British Labour Party, appealed to me. But initially the excessive centralism of the CCF and its ignorance of French Canada bothered me a great deal. And later, when it swung to the other extreme, the NDP's support for the "two nations" doctrine made me give up on it for good.

Like a number of my contemporaries, I therefore had to fall back on non-partisan action in organizations such as the Rassemblement, founded in September 1956. This fragile and short-lived body undertook to defend and promote democracy in Quebec against the threats posed by corruption and authoritarianism. There was also a later initiative, the Union des forces démocratiques, which I founded. Its aim was to create an effective coalition in time for the 1960 provincial election. We wanted to unite all the opposition parties around their principal shared objective: making Quebec a genuine democracy, and getting rid of the government machinations that were endangering people's freedom. Since the padlock law, the Roncarelli affair, and several punitive retroactive laws, no one could doubt that civil liberties were threatened in Quebec. And so it was a matter of having all the defenders of these liberties put aside their differences and unite to bring down the government.

Did these actions have the intended effect? It's difficult to say, because the death of Le Chef in September 1959 was to put an end to the abuses of the Union Nationale a few months later when it fell from power. Virtually without any transition, we entered the period of the Quiet Revolution. When the Liberals under Jean Lesage came to power in June 1960, the political situation took an entirely new and very positive turn, at least for the first two years. I was one of the very first beneficiaries of this change because, with Duplessis gone, the Université de Montréal offered me a position as head of an institute for public law. I declined this post, but accepted a chair as professor of public law in the law faculty to which this institute was attached. My old dream of being a teacher finally came true – twelve years late! But the joys of the Quiet Revolution weren't all so self-centred. For all of us who had fought for ten years for the modernization of Quebec, it was no small satisfaction to be governed at last by a young, competent, dynamic team urgently determined to move the clock forward and put Quebec onto the same time as the rest of the Western world.

During this period, I had a privileged vantage point on Quebec politics, thanks to a series of twice-monthly meetings. In the autumn of 1961, René Lévesque, the former Radio-Canada broadcaster who had been a minister for a year in the Lesage government, asked my friend Pelletier to bring together at his home a few Montreal friends: André Laurendeau, Jean Marchand (who lived in Quebec City but worked most of the time in Montreal), and myself. Over the next two winters, we would meet like this quite regularly and spend hours on end vigorously discussing all the issues confronting the world in general and our governments in particular. The times favoured change, pluralism,

René Lévesque (left) and Jean Marchand, two men whose lives were to have a great impact on mine, at the site of the great hydro-electric dam at Manicouagan. (NAC-TC)

tolerance, modernization. In short, politics was headed in the direction of which we had dreamed all our adult lives.

But why did this happiness have to be so short-lived? All this movement had barely started when people began hurrying to revive the old slogans. From 1962 onward, instead of becoming more open to universal values in Quebec, there was talk of nothing but being "masters in our own house." Instead of remaining committed to politics based on realism and common sense, we were plunged into the "politics of grandeur" whose main preoccupation all too often was rolling out red carpets. Were we so soon to retrace our footsteps, to once again turn inward on ourselves and on the concept of nation? Were we to leave the abusive tutelage of our Holy Mother Church and free ourselves from an atavistic vision, only to throw ourselves now under the shadow of our Holy Mother Nation? We had fought for

By contrast, here I am indoors, teaching, with chalk in hand.
(Trudeau Family)

ten years on behalf of all Quebecers: white, black, yellow, Catholic, Protestant, and agnostic; were we now to neglect all those others and devote all our attention only to old-stock Quebecers?

A province is not a nation but a mix of diverse people, differentiated by religion, culture, and mother tongue. Was it necessary to grind down all these differences and impose a dominating and intolerant ideology on all minorities? I found this change of direction aberrant. I knew that it led directly to doctrinaire separatism.

I have never denied the existence of the French-Canadian nation; nor do I deny the aboriginals led today by Ovide Mercredi the status of a nation in the sociological sense. What I rejected well before the advent of the neo-nationalism of the 1960s and still reject today is the doctrine that claims that every sociological nation must have political sovereignty and independence. If we were to promote the political independence of every sociological nation around the world, the planet would soon be torn by countless conflicts among ethnic and linguistic groups, each demanding sovereignty from the country in which it constitutes a minority.

I was also distressed by the attitude of certain students to whom I was teaching public law, young people who didn't even seem to be aware that we had barely emerged from a prolonged Great Darkness. Instead of taking advantage of being at university to open themselves up to universal values, they found nothing more pressing to do than to shrivel up intellectually with the notion of the "Quebec nation." Their approach to constitutional law could be summarized as rejecting anything that came from Ottawa and seeking only to increase the powers of Quebec. I found this moving backward very sad. I said to myself: "Here we go! It's starting all over again."

Unfortunately, the political context of the time encouraged such a turning inward, especially among the short-sighted, because there was nothing attractive about the political situation at the federal level. Starting in 1962, Ottawa offered the successive spectacles of a Diefenbaker Conservative government in full collapse and an extraordinarily accident-prone Pearson Liberal minority government. With the Conservatives, internal warfare was being waged in plain sight, with noisy resignations of Quebec and Ontario ministers. As for the Liberals, a succession of serious missteps, such as Walter Gordon's first budget, several pseudo-scandals exploited by the Opposition, and interminable debates (six months just to adopt a distinctive

*The so-called
"Three Wise Men,"
Gérard Pelletier,
Jean Marchand,
and me. In his
memoirs,
Mike, Lester
Pearson wrote:
"These were the
sort of men
I was looking
for: men of
quality and
standing in
Quebec, men
who inspired
both some
admiration and
some fear."
(NAC-TC)*

Canadian flag), all helped to create an impression of federal powerlessness at the same time as the Quebec government was pursuing its Quiet Revolution with an energy that was no doubt diminishing but was still present until its defeat in 1966. Such a contrast between the two capitals did nothing to demonstrate the benefits of federalism, to put it mildly.

It was at this point that I had my first discussions with Jean Marchand and Gérard Pelletier about what was to become the adventure of the "Three Wise Men." In 1962 Marchand, courted by both the Quebec and the federal Liberal parties, for the first time considered actively entering the political arena. In the autumn of 1962, at the time of the memorable Quebec election fought around the nationalization of electric power, he came within an inch of becoming a provincial candidate. At the last moment, for reasons too complicated to detail here, Lesage's party withdrew its invitation. But this setback in no way diminished Jean Marchand's extraordinary prestige as a champion of the people, profoundly rooted in the Quebec soil through his work as a labour leader. Emissaries of the federal Liberal Party intensified their efforts to persuade him to run federally. And he, for his part, began asking me to run with him. He did not want to leap alone into an adventure whose difficulty he clearly understood. We talked about this often and at length over the next three years, at the home of Gérard Pelletier. The two of us might have taken the plunge in the election of April 1963, had it not been for Mike Pearson's sudden about-face on the issue of nuclear weapons. Because of this unexpected stand against the strongly held convictions we had publicly expressed on a number of occasions, we refused at the time to associate ourselves with the Liberal Party.

It was only two years later, in the summer of 1965, when the Bomarc missiles had begun to rust in their underground nests, that we again considered the matter. Things had changed fast since 1963. In Quebec, sovereigntist nationalism had made striking gains in public opinion and, what was even more dangerous, Ottawa's weak federalism was being increasingly challenged even by the great majority of Quebecers who still believed in Canada. It was time for something to be done to restore the balance between the two capitals.

For all these reasons, no doubt, the Liberals were pressing Marchand harder than ever to join their ranks. Recruiting Guy Favreau as Quebec leader had not produced the anticipated results, and Jean appeared to be the saviour they were awaiting. But he refused to go it alone and insisted that the party also welcome Gérard Pelletier (who had just left *La Presse*) and me as candidates. Understandably, these latter two candidacies were of no interest to the Quebec caucus and its leaders Maurice Lamontagne, Guy Favreau, and Maurice Sauvé. Pelletier and I had on numerous occasions written scathing criticisms of the Liberals; I seem to recall one of my articles using the word "donkeys," not in a complimentary way. But Marchand was unyielding and he negotiated so well that at the beginning of September 1965, we three announced that we would run for Parliament in the November federal election under the Liberal banner.

The evening of November 8, the three of us were elected, Pelletier and I in what were called "safe" ridings, and Marchand in a Quebec City riding that he wrested from Social Credit in a fierce battle.

So here I was back in Ottawa after a fourteen-year absence, this time as a member of Parliament. It didn't take me long to realize that this new role was completely different from the one I had played as a bureaucrat. And I had to put aside the illusions I had entertained about life as an MP. Ever since I had decided to enter active politics, I had envisaged my first years in the House of Commons as an apprenticeship during which I would quietly learn my job as a representative of the people. But once I got there, my experience from the very beginning bore no resemblance to what I had imagined.

As a very new member of Parliament I expected to be given some time to learn the ropes. The prime minister, Lester Pearson, had other ideas and soon made me his parliamentary secretary. In his memoirs he described me as "a good Canadian and a good radical Liberal who had stood up to Duplessis." He went on to regret the limiting role of parliamentary secretary: "Trudeau had neither very much to do nor the opportunity to learn very much in my office. Nevertheless, I had enough contact with him to value his cool intelligence, his knowledge, and his very steady nerves." (NAC-TC/Duncan Cameron)

First of all, I almost immediately had to take on responsibilities I had not foreseen. Jean Marchand, who became a minister right off the bat after the election, told me within the first few months that Lester Pearson wanted to make me his parliamentary secretary. At first glance, this idea didn't appeal to me at all. I remember telling Marchand: "Give me time to get settled, to do my homework. You know I don't like to go into anything unprepared."

But he had an answer for everything. "We didn't come here to refuse to work, Pierre. What brought us here is that there's a job to be done, and we have to grab every opportunity to do it."

I had to admit that he was right and I accepted the position, not knowing what Mike Pearson was going to

In Paris, in April 1966, I (second from right) was a very junior member of the Canadian parliamentary delegation that was addressed by Premier Georges Pompidou. (NAC-TC)

ask me to do in that role. I vaguely expected some modest parliamentary chores and some pencil-pushing; he sent me running around the world.

First there was a stay in Paris to discuss certain questions with French parliamentarians, then an international congress of francophone jurists, then a trip to Africa to establish contacts with regard to the then-emerging idea of an international grouping of French-speaking countries, and finally a few months in New York as a member of the Canadian delegation to the United Nations General Assembly. During my first fifteen months as an MP, I wasn't around Parliament much. But I don't regret these various trips. No doubt Pearson felt I had a lot to learn about foreign policy. He was right. I knew the world at large fairly well, but I knew the world of diplomacy scarcely at all. My time at the United Nations and my visits to several African heads of state such as Léopold Senghor in Senegal, Habib Bourguiba in Tunisia, and Ahmadou Ahidjo in Cameroun were all part of a very helpful initiation for me. What's more, though I didn't know it at the time, this modest

*Addressing the
United Nations
as a member
of the Canadian
delegation in
the fall of 1966.
(NAC-TC)*

beginning of involvement in the executive work of government was intended to prepare me for appointment to the
Cabinet.

After only sixteen months as a member of Parliament
I got the call from the prime minister in April 1967; I was
to be the minister of justice. That September I presented
to Parliament a piece of legislation known as the Omnibus
Bill that attracted a certain amount of attention since it
involved a set of amendments to the Criminal Code. How
did I come to order the drafting of this bill and to present
it to Parliament? It was the most natural thing in the world.

Let me say first of all that I didn't hesitate for a second
before accepting the justice portfolio. It's a wonderful position, a powerful ministry whose decisions have considerable effect on the lives of the citizenry. What's more, this
position was right up my alley, as they say. I arrived there
feeling full of energy and said to the department's top
bureaucrats: "Right. Here I am. What needs to be done and

As justice minister I was pleased to modernize Canada's divorce laws in 1967. According to Don Jamieson, my Cabinet colleague from Newfoundland, "The enthusiasm and skill with which Trudeau chose to tackle the first of his projects as Justice Minister surprised Pearson, as it did many others."
(Canapress)

I learned a great deal from my time working with Lester Pearson, although our styles were very different. After my vigorous debate with Daniel Johnson at the 1968 federal-provincial conference, my Cabinet colleague Judy LaMarsh (who was not an admirer) wrote: "Unlike his predecessor's reputation for peace-making it was Trudeau's exercise in argumentation that led to his win." (Toronto Star)

where shall we start? What are our priorities?" They listed a number of issues that included such major ones as the constitutional problem but also some routine matters.

Then the civil servants added: "Of course, there's also the Criminal Code that needs to be brought up to date on a lot of sensitive and controversial issues such as homosexuality, firearms, abortion; there is also the divorce law, which is archaic....We need hardly tell you that several of these questions are quite delicate and politically dangerous. You know that as well as we do. You're a novice minister, so perhaps it would be better to start with a less thorny issue."

"No. I prefer to start with the most difficult one. Let's go with the Criminal Code and the divorce law."

Because of the succession of minority governments and other political problems in recent years, several of these issues had been neglected. Proposed amendments had been gathering dust for six years in the department's files. I needed first of all to persuade my Cabinet colleagues that it was appropriate to put these controversial subjects on the order paper in the Commons. Several of them objected strenuously, some for political reasons, some for moral ones. But I held my ground until finally, tired of arguing, even the opponents ended up saying: "If you want to risk destroying yourself, it's up to you." And I had carte blanche.

In mid-summer of 1967, despite all the commotion created by the Centennial celebrations, the World's Fair in Montreal, and the visit of General de Gaulle, we had in hand the final text of the two bills. Before launching the bills in the autumn, it was necessary first to prepare public opinion by drawing a very clear distinction between sin and crime. What is considered sinful in one of the great religions to which citizens belong isn't necessarily sinful in the others. Criminal law therefore cannot be based on the notion of sin; it is crimes that it must define. But I also had to make it understood that in decriminalizing a given action, the law was in no way challenging the moral beliefs of any given religion.

My bills nevertheless touched off some harsh debates in Parliament because the members, on both sides of the House, had very strong personal convictions on issues such as divorce and abortion. The same was true of homosexual practices – even between consenting adults, which was the sole focus of the amendment. Several of the other subjects we dealt with – including, for example, gun control

– interested some powerful lobbies that didn't hesitate to get involved. But public opinion, aware that the time had come to adapt the Criminal Code to the circumstances of our time and agreeing with my argument that "the state has no place in the bedrooms of the nation," supported us and the bill became law in December.

Just a few days before the bill's passage, Prime Minister Pearson announced that he intended to retire, which automatically touched off a leadership campaign within the party to choose his successor. Let me be very clear that I did not feel at all personally affected by this development. In my view, the obvious successor, if he was to be a Quebecer, was Jean Marchand. It was he who had dealt with all partisan party matters, it was he who had strong public support in Quebec and the rest of Canada, and it was his candidacy that prominent Liberals were promoting in Toronto and Montreal. The idea of running for the leadership myself never crossed my mind, not even for a split second.

It was only when Jean Marchand refused to run and pressed me to enter the race that I began to think about it. And even then, for several weeks I stubbornly resisted Marchand, Pelletier, and all the others who were pushing me. Was I playing hard to get? Not at all. Other powerful reasons were behind my refusal. First among them was concern for protecting my sacrosanct personal freedom. As justice minister, I had already discovered how much a Cabinet post monopolizes your life. I knew that in such a role, you no longer belong to yourself. And I was well aware that the position of prime minister demands even more of whoever occupies it. As well, I thought it

Four Liberal leaders – me, John Turner, Mike Pearson, and Jean Chrétien.
(Toronto Star)

inappropriate to seek the highest office after barely two years in Parliament and nine months in the Cabinet. And finally, before becoming a candidate in such a campaign, one inevitably assesses the risks.

First, running for the leadership seemed presumptuous for someone like me who had no deep roots in the Liberal Party, who barely knew the main party activists, and whose accomplishments to date were modest at best. That was certainly enough to give one pause! And even in the hypothetical event that I could win, the prospect of having to live under the constant eye of journalists as head of the government or of the Opposition didn't appeal to me at all.

But once I made up my mind, I resolved to forge ahead with all the energy at my disposal and never look back. On Friday, February 16, 1968, I announced my candidacy at the National Press Club.

In answering reporters who asked about my political goals if I became prime minister, I tried to express simple and widely understandable ideas, because I knew that if I became the leader those ideas would be the party platform

The leadership convention, Ottawa, April 6, 1968

In my box at the convention pretending nonchalance with the aid of a carnation, not a rose.

Mitchell Sharp (left) threw his support behind me before the start of the convention.

Addressing the convention as a candidate.

(NAC-TC)

Victory. The new leader of the Liberal Party and prime minister of Canada. Pearson wrote of this time: "The Trudeau campaign completely bewildered the old pros like Paul Martin, who could not understand the secret of its success. As Paul said to me: 'How can someone who knows nothing of politics or the party get so much support so suddenly, even from people like Joe Smallwood?' The answer was simple. Canadians thought of Paul Martin, or even of Paul Hellyer, in the context of Mackenzie King. They thought of Pierre Trudeau as a man for this season, uncontaminated and uninhibited." (NAC-TC)

in the general election that would follow. And so I based my campaign on the central theme of the Just Society. Achieving such a society would require promoting equality of opportunity and giving the most help to those who were the most disadvantaged. Social security and equalization payments, as well as a ministry of regional economic expansion, would give practical effect to these abstract principles. As well, I announced what we would do to redress the federal Canadian state's traditional injustice towards French, the mother tongue of 27 per cent of the

Canadian population. And when I was asked whether it was true that I wanted to "put Quebec in its place," I replied: "Yes. Absolutely. And its place is within Canada, with all the advantages and all the influence to which our province is entitled. There can be no question of Quebec standing apart or falling behind."

Once I had made this announcement, I found myself plunged into an indescribable whirlwind of activity: meetings, speeches, interviews, TV appearances, press conferences, and trips from east to west and north to south took up all of my days and part of my nights. The object was to make personal contact with as many as possible of the roughly 3,000 delegates who would vote at the convention on April 6. Those were intense weeks, a preview of the five election campaigns I was to experience between 1968 and 1984. I had stuck my finger into the machinery; I was caught in it for a long time.

The party's convention was held in Ottawa. After a lot of speeches, a lot of hoopla, a lot of cheering, a lot of applause – and three ballots – the majority of the delegates entrusted me with their confidence. I thus became leader of the Liberal Party and, because the party was in power and Pearson was resigning, prime minister of Canada.

PART 2

1968 – 1974
POWER AND
RESPONSIBILITY

After the leadership convention, Jean Marchand and I took off together for a two-week rest in sunnier climes. Then it was back to Ottawa to take up my duties as prime minister. The month of April drew to a close. The House went back to work.

I was also taking up residence at 24 Sussex Drive, the first time I would ever live in a house of my own. Until then, I had generally stayed at my mother's house when I was in Montreal. I had an office on Rue St-Denis, which also served as a kind of bachelor's digs. And then, shortly after I began teaching law, I had rented a tiny apartment on Sherbrooke Street, which allowed me to get to know downtown Montreal better. On the road, I had always stayed in students' quarters, at youth hostels, or at a YMCA. When I returned from my trip around the world, I stayed in various hotels throughout Quebec, at least during my

I was obviously happy to be in the seat of power in the Prime Minister's Office on April 22, 1968. But I was aware of what Lester Pearson in his memoirs called "a bitter reaction in the camps of some of the other candidates." After the celebrating, it was time to mend fences. (Canapress)

union activities, and when I became a member of Parliament and later a Cabinet minister, I stayed at the Château Laurier in Ottawa.

But from now on, for the unforeseeable future, I would be living at 24 Sussex Drive, in Canada's capital. The reason that the Canadian prime minister's residence isn't as well known as the Hôtel Matignon in Paris, or Number 10 Downing Street in London, not to mention the Élysée or the White House, is that it has only recently acquired its status as an official residence: 24 Sussex wasn't made available to the head of the government until 1955. It's a spacious and comfortable upper-middle-class house, admirably situated at the top of a cliff overlooking the Ottawa River. From the gardens that surround the house, the view takes in the river's Quebec side and, in the distance, the forests of Gatineau Park. My neighbour to the west was the French ambassador, and to the south, across Sussex Drive, are the immense grounds of Rideau Hall, the Governor General's residence. I arrived in early spring, suitcase in hand, with the federal elections coming up, not knowing whether I would be staying for a few weeks or a few months, or whether to take a more optimistic view and plan on being there for a few years. As it turned out, my lease at 24 Sussex would not expire for another sixteen years, except for what I might call a brief respite of nine months in 1979–80.

That spring, however, I had no time to admire the view nor to speculate about my own future, because I was immediately faced with two enormous challenges. The first had to do with the party of which I was now the leader. The election of a new leader and the campaigning that precedes it can have a fatally divisive effect on a party. Candidates who enter a leadership race spend a great deal of energy trying

The garden behind 24 Sussex Drive makes a perfect setting for informal receptions and parties, in this case for Liberals in September 1968.
(NAC-TC)

to win it, especially when the party in question is the party in power and becoming leader also means becoming the country's prime minister. In such a struggle, you draw not only on your personal influence but also on friendships you have acquired, and you keep going without calculating how much effort and energy you are using up. Some contenders get into extremely bitter battles: one candidate may, for example, hold positions that are diametrically opposed to those of his colleagues, or he may be the object of comments that are tough to take at the time and very difficult to forget afterwards. And a clique forms around each candidate that is opposed to other, similar cliques. The result is always friction, even splits, some of which can be very wide indeed, and can pose a grave threat to the party's overall effectiveness.

"The fact that you have won means that others have lost," I had to keep reminding myself in the days following my victory. "What state of mind will they be in now? Bitter? Spiteful? Vengeful? Discouraged? Whatever the case may be, it's up to you to pick up the pieces. If you don't, your ability to govern will be severely jeopardized." That, to me, was a particularly difficult task, because, as I have said, I had not yet had time to sink my roots deep into the Liberal Party. Some long-time Liberals felt that Marchand, Pelletier, and I had stolen "their" party from them, because we had been such merciless critics of its policies right up to the moment we had joined it. All of which made me realize that the first thing I had to do was restore party unity.

To do that, I had to establish contact with each of the other candidates, to heal wounded self-esteem and smooth over any lingering grudges and resentments as much as possible. Fortunately, a prime minister has at his disposal several effective ways of doing this. For example, when forming my first Cabinet I invited everyone who had been a candidate for the leadership to be part of it. And, except for one or two, they all accepted, which I found somewhat reassuring. If they were willing to be on my team, it showed that they at least intended to work with me rather than against me.

These problems arose in my relations with individuals, but similar questions came up with regard to the regions. The West considered me an Easterner, and the Atlantic provinces saw me as representing central Canada. The danger facing me on this front was that I would be cut off from the provinces that had provided candidates for the leadership. That's why I concentrated immediately on setting up "regional desks" in the Prime Minister's Office, whose job was to ensure that we did not lose touch with any part of the country.

The newspapers of the time took great pleasure in reporting how greatly I was extending the functions of the Prime Minister's Office, and I never denied the fact that I was increasing them considerably, compared with what they had been under my predecessors. And I don't apologize for it now, because at the time I was responding to entirely new circumstances. For instance, during Mr. Pearson's time, fifteen people were enough to look after his correspondence. When I came on the scene, the volume of mail increased fourfold. Perhaps that was the price to be paid for having preached participatory democracy, I don't know, but it meant that I had to respond to such uncontrollable situations by multiplying my staff by a similar ratio: I soon had about sixty people on the job. It may not be entirely out of place to note here that, at the time, the very same growth was taking place in prime ministers' offices wherever the British parliamentary system was in place, including (in her day) that of the very conservative and tra-ditional-minded Margaret Thatcher.

Throughout my mandate, I made a point of religiously attending our weekly Liberal caucus meetings. To my mind, these gatherings each Wednesday morning of all the MPs and senators that made up our parliamentary group were particularly important. It was there that all the caucus members would openly discuss matters of the day. In 1968, I saw in these meetings a way of deepening my rela-tionship with a party whose inner workings I did not know all that well. I am told that my predecessors often stayed away from caucus meetings, but I felt I needed to attend them without fail each week. Whatever reports may have come out of these get-togethers, nothing very sinister took place in them. We were among ourselves, with no public servants or advisers present. Caucus members could talk about anything that concerned them with complete can-dour. Proposals that senators or MPs could not make in public could be brought up there, in private. Harsh criti-cisms of the party and its government, of such-and-such a minister, or of certain Cabinet decisions could be aired. At these meetings, the prime minister could also report on decisions of the Cabinet and announce any new govern-ment initiatives, and he could gather reactions and sugges-tions from all members. First he would listen quietly as MPs and senators had their say, and only at the end would he respond, in an off-the-cuff speech, voicing his conclusions aloud. I have always respected that tradition. I made only one change. When my predecessors were in office, the prime minister would appoint a member to preside over the caucus meetings; I had the caucus itself elect a president, and I worked with whoever the senators and MPs had selected to represent them.

The second challenge was even greater. It was to encourage the general population to elect more Liberals. In my speech at the April convention I had promised that we would try to win a majority of the seats in every region, and put an end to the series of minority governments that had plagued Parliament since 1962. To this end, it was necessary to call a general election. But when? The mandate obtained by our party in 1965 would normally end in eighteen months. Should I first establish my credentials as a prime minister and government leader during the upcoming year? Or should I, on the contrary, strike while the iron was hot, and take our chances with the electorate right away while the leadership convention, with all the publicity that surrounded it, was still in the voters' minds?

If I took the former approach, I would be giving the electorate a chance to get to know me, and to judge my ability to govern the country, before letting them make their decision in a general election. But the head of a minority government never has it easy; we had all witnessed the problems confronted by Mike Pearson, a man who lacked neither experience nor talent. Should I expose myself to the erosion of a year in Parliament, with an Opposition that wouldn't hesitate to profit from any sign of weakness in myself or the party? Wouldn't it be better to face both challenges at once, to restore party unity by sending to the barricades together candidates who had so recently been rivals on the convention floor, and at the same time test public opinion as early as possible to find out whether the general populace had the same confidence in me that the party had just shown? This latter option had its disadvantages; the most important one was that it would mean sending back into battle people who were still exhausted from the leadership race. What shape would they be in for the long ordeal of an election campaign?

After considering the options, and holding consultations with the caucus as well as conducting a few private surveys among certain friends and many party members, I chose the second approach. When the House reconvened on April 23, I paid a formal visit to the Governor General, Roland Michener, and asked that Parliament be dissolved. My decision had been taken: Canadians would go to the polls on June 25. When I announced the election in the Commons that same afternoon, everyone was taken by surprise, because my visit to the Governor General had gone unnoticed, despite the fact that the press had been staking out my front door as well as that of Rideau Hall for the past twenty-four hours. Knowing that, I had left my office by a hidden staircase and, at the Governor General's residence, had entered by a gate that was always closed. I couldn't have the press announcing such important news before I did.

So there I was, involved in a general election for the second time in my life, this time not as a neophyte candidate but as the one on whom all the responsibility for the result would come to rest, whether it was defeat or victory. If the former, I would have been the most short-lived prime minister in Canadian history. If the latter, I would have four years to prove myself worthy of being the head of government.

My main opponent in the 1968 general election was Robert Stanfield (left), a quiet, decent man who perhaps entered federal politics at a time when his virtues were not appreciated. (Canapress)

If I had doubts about the party's readiness for an election campaign, they proved to be misplaced. No sooner had I announced the elections than the "campaign machine" that had so fascinated me as a child was set in motion. Members of Parliament, senators, and party workers climbed back on the hustings and the campaign got off without a hitch.

I have often been asked about something that became clear to the party leadership during the elections, the phenomenon the press dubbed "Trudeaumania." People want to know whether I was aware of it and, if so, what I thought about it at the time. It is extremely difficult to evaluate a shift of opinion when you yourself are the focus of it.

Almost everywhere I went, exceptional enthusiasm was apparent in the crowds that I found around me. People came in droves to rallies where I was speaking. As well as the phalanx of party members going into the meetings, the streets would be lined with masses of people of all ages and all races. I particularly remember two astonishing turnouts, one in Victoria and another in Montreal. In the British Columbia capital, a city of peaceful, respectable folk, many of them retired, I had to be lowered from a helicopter down to a park at the top of a hill that was totally surrounded by thousands of people. "No, this is not possible," I kept saying to myself. "Can this really be Victoria?" In Montreal, where the nationalist intelligentsia was already trying to make me into "the traitor of Quebec," the huge area of Place Ville-Marie was swarming with people. According to the newspapers, there were tens of thousands of them surrounding the podium from which I was speaking. Of course I was astonished, but I had no way of knowing what kind of audiences my colleagues were drawing. Were they comparable? Was such enthusiasm being directed at all of our candidates?

The real question, of course, was whether all those people had come to hear me, personally, or were they simply there to see this newcomer, this neo-politician who had made such a splash as the head of the party in power? I was inclined to the latter view when I was delivering my campaign speeches, which may have been enthusiastic but were not exactly masterworks of the orator's art. I had to believe, too, that the phenomenon was part of the spirit of the times. We had just come out of the Centennial celebrations; the year before had seen the remarkable success of Expo 67. The mood of the country was still one of festivity, and I happened to be there to profit from

Trudeaumania

Taking the plunge. On the campaign trail, June 14, 1968.
(Canapress)

Support is always welcome, and I was very glad to get all kinds of it, from a variety of sources. These included an enthusiastic young lady, my old friend Gérard Pelletier, and a few thousand Torontonians.
(NAC-TC/Duncan Cameron)

(Globe and Mail)

it. Of course, I wasn't about to complain! I may have been a bit concerned that people were responding less to my ideas than to "the Trudeau phenomenon," as the press called it. But I was in the middle of an election campaign, and I could only rejoice that so much interest was being shown by the electorate.

As for the rest, I have never been a great admirer of my own speeches. I much prefer discussions between two people, or talking in small groups. One doesn't really discuss ideas with a crowd. That's why I particularly appreciated the hecklers who came to my rallies to raise objections to my proposals. I could respond to them one-on-one, and our dialogues made the meetings a lot more interesting. As for the more rational speeches I made in the 1972 campaign, when Trudeaumania had calmed down somewhat, I tried to impose my own style on them, to my great disadvantage – but here I am anticipating; I'll come back to this point later on in my story.

For the time being, in the spring of 1968, the campaign was rolling along nicely, although not without incident. There were a few times when I was the target of insults, and even of violence. I am thinking of the funeral of André Laurendeau, who died at about that time. The three of us – myself, Jean Marchand, and Gérard Pelletier – were leaving Montreal's Saint-Viateur church together after the service had ended. Laurendeau had been an important figure for all three of us: Pelletier had worked under him at *Le Devoir* when he was just starting out in journalism and Laurendeau was the editor; Marchand had served under him when Pearson had appointed Laurendeau co-chairman of the Royal Commission on Bilingualism and Biculturalism; and I held him in very high esteem for the advice he had given me when I began to study law. After that, he had always shown me sincere friendship, despite our differences of opinion in many areas, and I had nothing but the greatest respect for him. We had therefore been profoundly grieved to see him go, and deeply moved at his funeral. But no sooner had we crossed the Saint-Viateur courtyard than we were met by loud accusations from a few people in the front row of a crowd that had gathered in front of the church: "Traitors! Goddam traitors! Go back to Ottawa!" What can I say? I found this reaction out of place, especially in view of the fact that, the same month, Robert Kennedy had been assassinated in California.

But that was not the end of my troubles. That same night, or the next day, I was speaking in a small village in the northwest part of the province when I became the target of a small handful of demonstrators who began to shout at me, calling me names and generally disrupting the audience, which was made up of a few thousand peaceful and attentive people. The demonstrators were grouped together in a corner of the arena. After a few minutes waiting for the cacophony to die down, I noticed that many of the attentive listeners were starting to get restless, and some were moving towards the demonstrators with the obvious intention of shutting them up. In order to prevent a fight, I spoke to the demonstrators: "Be careful," I said to them. "It's people like you who provoke violence. We are here to talk peacefully. Please respect the majority, who came here to take part in a democratic process. And take care: if you keep this up, you're likely to become the victims of the very violence you're provoking!" I think that they, too, had seen the way the rest of the crowd was moving; silence was quickly restored, and I went on with my speech.

What did I talk about in the course of my campaign? For the most part I spoke about the Just Society, about equalization payments, and about the Department of Regional Economic Expansion that I was proposing to create. I talked about language rights across Canada, about equal opportunity, and about the need for the government to protect the weak and to fight abusive speculators. Was the message received? I wouldn't go so far as to say it was universally accepted, but I have no doubt that it entered at least part of the consciousness of my listeners. When, for example, I would deliver part of my speech in French, in Edmonton or in Victoria, the message went out that the rights of French-speaking citizens were not confined to those living in Quebec. And when I spoke about the Department of Regional Economic Expansion, citizens in the Atlantic provinces certainly understood that we would be attentive to their needs if they told us what those needs were. Similarly in Quebec – the second most populous province in the country – when I invited my audiences to accept fully their role within Canada, to make their province's influence felt strongly in Ottawa, they could hardly ignore the fact that I was obviously determined to affirm the Quebec fact, the French fact, within the central government. Thus, when the audience was quiet enough to allow for a dialogue to take place, I tried to state clearly what would be the practical applications of the programs we were putting forward.

Alas, it wasn't always possible to discuss or exchange ideas. The night before the elections, June 24, 1968, was also the night of Saint-Jean-Baptiste, a major celebration every year right across Quebec. In those days, the traditional parade was still part of the festivities in Montreal, and I was invited to take my place on the platform reserved for dignitaries on Sherbrooke Street, in front of the municipal library. I don't know who sent me the invitation, perhaps the festival organizers, or perhaps it was Jean Drapeau, the mayor. Whoever it was, Drapeau changed his mind that very morning and busied himself trying to convince Gérard Pelletier that I shouldn't be at the parade. The two men met at Saint Joseph's Oratory, where a patriarch of the Eastern Church was conducting that day's service, and the mayor insisted that I be kept off the platform because my presence there, he said, would "run the risk of provoking separatist demonstrations."

"If you don't want to see him," Pelletier later told me he replied, "then you shouldn't have invited him. He's not the kind of man to back away from a threat."

Before the end of the day (the parade took place after sunset), a similar approach was attempted, this time without an intermediary, and it was me who replied: "You can't be serious. If you didn't want me to come, you shouldn't have invited me. Now that I have accepted, I'm certainly not going to admit, by backing down, that the prime minister of Canada can't watch the festival of Saint-Jean in his own home town! I've been watching this parade since I was six years old."

I showed up at the designated time and took my place in the front row of seats on the platform, flanked by the archbishop of Montreal on my left and Daniel Johnson, the premier of Quebec, on my right. A film of that evening's events tells the story better than I can. I only remember that after demonstrating loudly across the street, a group of agitators, most of them members of the Rassemblement pour l'indépendance nationale (RIN), the separatist clique of the day, threaded its way through the parade and ran towards us throwing rocks, bottles, and other objects that bore not the slightest resemblance to flowers out of the dark at our heads. There was "confused movement," as later accounts would phrase it, on the platform, perhaps even the beginnings of panic, as nearly all the dignitaries rose and started to leave. The plain-clothes Mountie whose job was to ensure my personal safety tried to persuade me to do likewise, but I would not have it. I had absolutely no desire to give in to such a ridiculous display of violence. I detest violence. As a democrat, I will never accept that a small group of agitators can make someone invited by the majority take to his heels by throwing a few stones at him. Perhaps the attack was also aimed at someone other than myself, but I was clearly the preferred target.

Before moving on from this incident, I want to clear up something else. As well as a few rocks and other projectiles, certain nationalist propagandists (aided by a few journalists) have thrown up a legend according to which Quebecers hate me and I, in turn, hold the citizens of my native province in contempt. This is clearly false. If they detested me, as has been said, would they have voted for me and the candidates of my party, in later years, to the extent of giving us seventy-four of the seventy-five Quebec seats in the House of Commons? And if I despised them, would I have devoted the better part of my adult life to urging them to play a greater role in the governing of their own province and of Canada itself? In my contacts with individuals, and in my relations with audiences in Quebec, francophone as well as anglophone, I have always felt a strong current running between us. It is true that I hold the theories of the ultra-nationalists in scorn, and that they feel more or less the same way about me. But the Quebec people? Not at all.

Certain nationalists, taking upon themselves the role of spokespersons for all French-speaking Canadians, gargle out a few gratuitous statements: "Quebec" wants more autonomy, and "Quebecers" feel humiliated by the federal government. Like hell they do. These nationalists are speaking only for themselves; they are not "Quebec." And the same Quebecers to whom they attribute so much hostility towards the federal government, or towards me, have voted overwhelmingly for my party; like us, the Quebec people rejected René Lévesque's concept of sovereignty-association in the 1980 referendum. Their actions, expressed formally at the ballot box, speak much more loudly than the words of a handful of journalists, or the self-serving declarations of a few political theorists, or even the rocks thrown by a few hundred demonstrators.

The day after Saint-Jean-Baptiste, my government was returned to power, this time with a clear majority: the Liberal Party won 155 of the 264 seats in the House of Commons. The election ended the series of minority governments that had been in place since 1962, and we had been handed the reins of authority in Canada for at least the next four years.

What were we going to do with them?

First, we would review the way government itself was run. When I had been appointed to the Cabinet in 1967, I had been struck by the amateurism that reigned in the upper echelons of the federal government. Until then I had always taken for granted that the Cabinet was well organized and efficiently managed. I assumed that a well-oiled electoral machine would produce a governing body that would run with equal precision. When I became a Cabinet minister myself, however, I discovered a few astonishing things. Agendas were hastily slapped together and followed only sporadically, if at all. As a result, the Cabinet wasted an inordinate amount of time discussing insignificant topics, and then had to whisk through questions of major importance, often without arriving at any conclusions. And all too often we would eventually learn that Mr. Pearson, with a handful of our colleagues, had already decided everything for us anyway. In short, the decision-making process was often rendered frivolous because of a lack of organization. As for the House, it was a noisy bedlam, and the disorder that ruled there bothered me a great deal. To give the prime minister his due, it should be said that all this was taking place in 1967, the year of Centennial and Expo, and Mike Pearson often had to leave in the middle of Cabinet meetings to run out to the airport to welcome some visiting head of state or other, which didn't help matters.

But still, I decided to introduce a measure of order and rationality to the whole question of procedure, and I undertook this reform at the very beginning of my mandate. Having worked twenty years earlier in the Privy Council (in other words, in the office of the executive arm of the government), I knew that committees of public servants prepared the work for the ministers, and I knew how daily agendas were established and memoranda were drafted. What I hadn't suspected was how badly organized the average minister's actual workload was. I therefore spent the summer after the election putting in place a more rational (my obsession!), better organized system of procedure, both by salvaging useful elements from the existing

I worked hard to make Parliament more efficient – but not at the expense of old traditions. Here the leader of the Opposition, Robert Stanfield, and I persuade the reluctant Speaker of the House, Lucien Lamoureux, to take up his duties at the opening of Parliament on September 12, 1968. (NAC-TC)

system and by introducing new methods better adapted to the work of the Cabinet. This job was made easier by two facts: Centennial year was over, and we had a comfortable majority in the House of Commons.

The reforms applied primarily to procedures affecting the decision-making process of the Cabinet. I began by making it clear to the ministers that the Cabinet could not consider a single question without having before it a formal memorandum drawn up on the authority of the minister responsible and signed by him or her. This document had to present a clear statement of the question, as well as a run-through of all possible solutions to it, including the one favoured by the signing minister after a careful analysis of the advantages and disadvantages of all of them. I recalled that in several departments (human nature being what it is), senior public servants would suggest to their minister the solution most favoured by themselves, and the minister would tend to adopt that solution without giving it much thought, since it had, as it were, been presented to him or her on a silver platter. I therefore took pains to involve the politicians more fully in the choice of proposed measures, because they, being elected, were better acquainted with the needs and aspirations of their constituents, and would generally be more sensitive to them. Finally, the memorandum in question had to take into account the consultations between the minister and the caucus, and had to propose the best means of making the public aware of the ins and outs of the decision that was made.

The memorandum had several advantages. First, it allowed me to get to know my ministers better, to assess their grasp of the portfolios they were handling, how well they could summarize and resolve a given problem, and the political thinking that inspired each of them. For the Cabinet members, it made the practice of ministerial solidarity much easier. This is the fundamental discipline for the coherence of any government: *all* ministers must be responsible for *all* decisions made by the government of which they are a part. Take the budget, for example: if a

A photograph from the days when it was possible to run the country with a Cabinet that could all sit around the Cabinet table.
(NAC-TC)

minister could declare himself in agreement with the reductions in taxes in a given budget, but at the same time dissociate himself from all of the tax increases, all hell would break loose. Each Cabinet member must share the collective responsibility for all decisions, not just the ones that affect the particular department of which he or she is in charge. And this solidarity necessitates a deep familiarity with the reasoning behind each decision, so that that decision can be effectively defended, either during an election campaign or on any other occasion when a minister is called upon to speak.

I am well aware that certain ministers – used to the previous system where ministers were left alone to run their own departments, often feuding with other ministers like medieval barons fighting for territory – regarded this process as a deplorable waste of time, or as an interesting but politically useless intellectual exercise. And it is true that preparing and reading these memos required many extra hours of work. But it also allowed us to address the major questions of the day in a rational manner, and it vastly improved the quality of the decisions taken by the government.

Another advantage of these reforms was felt in the area of ministerial committees. Several such committees already existed, but we had to form many new ones, and we conferred on all of them a level of authority they had never had before. There were eight groups in all, each comprising eight ministers, and each group was assigned to deal with specific questions pertaining to a particular field. No matter what the field was – Native affairs, culture and communications, external affairs, agriculture, social affairs, and so on – the subject would be referred to a specific ministerial committee that was already set up to deal with it. The frequency with which the committees met was determined by the number of questions that came before the Cabinet in each area. Each ministerial committee had at its disposal a public servant from the Privy Council Office. As well, ministers presenting their memoranda in committee could do so accompanied by their public servants. The committee would study the memo thoroughly and decide which measures to take. These decisions were communicated to the rest of the Cabinet, and if no objections were raised, the committee decisions were ratified at the next Cabinet meeting. The Cabinet would not discuss the question again unless a minister declared himself or herself to be in disagreement with the measures proposed by the committee.

Although these reforms may have added to the personal workload of each minister, the new, more active ministerial committees reduced the workload of the Cabinet. According to the reports of various ministers of the time, John Diefenbaker's Cabinet, for example, had to meet several times each week, very often at night, sometimes even on Sunday. During my several mandates, the Cabinet never met more than once a week, on Thursdays, and, except on very rare occasions, never sat longer than four hours.

This new system was not perfect, by any means, but it greatly improved the effectiveness of the Cabinet, and the quality of its decisions. I wouldn't say that that was true for every practice introduced by me. For example, we may have gone a bit overboard at times with certain new managerial methods, much in vogue at the time, especially among systems engineers – such as ergonomics, the use of mathematical modelling, new ideas in the management of large enterprises, and so on – the efficiency of which often turned out to be somewhat short-lived. But I do not include in that list the systematic improvements we made in the domain of public spending.

One example comes to mind. In the last months of his mandate, Mr. Pearson had the House pass the health insurance bill, but he refrained from having it proclaimed law because no one had any idea what its financial consequences would be. Now, during the election campaign, I had made two specific commitments: the proclamation of that act and, in a completely different area, the application of a tax on capital gains. But before proclaiming the health insurance act, I had to know what strain it would place on the federal budget, and not only for that year but for the next several years to come. I didn't want the minister of finance coming to us three or four years down the line and telling us that we could no longer afford to pay for health insurance. In such matters, a government cannot simply beat a retreat at the expense of the population. As a result of my questions, I found that no long-term provisional spending calculations were being done in Ottawa at the time. I therefore imposed them on all similar governmental programs, such as old age pensions, the financing of post-secondary education, and so on. I have never pretended to be a born administrator, nor to have acquired vast and arcane knowledge in this field. But a problem of such magnitude could not be left unattended, even by me.

I should add that the work methods in the House of Commons also needed to be overhauled and brought up to date. Six years of minority governments and their consequent instability had served to emphasize the weaknesses in our parliamentary procedures. No better example need be mentioned than the famous debate over the adoption of the Canadian flag that paralyzed Parliament for six full months. But that wasn't the only example. Bills that ought not to have taken up more than three or four days of the House's time dragged on for weeks and weeks, without any discernible advantage for anyone. In those days, the legislative assemblies of the larger provinces, such as Quebec and Ontario, were displaying more efficiency and achieving better results than were the federal institutions. It was our own Parliament in Ottawa that was dragging its heels; something had to be done to bring it up to speed, and it had to be done soon. We therefore introduced several procedural changes. For example, rather than have the House immobilized for days and weeks on end in the examination of every bill, article by article, right down to the last comma, the text could be referred to a parliamentary committee after the second reading. The committee could then study the bill at greater leisure and in greater depth without tying up the plenary session, which could then go on to address other issues.

The Conservative Opposition always went out of its way to portray me to the public as a prime minister who disdained Parliament and had no respect for the elected representatives of the people. To this end, they usually employed a remark that escaped from my lips in the course of a parliamentary debate. I said of a group of Conservative MPs who were refusing to adjourn on the eve of some holiday or other, "When they get home, when they get out of Parliament, when they are fifty yards from Parliament Hill, they are no longer Honourable Members – they are just nobodies, Mr. Speaker."

And to be honest, I was not all that impressed by the atmosphere in the House. I had put myself up for election in order to be able to discuss seriously the business of the state, and here I found myself interminably embroiled in shouting matches in which insults were hurled at anyone and everyone, and where precious hours were squandered deliberating over minor details at the expense of much more important questions. I certainly did not have a great deal of respect for MPs who believed that truth lodged with whoever had the loudest voice.

But if the critics considered the broad spectrum of improvements that I brought to parliamentary practice, instead of squabbling over isolated comments, they would have to admit that Canada's Parliament owes to my government some extremely beneficial reforms. The MPs I was accused of despising realized, over the course of my time in

Three grand old men of Parliament. On the left is Stanley Knowles (who always regretted that the NDP had failed to persuade me to join its ranks), with former Conservative prime minister John Diefenbaker in the centre and the NDP's David Lewis somewhat uncharacteristically on the right. Neither Diefenbaker, who worried about my profanity, nor Lewis, who felt that I lacked respect for the underdog, was an enthusiastic supporter. (NAC-TC)

office, an enormous improvement in their working conditions. Rather than being doubled up two to an office, which they also had to share with their secretaries, they were each given separate offices in which they could hold private discussions with their visitors. They were accorded substantial budgets with which to open offices and hire staff in their ridings, and to travel across the country to keep in touch with their constituencies.

Better still, the Opposition parties were granted research budgets out of public funds. This was a matter not simply of placating the Opposition, but, on the contrary, of making them more effective, so that the best interests of the people could be served. As I have already said, I believe that the existence of a strong counterbalancing force, a better political equilibrium, is an essential check against the abuse of power. I therefore insisted that the Opposition parties have at their disposal the means to mount an effective critique. In a parliamentary democracy, the government enjoys an enormous advantage: it has the public service, which provides it with competent and experienced advisers. It is therefore necessary to allow the Opposition a similar advantage. And that is what we did, so that our bills could be gone over with a fine-toothed comb, and any errors that may have crept into them, any shortcomings that may have weakened them, could be removed. Eventually, every member of the House was able to engage the services of a research assistant. Democracy demands that elected members be able to realize fully the role for which they have been chosen.

At the same time, we set about reforming the Elections Act from top to bottom. Before entering Parliament, neither my friends nor I had been sparing in our criticisms of the electoral process. We had often denounced the secrecy that surrounded each party's campaign funding, and the hidden role played by outside moneyed interests. When we came to power, we felt it incumbent upon us to take action, not only for the sake of our own internal logic, but more importantly to clean up the process by which universal suffrage is practised in federal politics. That's why I introduced a bill that permitted ordinary people who contributed to a party's campaign fund to deduct those contributions from their taxable incomes, and also obliged the party to make public its more sizeable donations from larger sponsors. The first measure was aimed at promoting participatory democracy; in the same way that by issuing tax receipts the state encouraged citizens to be more charitable, we wanted to use a similar method to stimulate their participation in the proper functioning of democracy. As for the second measure, its objective was to prevent any party from shielding the identities of its major contributors, thus rendering it less likely to bend its policies in the sponsors' favour if it became the party in power.

At the same time, we corrected certain other anomalies in the act, such as the prohibition against identifying candidates by their party affiliations on the ballots. This prohibition stemmed from an ancient theory that ignored the very existence of political parties. In practical terms, it allowed certain abuses, such as the listing of bogus candidates, or of candidates with similar-sounding names as legitimate candidates for the purpose of sowing confusion and possibly splitting the vote.

As can be seen, my supposed contempt for members of Parliament and for parliamentary life in general manifested itself in some very curious ways. Briefly, I think it can be said that I helped turn the Canadian Cabinet and Parliament into modern and effective governing tools.

Another subject demanded my attention at the beginning of my mandate, and that was the status of the French language within federal institutions. I had been aware of this problem for a long time. Earlier on, along with all my contemporaries in Quebec, I had been encouraged during my high school years to campaign for, successively, bilingual postage stamps, bilingual money, bilingual cheques, and other "table scraps," to borrow the phrase used by André Laurendeau in an editorial in *Le Devoir*, which shows just how complete was the contempt in which the federal authorities of that period held the language spoken by one-third of the Canadian population. And fifteen years later, in 1949, when I began working in the Privy Council Office, the situation was very nearly the same: before each federal election, a few "table scraps" were tossed to francophones. But to indicate just how thoroughly unilingual Ottawa was at that time, I can think of no better anecdote than one connected with the office of the prime minister, Louis St. Laurent. After he had been in office for some years, it was decided to stick a plaque on his door with the inscription in French: *Bureau du premier ministre.* Until then, the PMO had been identified only in English. Other public servants would come up to us and say: "Did you see that sign? Now it's in French, too!" How revolutionary! But English was still the only working language: a francophone public servant wishing to send a memo to another francophone public servant had to write that memo in English. French did not exactly enjoy the freedom of the city.

Unilingualism in Ottawa was not confined to the Hill; everywhere in the city it was English Only. If you wanted to speak French, you could go to Hull. Not that that was such a hardship for us young public servants, since all the best restaurants were on the Quebec side of the river.... But it didn't make things any more tolerable. Another fifteen years passed before I returned to Ottawa, this time as a member of Parliament. Had the situation changed? Hardly at all. A few more table scraps had been "conceded" to francophones: Mr. Diefenbaker had installed a simultaneous translation service in the House, for example, so that

Naturally, while we organized our internal systems, we continued to act as a government, at home and abroad. In spring 1969, when the White House held a reception for me they also invited the Canadian-bred singer Robert Goulet. Here he entertains a distinguished group including President Richard Nixon, myself, Defense Secretary Melvin Laird, and Vice-President and Mrs. Spiro Agnew. (NAC-TC)

members could follow debates in one or the other language, and Créditistes from Quebec, when they got to Ottawa, had managed to have the menu in the parliamentary cafeteria translated into French. But the situation in general remained unchanged. Even the parliamentary commissionaires were unable to reply to questions from visitors if they were addressed in French. The language of French Canadians was not being accorded equal treatment, a situation that could not be tolerated for long in the Just Society of which I dreamed.

With President and Mrs. Nixon and Don Jamieson in 1969 at the tenth anniversary of the opening of the St. Lawrence Seaway. New York State Governor Nelson Rockefeller is hidden behind me.
(Graetz Bros. Ltd.)

For one thing, such a situation created serious political problems. In Quebec, opposition to the Duplessis regime and the Quiet Revolution had changed many things; Quebecers were making great progress in the areas of self-respect and their cultural heritage. In Montreal, it was no longer acceptable to be told by a waiter in a restaurant, or a clerk in a department store, or an employee in some office: "Sorry, I don't speak French." We had tolerated such

I was pleased to receive John Lennon (a member of the Beatles) and his wife, Yoko Ono, in Ottawa in December 1969. He was kind enough to say afterwards: "If all politicians were like Mr. Trudeau, there would be world peace." I must say that "Give Peace a Chance" has always seemed to me to be sensible advice. (NAC-TC/Duncan Cameron)

things, in my view wrongly, for a long time, and the mood was changing. In government, things had changed significantly. Until 1960, bright young Quebecers wanting a serious career in the public sector had no other choice but to go to work for the federal government, because the Quebec civil service during the time of the Union Nationale was still a three-headed monster of patronage, incompetence, and menial wages. By 1965, that era was ended. Now it was Quebec that drew the best and brightest, since it was there that the most interesting changes were taking place. Also, some of the most brilliant young Quebecers already in the federal public service were being recruited by the provincial government, and the exodus back from Ottawa was decimating an already enfeebled francophone presence in the nation's capital. Could anyone blame Robert Bourassa, Jacques Parizeau, Michel Bélanger, and so many others for wanting to work in French?

We were thus in an emergency, as far as language was concerned, and the need to find a remedy played an important role for Marchand, Pelletier, and me in our decision to enter politics. I needed to apply myself immediately to the task of building up French in the institutions of the central government. But where to start? I already had an idea; all I had to do was put it into effect.

Within weeks of the federal election, I formed a work group that was to draw up, following the general outlines provided by me, a text that would eventually become the Official Languages Act, and would produce a veritable revolution within the federal public service in Ottawa. This act proclaimed first of all that Canada recognized two official

Davidson Dunton (left) and André Laurendeau did fine work in the 1960s on the Royal Commission on Bilingualism and Biculturalism in Canada.
(Canapress)

*Greeting Prime Minister Harold Wilson of Britain on a cold January day in
Ottawa, 1970. In his book* The Labour Government: 1966–1970, *Wilson
wrote kindly of me, noting that at my first Commonwealth Conference in
1969 I spoke "with an elegance of language and a willingness to understand
the African point of view which won for him a freshman's laurels." He notes,
correctly, that before the conference I was dubious about its value but by the
end I was "a committed Commonwealth statesman." Of our discussions in
Ottawa in 1970 he wrote: "It was interesting and instructive to note the
strength of Pierre Trudeau's feelings about ecological questions."* (Canapress)

languages within its borders, French and English, and that
the two languages were equal before the law. It also established the principle that every Canadian citizen had the
right to communicate with federal authorities, institutions,
and agencies in the official language of his or her choice.
The act also stipulated that both official languages be recognized and employed as working languages within the
federal government and its agencies. The aim of these
reforms was simple enough to grasp, but it postulated an
order of things that was in stark contrast to the way they
had been in the past.

I don't think I was under any illusions about the obstacles we would encounter in the promulgation and
application of this act. I was perfectly well aware that it
would upset a lot of people, not only those in the public
service, where unilingual anglophones occupied the vast
majority of important positions, but also in Canada as a
whole; Canadians still harboured many prejudices in
matters of language.

To calm the fears of unilingual public servants, I speci-
fied an adjustment period long enough that no one would
be immediately threatened. Existing rights would be protected. We undertook not to fire anyone on linguistic
grounds; it was at the bottom of the ladder that we wanted
to require a working knowledge of both official languages,
among the young candidates for jobs in the public sector.
For public servants already in place, however, we offered
free language courses to anyone whose job required knowledge of the other official language. It was never our intention, as some have maintained, to hand every fully bilingual
employee in the public service a senior position on a silver
platter. As for public opinion, I counted on members of

Parliament to explain the ins and outs of the law to their constituents, and to communicate not only the urgent necessity of preserving national unity but also the concept of complete equality.

Despite all these precautions, I was expecting resistance from certain quarters; you don't overturn the habits of a lifetime without drawing some hostile fire. But I never thought that the opposition from the anglophone community would be so shrill and so stubborn, nor that the ultranationalists within the francophone community would seize the opportunity to brandish the tomahawk rather than bury it. But of course, that is exactly what happened.

In the House of Commons, the bill occasioned some serious debate, but there was none of the emotional and strident opposition to it that had characterized the debate over the Canadian flag. The majority of the Official Opposition, led by Robert Stanfield, voted with the government. Only a handful of Conservative members – twenty or so – and two or three NDPers refused their support. The principle of *institutional* bilingualism (and I insist on that qualification) seemed firmly established.

But no sooner was the act in force than a group of anglophone journalists, a noisy bunch of provincial politicians, and a great many ordinary citizens following in their wake began to rage against its effects. They did not attack the principle of institutional bilingualism, and they did not criticize the text of the act itself (which was, in any case, unassailable). It was not "politically correct" to question whether the government actually had the right to accord the same, equitable treatment to the two major language groups in the country. So it was always the "wrong application" of bilingualism that was attacked. Objectives were attributed to us that we had never set out to achieve, the very sense of our policies was twisted out of recognizable shape, and straw men were set up and then massacred with great enthusiasm.

First, they stated that we wanted to "force French down the throat of every farmer in western Canada." Then they said we had some kind of "hidden agenda" to turn Canada into an entirely French country ("Bilingual today, unilingually French tomorrow!"). I am, of course, citing only a few of the major objections raised by the opponents of our policy; to go through them all would take up a whole volume. Even respectable daily newspapers in western Canada predicted that, given time, all the senior positions in major corporations as well as in the government would be filled only by those able to communicate in both official languages. And in support of this apocalyptic prophecy, they pointed out that bilingualism was like pregnancy, and that a country could no more be half bilingual than a woman could be half pregnant. After a quarter of a century, we can smile at the alarmism that gave rise to such predictions – "unilingually French tomorrow!" However, that opposition to the policy we set in motion in 1968 has not died down yet.

By way of making excuses for the anglophone extremists who accused us of intolerance, if not of cultural racism, moderate anglophone Canada continues to believe that "the government did not explain its official languages policy very well." After twenty-five years of discussions, countless interviews, dozens of debates, and hundreds of official statements, this excuse must appear somewhat lame, not to say grotesque. What about the tens of thousands of anglophones who have gathered together under the banner of

Canadian Parents for French, voting, as it were, with their children's feet? As often happens, ordinary people caught on much faster than journalists and politicians. Opponents can no longer hide the fact that, in fighting our policy, they are opposed to the idea that francophone Canadians should be able to communicate in their own language with the federal government and its agencies, as their anglophone fellow citizens have been doing since 1867.

As for opposition from the Quebec secessionists, reasons for it fairly leap to mind. In effect, the language question has always been their best weapon for discrediting Canadian federalism. In the early 1960s, the interim report of the Laurendeau-Dunton commission identified the language situation as the major source of discontent among francophones in the country, and discontent is exactly what the separatists have shamelessly exploited in order to advance their cause. It was therefore quite right for them to become worried when we began correcting the language situation in federal institutions. And of course they, too, were not above distorting our policy in order to make it an easier target. They thundered from the start against the Utopian aspects of our attempt "to make the population of a whole country bilingual." They knew full well, of course, that that was never our objective, but ridiculing Utopia was a lot easier and ran fewer risks than discrediting measures aimed at strengthening Canadian unity in the service of justice and equality.

Needless to say, I had many other reforms in mind at the time, but in 1970, a major crisis presented itself that complicated our lives for many months. I am referring, of course, to the October Crisis, or the crisis of the FLQ.

A job for all seasons

In the Arctic in March 1970 I was able to try my hand at igloo-building and coping with huskies – and also at traditional Inuit drumming.
(Canapress/Peter Bregg)

The American singer and actress Barbra Streisand was my guest at the National Arts Centre in Ottawa in January 1970.
(Canapress)

Surfing off the west coast of Vancouver Island in the Pacific breakers is a good way to clear your head of parliamentary wrangles – but autograph hounds will seek you out anywhere!
(Canapress)

James Cross (left), a British diplomat stationed in Montreal, was kidnapped by the FLQ, a Quebec terrorist group. Pierre Laporte, a member of the Quebec Cabinet, was kidnapped and later murdered.
(Canapress)

We were severely criticized at the time for not having anticipated this highly unforeseeable series of events. To govern is to foresee, we were reminded, and we had failed to see the storm on the horizon, which ought to have been easy to forecast after seven years of terrorist assaults in Montreal and Ottawa. Today, the same critics reproach us for exactly the opposite reason, for sending in federal forces to search for information about illegal activities, thus inciting violent reactions from within the separatist movement and some other political parties. Thanks to the Freedom of Information Act introduced and adopted by my government, however, I have recently obtained a copy of a memorandum in which my exhortations to the police are preserved.

In fact, in December 1969, nearly a year before the October Crisis, a Cabinet committee – one of the new committees – was deliberating over problems of public security in general, and those raised by the FLQ in particular. Among other things, I said to those responsible at the RCMP that I was counting on them to "gather information on the sources of financing for the separatist movement in Quebec, on separatist influence within the government of Quebec, the public service, political parties, universities, unions and professions, and on the political troubles in Quebec." It seems to me quite clear, upon reading that quotation, that I had two things in mind: certainly the activities of terrorists and other advocates of violence who, since 1963, had been increasing their assaults; but I was also thinking that it was important that the higher levels of the RCMP become better educated about the very nature of separatism, about the circumstances that gave rise to a movement the goal of which was the dissolution of Canada, either through the democratic process or by means of violence and terrorism. Until that time, the RCMP seemed to believe that Canadian unity could be threatened only by outside ideologies: fascism, communism, Trotskyism, Maoism, or anarchy under any of its known forms. It was necessary to make them understand that violent separatists could come from and find support in good, middle-class Quebec, and that they must not hesitate to pursue their inquiries within that milieu.

Of course, there was no question of encouraging the police to make inquiries into legitimate democratic opposition parties as such, and even less of encouraging them to resort to illegal methods. When I spoke to them of "political troubles in Quebec," I had in mind such things as the bombing incidents, of which there had been more than sixty at the time, and which could easily have resulted in the deaths of many people. I was also thinking about the theft of weapons and dynamite, which had been on the increase, and a number of armed robberies (responsibility for which had been claimed by the FLQ) of banks, credit unions, and gunsmith's shops – and all of these crimes, it seemed, had been perpetrated to promote the cause of Quebec independence. It would have been wrong for us to ignore the problem when we were faced with a movement that was growing so rapidly that there were more bombing incidents in one year – 1969 – than there had been in the five previous years combined. The stated objective of the terrorists was the violent destruction of the Canadian federation – the disruption, through criminal activity, of a country whose population had conferred political responsibility on us.

I had been fighting separatist ideology for years without once considering asking the police for assistance. As long as the secessionists limited themselves to democratic methods to promote Quebec's withdrawal from the country, there was never any question of putting the police on their trail. But the moment they resorted to using bombs, or theft, or assassination attempts, we were no longer dealing with democratic opposition, and it became our duty to hunt them down, or at least to identify them, so that we could put an end to their criminal activities. At the time, not only were they increasing their own illegal pursuits, they were also encouraging others to do the same. The FLQ was inciting militants to infiltrate the Parti Québécois and other peaceful political organizations, as well as the public service and the provincial government. How successful their campaign had been we could not be sure, but we had to find out, using every means the law put at our disposal, who it was who was promoting violence. When supposedly serious journalists termed our inquiries a "witch hunt," they were merely demonstrating either incompetence or else their own bad faith – if not both. In fact, as every janitor knows, it is the duty of any democracy to protect itself against the forces of dissolution as soon as they raise their heads.

Under common law, the mandate of the RCMP is to ensure the safety of Canada. They had been doing that until then by remaining informed about the comings and goings of Maoists and Trotskyites. Suddenly, they had to realize that even the most detailed knowledge of the extreme left would tell them nothing about the FLQ, or about the other agitators who, at that moment, were at large in the city of Montreal. There had been the demonstration by a group known as "French McGill," which had degenerated into a brawl; there was a call for "taxi liberation"; there were the riots incited by the Murray Hill affair when a strike at the bus company of that name turned ugly and violent; and finally the Montreal police strike, which took place a few weeks before the committee meeting I referred to above. This strike also turned into a riot: department stores on St. Catherine Street were looted, and the Quebec government had to ask for the intervention of the Canadian army to protect City Hall.

It was in such a climate that I made my pronouncement. When certain police officers concluded from my words that they had to spy on every activity of the Parti Québécois, they were mistaken. The Mounties had the right, and even the duty, to keep track of anyone they suspected of treason, even if such suspects were members of a democratic party. But they ought not to have targeted the party as a whole. As soon as I learned about any case of abusive surveillance, I demanded that it be stopped. I even brought that order to the attention of Parliament, as a reading of Hansard will attest.

That being said, I have to confess that we were

completely stunned by the kidnapping in Montreal of the British diplomat James Cross, and his detention as a hostage by a cell of the FLQ. Nothing like it had ever happened in Canadian history, and the sheer senselessness of it caught us off guard, which meant that we were badly equipped to deal with it. The action of the terrorists, and the threat they made to kill their hostage if their demands were not met, created a sudden and brutal emergency. We had no laws in our Criminal Code covering such exceptional measures in times of peace, and none of those "specialized teams of police that seem to fascinate certain democracies," as Premier Robert Bourassa noted at the time, existed in Canada. But I'll return to that later on.

My first reaction was unequivocal, and I have maintained the same position ever since: there could never be any question of negotiating with terrorists, not even to obtain the release of a hostage. Must I explain myself here yet again? The reason is simple: if we had agreed, as the FLQ demanded, to release from prison FLQ criminals who had been convicted of murder, armed robbery, and bombings, we would have been putting our finger into a gearbox from which we could never get it out. Puffed up by the success of their tactic, they would have no reason to hesitate to murder, rob, and bomb again, since if they were caught, all their pals would have to do is kidnap someone else to have them released from prison – and on and on indefinitely. The only action to which we could give our consent was to satisfy a few of the FLQ's minor requests in order to give the police time to track down the kidnappers – as Mitchell Sharp did when, as secretary of state for external affairs, he authorized the reading of the terrorist manifesto over Radio-Canada.

Even that concession seemed to me at the time to be too

much: as soon as I heard about it I remember thinking: "He's made a mistake!" I had already told the Cabinet: "We will not give them an inch." But upon reflection, it seemed to me that Mitchell had done the right thing. He had taken the decision on his own, since he was in charge of the department that was brought directly into play by the kidnapping of a foreign diplomat. He was responsible for the safety of members of the diplomatic corps when they were in Canadian territory. Just as our government counted on foreign governments to protect Canadian representatives when they were on their soil, so it was our duty to protect their diplomats on ours. Which is why the kidnapping of Mr. Cross from his home in Westmount brought the federal government into the picture even more directly than all the bombings and other acts of violence committed in Quebec's jurisdiction had until that time. Also, the reading of the FLQ manifesto did not present the obvious dangers to which negotiating over the question of FLQ prisoners would have exposed us. It was entirely consistent with the very firm position we had adopted: being democratically elected, it was up to us to decide whether justice would follow its own course or that dictated by the FLQ. Our option was obviously the former, and reading the manifesto did not affect that.

The kidnapping of Pierre Laporte, a member of the Quebec Liberal Cabinet, one week after that of Mr. Cross, seriously aggravated the situation. This second crime touched me personally: Laporte had sat on the same school benches as I had at Brébeuf, and his father and mine, both bright lights of a former age, had attended the same college, Sainte-Marie. I had been an admirer of the fight Laporte had waged as a journalist against the abuses

A decade earlier, I had appeared on a panel with Pierre Laporte, who is flanked here by Jean Drapeau and Gérard Pelletier. We knew each other, so his kidnapping touched me personally. (NAC-TC)

of the Duplessis regime. We had lost touch with each other a bit since he had become a Cabinet minister in Bourassa's government, but I still had very fond and friendly memories of him.

The kidnapping in broad daylight of a Quebec Cabinet minister in front of his own South Shore residence had a dramatic effect on our view of the crisis we were facing. We began to believe that perhaps the FLQ was not just a bunch of pamphlet-waving, bomb-planting zealots after all; perhaps they were in fact members of a powerful network capable of endangering public safety, and of bringing other fringe groups – of which there were a large number at the time – into the picture, which would lead to untold violence. If all these groups coalesced, the crisis could go on for a very long time, with tragic consequences for the entire country.

It has been reported that I was furious with the police for not anticipating these actions, but that is not true. I was certainly impatient, but I also had good reasons for keeping my impatience in check. Until then, the police had done an excellent job of disarming the most powerful bombs, often at great personal risk, and some brave men had died in the course of this duty. They had also exposed two other kidnapping plots – one against the Israeli consul in Montreal, the other against the consul of the United States – and in both cases had prevented the crimes from taking place. What I couldn't understand, however, was why, when left to their own devices, the police continued to hunt for villains among such extreme leftist groups as Maoists and Trotskyites, when all the FLQ members arrested until then had come from middle-class families with more connections with the Société Saint-Jean-Baptiste than with international communism.

Police action against the terrorists was not my only worry, however. Barely a few hours after the kidnapping of Pierre Laporte, Premier Bourassa telephoned me from Quebec City and said: "Pierre, you are going to have to send in the army, and you should think about invoking the War Measures Act."

My reply to him was in two parts: "As far as the army is concerned," I said, "you know the National Defence Act obliges us to respond positively. All your attorney general has to do is request, in due form, the intervention of the Armed Forces and they'll be on their way as soon as possible. But invoking the War Measures Act, the only means at our disposal of declaring a state of emergency, that's a completely different story. The consequences of such a measure would be extremely serious, and we have no proof that it is necessary. I prefer not to think about it." In short, I answered yes to his first request, as the law obliged me to do, and no to the second. "Let's wait and see how the situation evolves," I added. And Bourassa agreed.

From that moment on, telephone conversations with Bourassa became an almost daily ritual. I also spoke with Jean Drapeau, the Montreal mayor, and Lucien Saulnier, the head of the executive committee at City Hall, although not as often. And the impression I received from these conversations, as well as from all the other information coming out of Montreal, was that the situation was getting out of control.

The police were out of their depth, and were on the verge of physical and mental exhaustion. Every lead they followed had proved to be false, and the disturbances were continuing unabated. The city of Montreal had no legal authority to control the demonstrations or gatherings of support during which thousands of people, fists raised defiantly, were shouting "Vive le FLQ!" while speakers hurled the most injurious insults not at the terrorists, but at the politicians.

So for the second time in as many years the Canadian Armed Forces were called in, at the request of the Quebec government, "in aid to the Civil Power." Since the kidnapping of Pierre Laporte, soldiers had been ensuring the safety of federal ministers, including the prime minister. I spent the weekend at Harrington Lake, in the Gatineau Hills, and both military and police personnel kept my country house under surveillance. And official communications continued to flow in, from Montreal and Quebec City, clamouring for the proclamation of the War Measures Act. I resisted for several more days, conscious as I was of the consequences of such a move. I kept putting it off from one day to the next, but those from whom I was hearing in

"Just watch me," I told an interviewer who asked how far I would go to fight terrorism. The army was called out to guard Parliament. Here Cabinet minister John Munro encounters a soldier on Parliament Hill.
(NAC-TC/Robert Cooper)

Montreal and Quebec City would not let me stall any longer. In the end, I had to recognize that they were in a better position than I was to judge the urgency of the situation.

In the final analysis, what made me come to a decision was the fact that the crisis had begun to cause a lot of irrational behaviour among people I had assumed to be more reasonable. I am thinking now of a declaration, signed by a group of Quebec leaders, that appeared in major newspapers in Montreal.

Le Devoir published this incredible document on October 15, 1970. It ended with the names of the signatories: René Lévesque, president of the Parti Québécois; Alfred Rouleau, president of Desjardins Life Insurance; Marcel Pépin, president of the CSN (Confédération des

The troops in Montreal had a tough time hunting down the kidnappers, even conducting fruitless house-to-house searches in bitter weather. (Canapress)

syndicats nationaux); Louis Laberge, president of the FTQ (Fédération de travailleurs du Québec); Jean-Marc Kirouac, president of UCC (the farmers' union); Claude Ryan, editor of *Le Devoir*; Jacques Parizeau, president of the executive council of the Parti Québécois; Fernand Daoust, secretary general of the FTQ; Yvon Charbonneau, president of the CEQ (Centrale de l'enseignement du Québec); Mathias Rioux, president of the Alliance des professeurs de Montréal; Camille Laurin, parliamentary leader of the Parti Québécois; Guy Rocher, sociology professor, Université de Montréal; Fernand Dumont, director, Institut supérieur des sciences humaines, Université Laval; Paul Bélanger, political science professor, Université Laval; Raymond Laliberté, former president of the CEQ; Marcel Rioux, anthropology professor, Université de Montréal.

And what did this document say? After giving some consideration to "the atmosphere of semi-military rigidity that can be detected in Ottawa," and the grave fear that there existed "in certain non-Québécois quarters in particular, the terrible temptation of a policy for the worst, i.e., the illusion that a chaotic and well-ravaged [*bien ravagé*] Quebec would be easier to control by whatever means," the group went on to its main proposal, soliciting the support of the population (which, to judge by the number of signatures appended, it had received) for the Quebec government's willingness to negotiate. The signatories urged the government to be flexible and provided "essentially our most urgent support in negotiating an exchange between hostages and political prisoners."

Yes, they were using the term "political prisoners" to describe condemned terrorists, people who had been convicted of criminal acts, and they were calling for their release from prison, thus sticking their heads right into the trap set for them by the FLQ. The members of the FLQ who had been imprisoned were not there because of their opinions, which would indeed have made them political prisoners. From all the evidence, these young people were behind bars because they had been convicted of criminal acts. Such confusion in the minds of otherwise well-informed people seemed to me to be the obvious symptoms of an alarming state of affairs. I might have understood the man in the street holding such opinions. But when university professors, leaders of a democratic party, and labour union leaders displayed such twisted logic, such willingness to capitulate to the demands of the FLQ, it suggested an extremely disordered state. Had the terrorists succeeded in confusing Quebec's intellectuals and opinion leaders? From the evidence, some of them at least were in the process of losing their perspective, which to me was a measure of the general disarray.

That October 15, I ended up giving in to the representations of my Quebec counterpart and of the mayor of Montreal. "But be careful," I stated. "The War Measures Act cannot be invoked for just any reason. The law specifically states that only a state of war, real or apprehended, or insurrection, real or apprehended, can justify having recourse to the War Measures Act. Are you, Bourassa, and you, Drapeau, ready to declare, in writing, that you are under such an apprehension? If you are not, it is impossible for me to go ahead. The law itself prevents me from proceeding."

Their affirmative response was immediate. Was I wrong in acceding to the reasons they presented to me? I don't think so. And I am certain that, had I not declared the War Measures Act when I did, I would be accused today of having played the "Big Brother in Ottawa" by placing my own judgment ahead of that of more interested parties, ignoring the repeated appeals of the premier of Quebec and the mayor of Montreal, thus demonstrating my own contempt for the competence of the government of Quebec as well as for the administration of Montreal, and finally acting as if the federal government knew the situation better than anyone else, as if we alone were capable of rational judgment. And at the same time, I would be held responsible for the eventual death of Pierre Laporte.

On the night of Thursday the 15th and Friday the 16th of October, then, the government decided to resort to the War Measures Act. We did not take this decision lightly. For my part, I was deeply disturbed by it, and extremely apprehensive about what would ensue. I was afraid that it would lead to abuses, and I was worried about the political consequences. I knew that we would be reproached most severely by some people. But when you have been elected to govern, you have to do so to the best of your ability, without worrying about the condemnation that might later be levelled at your actions. What was important was to pre-vent the situation from degenerating into chaos, and the conduct of the elected representatives of the people from being dictated by terrorists.

So we acted. And the population immediately sup-ported our action. We read in *La Presse,* a few weeks later, that, according to a Gallup poll, "87 per cent of Canadians support the application of the War Measures Act decreed during the crisis provoked by the FLQ. That is the most sup-port a government has received in any opinion poll taken over the past several years. The support given to Trudeau and Bourassa *came almost equally from francophones and anglophones."* (My emphasis.)

One of the main criticisms levelled at us at the time, and which to a certain extent is still heard today, is that, in the words of NDP leader Tommy Douglas, we "used a sledge-hammer to crack a peanut." This criticism doesn't take the facts into account. First, peanuts don't make bombs, don't take hostages, and don't assassinate prisoners. And as for the sledgehammer, it was the only tool at our disposal. "The government," I stated at the first session of the House that followed our decision, "recognizes that the authority contained in the act is much broader than is required in the present situation, notwithstanding the seriousness of the events. For that reason the regulations which were adopted permit the exercise of only a limited number of the powers available under the act....

"Following the passage of enough time to give the gov-ernment the necessary experience to assess the type of statute which may be required in these circumstances, it is my firm intention to discuss with the leaders of the Opposi-tion parties the desirability of introducing legislation of a less comprehensive nature."

The terrorists apparently did not have the same concern for personal freedoms and human rights as we did. The next evening, on Saturday, October 17, while Parliament was in special session, holding an emergency debate over the imposition of the War Measures Act, we learned from the press that the body of Pierre Laporte had been found in the trunk of a car in the parking lot of the Saint-Hubert airport. The news produced in me the mixed emotions of horror, sorrow, and anxiety. To lose an old friend, and in such a manner, just when we were trying to come to his aid, to come face to face with the inhuman cruelty of these anonymous assassins, was atrocious. I still have a very sad memory of my meeting with Françoise, Pierre Laporte's widow, and his children at the funeral services held in the church of Notre-Dame, in Montreal.

I was heartbroken, but I was also extremely worried: were we in for a series of assassinations, as the FLQ had been warning us for a long time – warnings (such as the article in *Victoire*, the in-house publication of the FLQ, that appeared in March 1964 under the title "The FLQ Will Kill") that we had never, until now, taken seriously?

The imposition of the War Measures Act was followed by an unprecedented flurry of arrests, most of them in Montreal, but a few in other Quebec cities as well. Within hours of the vote in the House, more than 400 people were locked up and kept behind bars for longer than the forty-eight hours prescribed by the Criminal Code. Some of them spent weeks in jail. And most of those arrested were never charged. They were eventually

We were too late. This note from the "Dieppe cell" of the FLQ told police of Pierre Laporte's "execution," and told them where to find the body.
(Canapress)

FACE À L'ARROGANCE DU GV FÉDÉRAL ET DE SON VALET BOURASSA, FACE À LEURS MAUVAISES FOI ÉVIDENTE, LE FLQ A DONC DÉCIDÉ DE PASSER AUX ACTES.

PIERRE LAPORTE, MINISTRE DU CHÔMAGE ET DE L'ASSIMILATION A ÉTÉ EXÉCUTÉ À 6.18 CE SOIR PAR LA CELLULE DIEPPE (ROYAL 22ᵉ).

VOUS TROUVEREZ LE CORPS DANS LE COFFRE DU "CHEVROLET VERT (9) 2420) À LA BASE DE ST HUBERT.

NOUS VAINCRONS
FLQ

P.S. LES EXPLOITEURS DU PEUPLE QUÉBECOIS N'ONT QU'À BIEN SE TENIR.

released, and the Quebec government compensated them for the inconvenience.

It is, of course, very regrettable that a number of innocent people were swept up in the police net. Without wanting to turn this account into a plea of self-defence, I nonetheless feel that I should present some of the evidence in the case, because the arrests had hardly stopped before we came in for some harsh criticism. The targets were not only the federal authorities but me, personally, and the attacks came not only from separatist sympathizers but also from certain editorial writers who were not particularly scrupulous about verifying the facts on which they based their condemnations. One of these actually accused us, just last year, and without offering even a modicum of proof, of having imprisoned people *we knew to be innocent*. I pick that particular statement because dozens of similar accusations appear in the October Crisis file, and I do not want to pretend that I am ignorant of their existence. Nor am I unaware of the hypothesis advanced by certain university professors, according to which the War Measures Act was invoked as a political manoeuvre designed to crush the very idea of Quebec sovereignty. Some even go so far as to say that the terrorists were invented by the federal government; those who still maintain radio contact with reality content themselves with the charge that we "jumped at the chance" provided by the FLQ to discredit the Parti Québécois.

Let me address the question of the arrests first. I can attest without fear of contradiction that the vast majority of arrests were made by the Quebec Provincial Police and the Montreal police, on information gathered by those two forces. The role played by the RCMP in that operation was a very minor one. I know that because I obtained, a short time before the arrests, a list of the people the RCMP wanted to keep under surveillance. I wanted to see the list not so that I could substitute my own judgment for that of the police, which was not my role, but simply to inform myself about the kind of information the RCMP was gathering. Now, this list consisted almost entirely of the names of members of Maoist and Trotskyite groups, none of which reappeared later on lists of prisoners arrested under the War Measures Act, from which I conclude that those on the RCMP list were never bothered. As for the dozen or so other names on the first list, they belonged to people who were relatively unknown and who, once again, were never arrested. Those who have repeatedly accused the federal forces of having arrested "singers and poets" are barking up the wrong tree.

From all the evidence, it was the Quebec Provincial Police and the Montreal police who made up a list that was too long and badly verified; it included the names of activists and protesters who were vociferous, certainly, but not guilty – or even capable – of criminal activity. I'm not throwing stones at these police forces; while we were sitting peacefully up on Parliament Hill, they were down in the thick of it, in an atmosphere charged with emotion, and surrounded by an impatient populace on the verge of panic, who were demanding that the police do something to get the terrorist situation under control, and do it quickly. It's not easy in such circumstances to keep a cool head. But mistakes are mistakes, and they were recognized as such by the Quebec government, which, as I've mentioned, recognized its responsibility to compensate those who were unjustly arrested.

As for the supposed manoeuvres attributed to us, aimed at "crushing Quebec separatism," I will first say that the accusation is completely without basis, the pure product of overwrought or spiteful imaginations, and attributable to an attitude of mind, common among ultra-nationalist groups, that sees plots and counterplots everywhere. I know that one can find support for this thesis in the entries that Don Jamieson made in his journal at the time, and that were published posthumously twenty years later by the Toronto magazine *Saturday Night*. But in order to give proper weight to Jamieson's unique version of the events, it must be remembered that he was in London at the time when the crisis reached its peak, and for the fifteen days that followed. He therefore participated in none of the crucial exchanges in the Cabinet, during which our reasons for invoking the War Measures Act were put forward and the attitude the government had decided to take was defined.

Furthermore, it is well known that, when it came to fighting separatism, we in Ottawa had always done so openly, without dissimulation. Any sovereigntist who

A placard-carrying young woman wears a shirt calling Paul Rose – one of the FLQ kidnappers – a "Quebec patriot." I am reminded of my friend Eugene Forsey's summary of those terrible days in his autobiography, A Life on the Fringe: *"In my judgment Pierre Trudeau kept Quebec in Canada when no one else could have done it. In my judgment also, he saved us from Baader-Meinhof gangs and Red Brigades." (Canapress)*

doubts that need only take a look at the referendum campaign conducted in 1980. And anyone who doubts my own resolve to fight openly to maintain the rule of law has only to recall the interview on the steps of Parliament when a hostile interviewer asked me how far I was prepared to go with the use of armed force. I replied: "Just watch me."

The Parti Québécois no doubt suffered greatly from the October Crisis, but it did so because of the separatist proclamations of the FLQ, because of the sympathy with terrorist tactics displayed by many Parti Québécois supporters, and because an irresponsible wing of the party later staged a delirious welcome-home for released FLQ members, including one member of the FLQ cell that had kidnapped and assassinated Pierre Laporte. To be fair to their leader, René Lévesque never excused, much less approved of, the actions of the FLQ; but it must be said that members of his party did not always follow his example.

I could go on to give an account of the events that followed the police round-up – the liberation of James Cross, the departure for Cuba of his captors – but the facts are well enough known, and I have nothing to add to the many pieces that have been written on that subject. I would only like to point out that by the end of 1970, as promised, more limited legislation had replaced the War Measures Act. If we had possessed the slightest dictatorial tendencies, as certain of our adversaries claimed we did, then we would not have made such haste to erase all traces of the special powers we were made to adopt at the express request of the Quebec authorities. It should also be noted that in the quarter-century that has followed the October Crisis, the country has seen no resurgence of terrorism. "One day, the police and the army will be gone," René Lévesque predicted in *La Presse,* "and Trudeau's stupidity will not have prevented more kidnappings." The facts have proven otherwise.

I have often been asked whether I have any regrets about the October Crisis, and I have always responded in the negative. We made it through the crisis. Naturally, I would prefer that it hadn't taken place, that the FLQ had never seen the light of day, and that Pierre Laporte were still among us. But wishes do not change reality.

I am sometimes also asked whether the October Crisis taught me anything about the art of governing, or about the means that were at my disposal for defusing the crisis. First of all, it taught me that you can be the most prescient futurologist in the world, you can lay out the best-made plans and define your priorities with the utmost care, but if you show yourself to be incapable of managing a crisis when it arises, you will lose your right to govern and the whole thing will blow up in your face. Under normal circumstances, the art of governing consists in preventing crises, in spiriting them away before they even arise.

In the socio-economic sphere, for example, you anticipate a period of recession by beefing up the unemployment insurance program to prepare for massive unemployment, and by putting in place as many measures as possible to create jobs. In the Quebec context, the emergence of the FLQ and its terrorist activities had been threatening the Quebec economy for years. Corporations hesitated to invest in the province, certain industries that had intended to locate factories in Quebec decided to look elsewhere. Our response to the FLQ prevented the situation from deteriorating further into recession, and avoided wide-scale unemployment that would have created much social hardship, leading perhaps to anarchy and a general disaffection with the workings of democracy.

When everything is quiet, it's easy to see ahead and to take certain steps. But crises cannot always be anticipated. When a crisis hits, it has to be faced with all the means and personnel at your disposal. My opinion of the means available in 1970? The Cabinet, Parliament, and the army carried out their roles extremely well. The police? In the end, the police were successful: they captured the kidnappers and murderers, but only *after* there had been kidnappings and a murder. In any crisis, there comes a time when everyone is shouting in the dark, demanding to know what's going on. What the October Crisis taught me was that it is absolutely essential to have, at the helm of state, a very firm hand, one that sets a course that never alters, that does not attempt to do everything at once out of excitement or confusion, but that moves along slowly, step by step, putting solutions in place. As I have said many times, "The first duty of government is to govern," which means never giving in to chaos or terror.

As for the long-term effects of the October Crisis and the methods we used to bring it to an end, they seem to have shut down the activities of the FLQ for good, which is no small thing. Shortly after the crisis, even Pierre Vallières – who in the 1968 edition of his *White Niggers of America* called upon a guerrilla force made up of "workers, students, young people and intellectuals" to fight "first with placards, then with stones, Molotov cocktails, dynamite, revolvers and machine-guns" – even this former FLQ theoretician realized that violence would never succeed in Quebec, and that in order to gain power it was necessary to resort to legal, democratic means.

Other analysts claim to have perceived that the episode actually strengthened the position of the Parti Québécois, and to have increased its influence. Is that the case? If the October Crisis strengthened the Parti Québécois, it certainly did not reinforce separatism. Quite the contrary. It is true that six years after the crisis, the PQ assumed power in Quebec. But how did it do so, and what price did it pay? By obscuring, for the purposes of winning an electoral campaign, the first article of its constitution. Twice in a row, in 1970 and 1973, the party placed its separatist plank at the top of its electoral platform, and twice in a row it was thoroughly demolished by Robert Bourassa's Liberals. By 1976, the Parti Québécois had learned its lesson. It finally had to admit that the people of Quebec were not in favour of the secession of their province, which is why in 1976 the PQ said: "This election is not about sovereignty. It is only about bringing good government to the province, a better government than the current administration. Elect us, and you will be better governed. As for independence, we can talk about that later, and only after we have consulted you again." That is why I said at the time that separatism was dead, because its official representatives themselves had given up on it; they considered it an obstacle to being elected.

Separatism died in 1976, but its funeral was the referendum of 1980. It's true that the Parti Québécois was re-elected in 1981, but as René Lévesque said in 1985, it was elected to take "the beautiful risk of federalism." And when the Quebec government tried to block the patriation of the constitution in 1982, it was repudiated by a clear majority of the members elected by the Quebec people to sit in Parliament in Ottawa and the legislative assembly in Quebec City. What is more, in three by-elections held at the time, the Quebec people chastised the PQ government for having rejected patriation in 1982. And shortly after that, they rejected the PQ government itself.

With the FLQ crisis over, I was able to continue my work in a more relaxed atmosphere, and could resume my apprenticeship as prime minister in relative peace. There were fewer than twenty-four months left in my first mandate: I was determined to put them to good use.

During our first two years as a government, we had made some important progress: examples include the Official Languages Act, diplomatic recognition of mainland China and the Vatican, lowering the age of majority from twenty-one to eighteen, and so on. But our efforts had been

This personal photograph, taken at the Grey Cup game in Toronto in November 1970, may be a little blurred, but all is explained by the message that it comes "avec les amitiés chaleureuses d'un photographe très, très amateur." The very amateur photographer's name was Jean Drapeau.
(NAC-TC)

In 1970, I fell in love with a very beautiful girl. March 4, 1971, was the date that Margaret Sinclair and I married in Vancouver.
(Trudeau Family)

At work and at play

The Common-wealth Conference in Singapore in 1971, although it was overshadowed by a somewhat acrimonious debate about U.K. arms sales to South Africa, served to remind me of the wide range of nations who belong to the organization, making it a useful forum.

Visiting an English-language classroom in the course of our tour of the Soviet Union in 1971.

(NAC-TC)

This photo is an official souvenir of my visit in 1971 to what was then Ceylon. The caption is simply: "Riding an elephant at Katugastota."

This caption is equally simple: riding a camel in India.

British prime minister Edward Heath, who visited India at the same time, wrote that my "élan and exuberance captured public attention and press headlines."

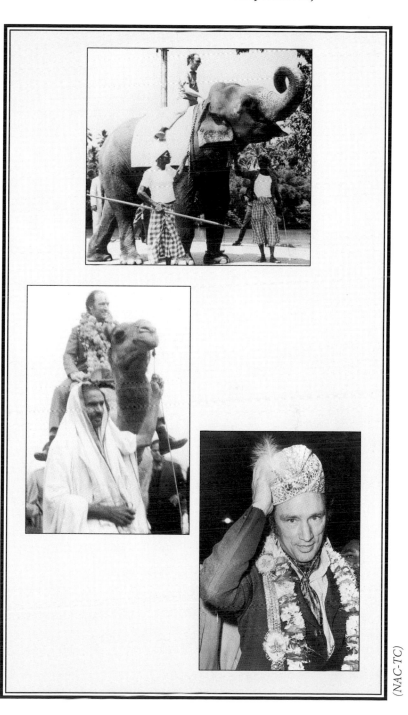

(NAC-TC)

based primarily on the functioning of Parliament and the government, on internal policy questions that were of little interest to the general public. The next two years would be marked by many more important decisions, a few of which I will mention here, one of which was a resounding failure and another only a partial failure, but that proved to be almost fatal to us.

But first, a personal note: 1970 was also the year I fell in love with a beautiful girl, Margaret Sinclair. On March 4, 1971, we were married in Vancouver. The romance took the press by surprise, which was the way we wanted it.

In June 1971, my government created the Canada Development Corporation and the first ministry of the environment ever set up in Canada, and probably any-where. In August of the same year, we undertook, with Ontario, the clean-up of Lake Erie. In April 1972, I signed an agreement with U.S. president Richard Nixon on water quality in the Great Lakes. In the meantime, we voted in a capital gains tax and created a young people's summer employment program, called Youth Perspectives, and a leisure activity program for the aged, called New Horizons.

The previous year, I also made my first official visit to the Soviet Union, a two-week tour that took me to the far reaches of Siberia, accompanied by my wife Margaret, who was pregnant with our first son. When I signed an agreement on cooperation and fair dealings with General Secretary Leonid Brezhnev, I laid the foundations for what would later be called the "détente" in East-West relations, which would be crowned in 1975 by the Helsinki Confer-ence on Security and Cooperation in Europe.

Within the Liberal Party, I had instigated a series of meetings, which were intended to break with old habits and traditional ways of formulating policy. I wanted the party to turn its face resolutely towards the future, while at the same time practising participatory democracy. All party members were invited to present their ideas and projects to us for study at regional and national conferences.

The failure mentioned above happened to us in Victoria at the end of a series of federal-provincial conferences on the constitutional question. I'll return to this episode later on in this account. The half-failure was more serious, since it occurred during the general election of October 30, 1972, which reduced the Liberal seats in the House of Commons from 155 to 109 and all but swept us out of power. For a day or two, while recounts were going on, I didn't know whether my party would be called upon to form the next government or not.

I must accept responsibility for this half-failure. I may not have been solely responsible, but I was certainly mainly to blame. Looking back on it, the errors I committed at the time seem startlingly clear to me. The campaign had gone badly from the beginning. The party had chosen an English slogan – "The Land Is Strong" – that was both inept and untranslatable. As for me, I got off on the wrong foot by having a confused idea of my own role. I put myself at the head of the campaign, but I treated it not so much as an election battle as a simple appeal to the voters: "Here is the record of our four years in power; tell us what you think." I wanted to make a clean break between these elections and the emotionalism of Trudeaumania that had characterized the previous campaign. At one time I even said, during a

campaign speech, that I had no quarrel with the Conservatives or the New Democrats, I was only presenting our
ideas and allowing the other parties to present theirs, and
leaving it up to the voters to choose which were the best. I
described the exercise as "a conversation with Canadians."
"Here's what we've accomplished in the past four years,"
I said to them, "and here are our plans for the next four
years. If you like them, if you approve of them, then vote
for us." I was counting on the infectious nature of good
ideas to bring us victory.

Well, as I soon realized (but not soon enough!), the
approach was too cerebral. Politics can't be conducted at
such a rational level, devoid of all emotion. The voters
wanted a leader to guide them, and I was giving them a
professor. The members of my party wanted to jump into
combat, and I was giving them a lecture. The electorate
was eager for its regular dose of eloquence, attack, riposte,
cheers, and rallies, and there I was giving them calm, lucid
propositions in pedagogical tones. That is not how you
win elections. That is how we came within a hair's breadth
of losing this one. I had forgotten all about the famous
Liberal campaign machine that I had heard my father
talking about with his friends when I was five years old.

As you can imagine, election night was a long, hard
vigil. For several hours I was convinced that my brief career
as prime minister might be over. I wasn't discouraged by
the thought, much less depressed. But it seemed entirely
possible that my life was about to take another turn, and I
began running through my mind the various prospects that
were opening up before me. The next morning, with the
results of the election still uncertain, the mood of those
around me was sombre. A few of my Cabinet ministers

My aide, Timothy Porteous, is about to close the door of the Prime Minister's Office. Meanwhile the poster in the office hallway sums up our attitude towards our precarious minority government position. (Canapress)

thought that whatever happened we would have to hand power over to Robert Stanfield, whose party seemed to be gaining in strength. But I refused to see myself as a loser, and at any rate didn't want to decide anything before knowing the final results of the recounts.

As time passed, our half-failure began more and more to take on the aspect of a challenge that had to be met, and I found myself mentally rolling up my sleeves; I felt charged with the spirit of combat that had eluded me throughout the election campaign. From that moment on, I was ready for action, ready to erase all traces of the miscalculations that seemed to have damaged us. The final result confirmed that we were still in power, even though we would be going back into the House barely two seats ahead of the

Conservatives. At least I was entitled to form the government, and I drove up to the Governor General's residence full of confidence, dressed in a Native buckskin jacket and driving a sports car, to show that we were treating the results not as a defeat but as a challenge, and there was no question in my mind of giving up.

All the same, I decided to conduct a thorough housecleaning within the Cabinet and my own office. I asked all the Cabinet ministers, senior as well as recent appointees, to change their posts. Only one, Bryce Mackasey, refused, and was excluded from the Cabinet. In my office, I changed the team of my closest advisers from top to bottom. Instead of intellectuals like Pierre Levasseur and Jim Davey – who remained friends, of course, and favoured me with their advice – I surrounded myself with more politically minded advisers, people like Keith Davey, Jim Coutts, and Tom Axworthy, who had proven themselves during Pearson's time in office. I wanted the change in style to be obvious to everyone, proof that, first of all, I was aware of the errors I had made during the campaign, but more importantly, proof that we were re-entering the political arena with more aggression and determination than we had ever shown before.

As for me, who had spent most of my time until then in the rarefied upper strata of politics, I wanted to ground myself in the art of the politician. To my great surprise, I found this new apprenticeship more interesting and more stimulating than I would have thought possible. Ever since my youth I had been a loner, very jealous of my freedom. I had carefully kept my distance from my colleagues, no matter who they were. Even among friends, for example during expeditions into the bush, I instinctively took the lead, where I would be alone. If my companions caught up with me I would slacken my pace until I was trailing far behind, once again alone. I am not describing this character trait in order to make it seem that I thought of myself as superior; on the contrary, I am trying to explain the deficiencies I discovered in myself when I took on the job of party leader.

In politics, a healthy dose of gregariousness is not a fault. When you are at the head of a party, it becomes a necessity. I learned that lesson the hard way when Liberal Party members began to get the impression that they were members of a party without a leader. From then on, I resolved to demonstrate the qualities of leadership that were expected of me. Without my really being aware of it, I had not yet fully accepted the role. I even found it a bit repugnant. Personally, I have never felt that I was in need of a leader, perhaps because of the authoritarianism that was so rife in Quebec during my youth, and I must have assumed that everyone else had the same feeling as I did. But I now realized that that was an illusion; I jumped into action feet-first, by which I mean I entered more energetically and completely into the fulfilment of the mandate that had been given me, and I accepted fully all the responsibilities that went with it.

The next twenty months of minority government, during which survival was constantly under threat from the first important vote that would coalesce the Opposition parties, taught me an excellent lesson. On the one hand, we relived the inconveniences we had gone through from 1965 to 1968; on the other hand, we also learned how to live dangerously, how to savour the pleasures of running risks and overcoming perils. We could govern, but we were continually aware of the sword that the majority of Opposition

Ottawa Commonwealth Conference

Welcoming the Queen and the Duke of Edinburgh to Canada on the occasion of the Commonwealth Conference in Ottawa in August 1973, and presenting Margaret to them.

As host I chaired the meeting with the Commonwealth Heads of Government. Edward Heath's memoirs contrast this meeting with the unsuccessful one at Singapore, noting, "under the chairmanship of Pierre Trudeau, a happier atmosphere prevailed and more business was done."

(NAC-TC)

The official photograph was signed by the Queen and the Duke of Edinburgh.
(NAC-TC)

members dangled over our heads. Today we were the government, but tomorrow our governing days could be over. My role was both that of the tightrope walker, who could at any moment plunge to the ground and break his neck, and that of the boxer permanently awaiting the knockout punch. It may not have been a secure position, but it certainly was an exciting one, and at times even amusing.

I should mention that being a minority government allowed us to engage in a new form of politics that attracted me greatly. Throughout my first mandate, the "leftist" reputation I had earned in Quebec during my days in opposition to the Duplessis regime imposed a certain reserve on me. In North America, every major political party in power over the centuries had been made up of a balance between a left wing and a right wing, and the Liberal Party was no exception to that rule. I had to be very circumspect from 1968 to 1972. Still somewhat shakily established at the head of the organization, I had to be constantly aware of the possible risks involved in ranging the more traditional Liberal members against me, and of provoking a rift between the two wings. That didn't prevent me from recognizing mainland China, to the displeasure of the United States, nor from putting into law the health insurance act. But I had to be on my guard all the time to maintain a careful equilibrium between progressive measures and more moderate ones.

From that point of view, the minority government allowed me to put forward more advanced "left-wing" projects. I knew that the NDP, under David Lewis, would back me up – in fact, the NDP supported me when some of the more conservative members of my own party did not. I was thus able to institute policies that I had been dreaming about for a long time, and the social-democratic faction of the Opposition was forced to support them, or else deny their own social program. What was more, the constant threat of a negative vote in the House reminded me of the advice of an old friend in Paris, the great medievalist Paul Vignaux: "If you have to fall," he said, "be sure to fall to the left." I was much more inclined to heed his advice than was the rest of my party, which, at the provincial level, had for years tended to fall to the right. As a result, in Saskatchewan, Manitoba, and British Columbia, the Liberal Party had all but disappeared from the political stage, to be replaced by the NDP. As federal Liberals, we were worried that we might share the fate of our British counterparts, who had let themselves be pushed so far to the right by the Labour Party that there were only a handful of Liberal members left in Westminster, none of whom exerted much influence on the course of events. We were determined not to let that happen to the Liberal Party of Canada.

The answer, I was convinced, was to formulate a left-of-centre policy that would split the Opposition into two camps: Conservatives and Socreds on one side, New Democrats on the other, and then to count on the Conservatives from time to time to adopt measures refused by the NDP. This, I felt, would create a split in the Opposition that I could use, when the time came, to go to the people to ask that our majority be restored. Half jokingly, at a caucus meeting, I compared our strategy to that of Napoleon at the Battle of Austerlitz; he had divided the armies of the two emperors, first by feigning a long retreat, then by luring one of the armies into a swamp to slow down its manoeuvrability. He then struck right down the centre, his forces annihilating first the Austrians, and then the Russians.

Although my relations with Indira Gandhi were later to chill over India's use of the Candu reactor, Margaret and I enjoyed meeting her in Ottawa in 1973. (NAC-TC)

Greeting Prime Minister Michael Manley of Jamaica in Ottawa in 1974. He and I enjoyed what he described in his book Jamaica: Struggle on the Periphery *as "a warm relationship." He writes of me: "By training and instinct, he believes mankind's best hopes lie in reason, persuasion, accommodation, seeing the other fellow's point of view. To these qualities he adds the breadth of vision and sense of history that make the true internationalist." Obviously, a very generous description. (Canapress)*

Henry Kissinger, Nixon's secretary of state, is greeted by me on a 1974 visit to Ottawa. Kissinger's book The White House Years *tackles my relationship with Nixon: "It cannot be said that Nixon and Trudeau were ideally suited for each other.... Trudeau was bound to evoke all of Nixon's resentments against 'swells,' who in his view had always looked down on him. He disdained Trudeau's clear enjoyment of social life; he tended to consider him soft on defense and in his general attitude toward the East. And yet, when they were together, Trudeau treated Nixon without any hint of condescension and Nixon accorded Trudeau both respect and attention. They worked together without visible strain."* (Canapress)

In this way the minority government allowed us to get social legislation through Parliament that helped less-advantaged Canadians, such as the increasing and indexing of old age pensions, higher unemployment insurance benefits, and the creation of several institutions that consolidated Canadian autonomy, such as Petro-Canada – a response to the oil shortage of 1973 – and the Foreign

Investment Review Agency. It also permitted me to blow the dust off some of our original objectives, such as the consolidation of institutional bilingualism in the federal government.

There were those who took it for granted that our quasi-defeat in the fall of 1972 was due to some extent to our official languages policy. According to an enlightened commentator from the Conservative Party, Dalton Camp, we had "lost [our] constituency" because "the persistence and growing pervasiveness of bilingualism had alienated English Canadians from their federal government." To be honest, I was never able to be certain whether that was the cause of our semi-stumble, but I determined nonetheless to make it quite clear that we were not reneging on our major objectives. That is why I presented to the House a resolution that fixed 1978 as the year in which the federal public service must become effectively bilingual. That resolution was voted through Parliament on June 6, 1973.

My first official visit to China also occurred during that time of minority government. On October 10, 1973, I boarded a jet for Beijing, once again accompanied by Margaret, who this time was pregnant with our second son. I had a long meeting with Mao Zedong, after which we spent two days travelling in the provinces with Prime Minister Chou Enlai. Two days later, Chou Enlai handed us over to a victim of the Cultural Revolution whom he had helped to become rehabilitated: his name was Deng Xiaoping, and he has gone on to become the supreme leader of the government of the People's Republic of China.

Visit to China

(NAC-TC/Robert Cooper)

Inspecting the guard of honour as we arrive in China in October 1973, escorted by Chou Enlai.

"Let a Hundred Flowers Bloom" – and Canadian flags – as crowds stage a "spontaneous" welcome for me, Margaret, and the rest of the Canadian party.

(NAC-TC)

Chou Enlai introduced me to a victim of the Cultural Revolution whose rehabilitation he had helped. His name was Deng Xiaoping, and he went on to become the supreme leader of the People's Republic of China.

Escorted by Chou Enlai, we travelled widely to see many of the great sights in China. Here we are shown visiting the Luo-Yang caves.

With Mao Zedong and interpreters in the course of private talks.

(NAC-TC)

When we returned from China, nine months still separated us from the event that had been threatening us since we lost our majority in 1972: defeat in the House of Commons.

Personally, I had not been dreading such an eventuality. As I noted above, directing a minority government is uncomfortable enough from a variety of points of view, exciting though it can be, even passionately so, given the tensions and difficulties to which it exposed us. Also, as I have already explained, I had nothing to be ashamed of regarding the balance sheet of those minority years. Quite the reverse. I wasn't the only one to feel positive about it; there was no shortage of observers praising the policies we had undertaken since the autumn of 1972. I had been ready to go to the people to solicit a new mandate, on whatever day the Opposition parties might commit the mistake of uniting against us. In fact, I had even been asking myself whether it wouldn't be necessary to incite our opponents into making that fatal error.

PART 3

1974 – 1979
VICTORY AND
DEFEAT

The minority Parliament that began in October of 1972 had been an exciting time for me, because we were fighting for our lives every day of the year. We were looking for a result not somewhere in the distant future, but here and now. Every day over our heads hung the Damoclean question: will we still be the government tomorrow morning? That sort of existence "concentrates the mind wonderfully" and excites the imagination. I enjoyed myself more; I took myself less seriously. I knew I had almost lost, and I knew I had a major battle on my hands if I didn't want to really lose the second time around.

But by the spring of 1974, it was time to move that battle to its next phase. We knew by then that we had succeeded in regaining the people's confidence to the extent that we could win an election. So rather than being tempted to say, "Well, let's just go on until they defeat us in Parliament whenever they feel the time is right," we decided that we had to choose the exact time and place of the battle. And we did. We actually engineered our own defeat in the House of Commons.

John Turner, the minister of finance, and Allan MacEachen and I got together for lunch in a private room at Le Cercle universitaire in Ottawa. Turner, a former Rhodes scholar who had entered Parliament as a young man, was a smart politician who certainly knew the party better than I did. Although I can't say we were ever close personally, I think we both made efforts to become so. He had a different view of Quebec than I did, but I can't remember our ever having a fight over anything. As for MacEachen, known throughout Cape Breton simply as "Allan J.," I recall him as a very private person – not someone you could get to know very well. He had a very good strategic sense, both in and out of Parliament, and he lived and breathed politics. MacEachen was certainly a character I liked, in part because he was unpredictable: I knew he'd generally be on the side of the people as he saw it, but I couldn't always foretell the direction his decisions would take. But he was the kind of man I respected, because he had no ulterior motives; he said what he thought, and the reasons he would give were always his real reasons.

In any event, at that lunch I had with Turner and MacEachen, we put things in Turner's budget that we knew the NDP couldn't support and others that we knew the Tories couldn't support. We made sure, in short, to produce a budget that would get both of them to vote against us. But we also put in the kinds of things that would let us go to the people and say: "See, these guys defeated us, they're just hungry for power, we were going to do this

Allan MacEachen was always a source of shrewd advice.
(Canapress)

for you." And we went in knowing that we would be defeated when the budget came to a vote.

Some people might say that this was being too political, that this kind of manoeuvring breeds cynicism about politics. My answer is that if it does, it shouldn't – any more than we should be cynical about Napoleon having won the Battle of Austerlitz. What did he do? He divided the enemy. If you can't do that when you are in a minority government, you shouldn't be in politics. If it's called manipulative, then so be it. I had learned in 1972 that I almost threw the election away because I had been too theoretical, too unconscious of the need for a political machine, too oblivious to the needs of the people working for us and to the need for the stimulation of the party. So I wasn't about to commit the same mistake in 1974.

One way to avoid that was to make it a different kind of campaign – a more lively one, centred on one or two issues. That came easily enough to me, because I did enjoy campaigning, up to a point. Some things I never learned to like. I didn't like to kiss babies, though I didn't mind kissing their mothers. I didn't like to slap backs or other parts of the anatomy. I liked hecklers, because they brought my speeches alive. I liked supporters, because they looked happy. And I really enjoyed mingling with people, if there wasn't too much of it. I think those who organized my campaigns realized that there are just so many hours and minutes a day I can spend in crowds and love it, but after that point it breaks and I don't love it. So if they didn't want me to start making faces and so on, they had to limit the time.

Another element of difference in the 1974 campaign was that Margaret participated actively in it, for the first and only time. Right from the beginning, when we campaigned by train through the Maritimes and on to Montreal, I had the pleasure of seeing my wife and baby on the train. I'm not sure if it was the right or the wrong thing to do. People wanted to see her and she would make the occasional speech, which was well appreciated. I think Margaret did, in fact, help with the public. I can't say I was all that comfortable with the approach, but why not try it once? But that was an exception.

For the most part, I kept a watertight seal between my private life and my public life. I never brought my family problems into my job as prime minister, and I tried never to bring my prime ministerial problems into my life as a parent and husband. I remember when I'd go home and play with my children, it was almost as if "the Prime Minister" was someone other than me: "Those are the things he's doing, but I'm doing something else." I wouldn't spend a moment worrying about the silly mistakes I had made during the day, or the unfortunate incidents in Parliament, or the defeat or failure of this or that policy. I would start worrying about that only after breakfast the next morning, when I had woken up well-rested and had seen my kids off to school. It really was almost schizophrenic – and it helped me a lot.

But, unknown to me, some of the political life may have spilled over onto the family life. I suppose that was inevitable, because one of the problems of being in politics is that it is not always a good life for the spouse. The man or the woman in it is fighting all the time, with the excitement that goes with active involvement in any contest; but the one who stays back home with the kids is stuck on the side-lines just hearing about the nasty aspects of it all, and not enjoying the fight. In my case, what's more, I was a neo-phyte at both politics and family life at the same time. I married late in life, our three boys – Justin, Sacha, and Michel – arrived fairly quickly, and I was learning about marriage and parenthood at the same time as I was learn-ing about the workings of politics. So perhaps it was a lit-tle too much for me and, regrettably, I didn't succeed all that well.

But coming back to the 1974 campaign: our plan to keep it lively and focused on one or two issues became much easier when Tory leader Bob Stanfield handed us what became the key issue of the campaign. His advocacy of a wage and price freeze, to be followed by wage and price controls, was in military terms the mistake an enemy makes when he puts an army in the field in such an exposed posi-tion that you can snipe at it from everywhere. My attack was to say: "Look, we're just a few months after the OPEC oil

A family album

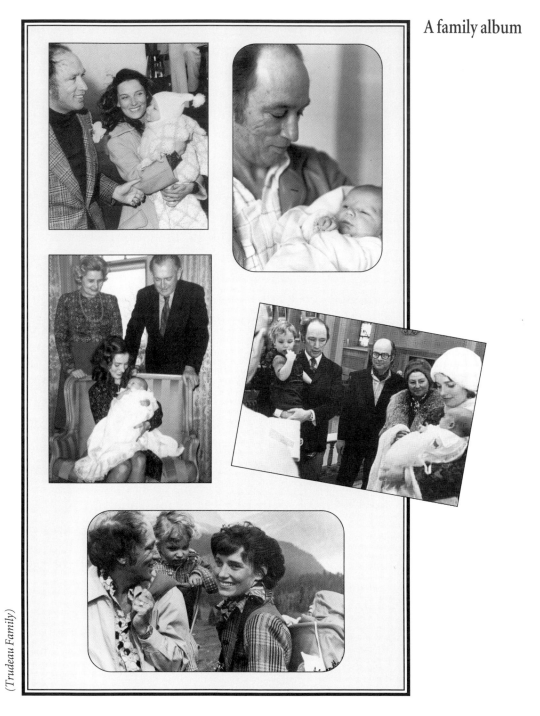

crisis. The price of energy looks as though it's going to go through the roof. How are you going to control that? How are you going to freeze the price that is being set in the Middle East by the OPEC cartel? You can't just say 'Zap! You're frozen, and we're not going to pay more for your oil.'"

I saw that it was a successful line and that he was getting into the mud in the field: for an Opposition leader it's always a disaster to be put on the wrong foot in a campaign, defending your proposed policies, not attacking the government's flaws. On my part, it was a simple message, a tactical use of the error of an opponent. Later, of course, we paid a price for this, when we brought in controls ourselves in 1975. All I can say is that we didn't explain it well enough, because these were two entirely different sets of circumstances. In the first case, in 1974, OPEC – outside Canada – was setting prices and you couldn't freeze the price of oil unless you didn't want to buy it. In the second case, a year and a half later, it was expectations, within Canada, that were causing inflation. We didn't make the distinctions sufficiently clear, and we paid a stiff price in lost credibility. But in 1974, I kept up my attack on Mr. Stanfield's proposal, and I won the election.

That was the last of my campaigns against Bob Stanfield, an opponent I liked and respected. In a sense, I felt that sometimes he was being treated unjustly, indirectly by myself and more directly by the media. He was intelligent, and reflective, not aggressive. When he played the aggressive role as leader of the Opposition, I could sense it was just that – a role – and he was doing it because that was his job, rather than because he was an aggressive man. In certain respects, I felt I had an unfair advantage over him. He had been chosen to succeed the tempestuous John

Diefenbaker as Conservative leader for a certain set of reasons, which were perhaps no longer in the public's mind by the time I was chosen. It seemed that Canada was no longer inclined to vote for a quiet man. People wanted somebody new and fresh who would rise above the image of bumbling parliamentarians that was generally held. Stanfield had been a good premier of Nova Scotia, quiet and competent, but he was still an old-time politician.

I feel that, overall, he was badly treated by the media. This troubled me because although I liked to win, I didn't want to win with the other man's hands tied behind his back. That's why when they ran the famous photo of him fumbling a football, after several successful catches, I didn't think that was fair play. My only real dispute with him, in fact, was purely ideological. I thought it was a mistake for him to talk of Canada as being composed of two nations. I always had a quarrel with those Anglo-Canadians who felt you had to bend over backwards to "understand" Quebec. I think that Stanfield – because he didn't know Quebec well – was a victim of that tendency. I had entered politics with my friends to prove that French Canadians are as good as anyone else: they have no need to be ghettoized by special status or a two-nations theory.

On our side, the 1974 election saw the emergence of Keith Davey, Jim Coutts, Tom Axworthy, Jerry Grafstein, and Martin Goldfarb as key election strategists. They joined Marc Lalonde and Jean Marchand, who had both been with me since 1968, as the most important members of my campaign team. During the 1972 campaign, Keith Davey had sent me a letter warning that I was doing it all wrong, and he correctly forecast many of the unpleasant results. After that near-defeat, I made Keith the campaign chairman, and he was largely responsible for recruiting my successful new team. Soon after the election, I invited the campaign committee for dinner at 24 Sussex Drive to thank them for their efforts. I told them the story of my father, an ardent Conservative, whom I had often heard during my childhood damning the "Liberal machine" for producing victories for Mackenzie King. To great laughter, I said that for many years thereafter I thought that the Liberal Party had some huge magic device that whistled and snorted and threw off enough sparks to attract the voters. There was even greater laughter when Jean Marchand called out, "But Pierre, haven't they shown it to you yet?"

The 1974 election opened the door to a turbulent five-year period, until the end of the mandate in 1979, during which we had our hands full with major developments in the economy, foreign policy, and the national unity debate. These years were also ones of great domestic difficulty for me. The bare facts are that in March 1977, Margaret and I separated. Eventually, in 1984, we were divorced. Anyone who has gone through the breakdown of a marriage – perhaps without three small children, and perhaps not in the glare of the public spotlight – will understand why I choose to write no more about the matter.

As soon as we finished celebrating our election victory, the government entered what seemed to the public and certainly to the news media a very quiet period. Actually we were very busy, but not in ways that were outwardly visible. It was largely a matter of the re-emergence of my famous obsession with creating counterweights. To counter the frenetic pace of minority government and the rough-and-tumble, very political election campaign I had just completed, I saw a need for some calm long-range reflection.

With trusted lieutenants Tom Axworthy (left) and Jim Coutts.
(J.M. Carisse Photos)

At the same time, I wanted to avoid indulging in too much reflection at the expense of action. And so I said: "Now that I've got my majority, I won't repeat the mistake of 1968 of being too philosophical, but I will do things seriously, the way I believe they should be done." This entailed giving ourselves six months or so to develop a thoughtful program and timetable for the next four years.

That was perhaps a mistake, because it did in fact allow our momentum to dissipate, and it disappointed a public that had been led by the election campaign to expect dynamic action. But when you are in a minority government that is fighting every day for survival, there isn't much time to plan in detail what you are going to do if you are re-elected. So I launched what may have been a rather tedious process of telling my people to go out and talk to all the ministers one by one, find out their priorities, and make a list in order of importance. And I should note that we had some very able ministers in that Cabinet.

We did roughly the same thing with key people in the party. It was an attempt to move back in the direction of participatory democracy. I recognized that I had priorities of my own in three, four, or five fields, but that a government must have twenty or thirty priorities it should be pursuing. This was a way of establishing what they should be. The process was carried out well enough, and produced useful new strategies for the future, but the snag was that by the time we were finished, the economy had changed.

The inflation that was already a problem at the time of the 1974 election had become almost runaway, while unemployment was growing at the same time. Industrialized countries were discovering for the first time that it was possible to have inflation and unemployment simultaneously, in a new phenomenon known as stagflation. No economist anywhere in the world had any experience in dealing with both problems at once, because the economic remedy for inflation is precisely the opposite of the economic remedy for unemployment. All of a sudden we had both problems on our hands at the same time, and all the careful long-range plans we had been developing were swept away by the need to act urgently. The result was that issues of economic management took up an increasing proportion of my time and attention in the years following the 1974 election.

In one sense, this was nothing new for me. Economics, as I have recounted earlier, was one of my major preoccupations as far back as my student days. I recognized early on that the concepts of justice and of the freedom of all individuals to fulfil themselves to the best of their ability, to which I attach such fundamental importance, have little practical meaning in the absence of economic opportunity. Where is the justice in a country in which an individual has the freedom to be totally fulfilled, but where inequality denies him or her the means? Absolute freedom, in fact,

At work and at play, at home and abroad

1. Visiting workers at the massive James Bay project in the North, 1975.

2. Skiing in Bavaria, 1975…

3. …and enjoying another great Bavarian tradition.

4. Relaxing in a waterfall in Guyana, 1975.

5. At home, rallying the troops. The organizers were perhaps concerned that the audience might not hear the speaker's name clearly.

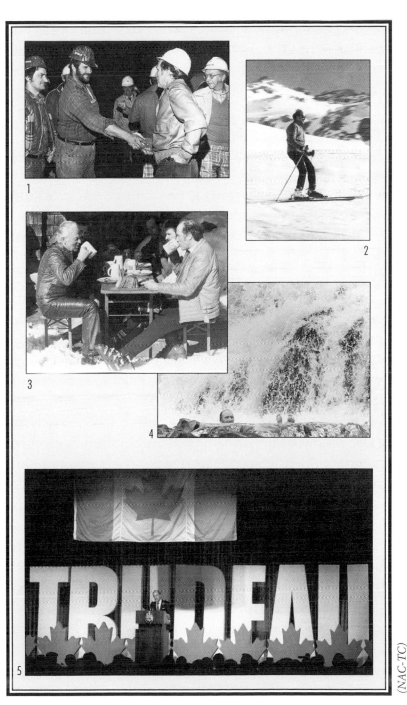

(NAC-TC)

tends to create inequality because there are the strong and the weak, the sick and the healthy, and the rich and the poor. Those who have greater resources go to the best schools, have the best health care, acquire the most influential friends, and wield the most power. It is not an equal race if many of the contestants are lame.

This question of fairness began to strike home in a personal way when I competed with my fellow students at Brébeuf. Many of my classmates came to Brébeuf from Saint-Ignace, a poor man's classical college. At home they had to do their schoolwork on the kitchen table, with their mother cooking and the family milling about. I felt it was unfair that I should have a private room at home to do my work. I was ambitious and wanted to be at the head of the class, but I didn't want to win any contests because I had special advantages. The contest would be fair only if the playing field was level.

I remember, too, being very much influenced in this regard by a powerful story by Antoine de Saint-Exupéry. Travelling by train from France to Poland with a coach full of immigrants who were being sent back home because there was little work in France, Saint-Exupéry noticed a beautiful child with large sad eyes. The thought suddenly struck the writer that this little boy might be as talented as Mozart, but he would never have a chance. His parents were poor; it was obvious that they had little to eat. He would never be able to learn a musical instrument. Saint-Exupéry called this story "Mozart Assassinated," and I remember thinking that Canada must organize itself so that we stop assassinating our Mozarts – that all Canadians should have the opportunity to fulfil themselves to the best of their ability.

This notion of personal fairness was expanded into a

more developed theory of the economy and the state during my studies in the 1940s. Before going to Harvard, I had been quite a conventional thinker on economics: business was there to produce the goods and services, and the state was there to provide the proper environment for the production of wealth – but not much more. During my graduate studies, I began to favour a balance between the role of the state and the role of the private sector. You need a state strong enough to provide the counterweight to the profit motive and to make sure that once the wealth is produced, it is distributed with fairness: in sporting terms, you need a referee to see fair play. The state has an active role to play in ensuring that there is equilibrium between the constituent parts of the economy, the consumers and the producers.

In my opinion, the recent changes in many Western countries exalting the free market and weakening the counterbalancing role of the state have not been a notable success. When I saw Thatcherism and Reaganism and later Mulroneyism become all the fashion and then spread even to the East European countries, I just felt that this was wrong, wrong, wrong. Though the market is certainly the most efficient way of ensuring an economically ideal distribution of inputs, it isn't designed to ensure that this distribution is effected fairly. In other words, reliance on market forces makes the economy work well in strictly economic terms, but it doesn't necessarily prove beneficial for a society because there is nothing to control the excesses of the market.

That should be obvious from the history of the industrial revolutions of the nineteenth century in Europe. We know the excesses in France through reading Zola, and we know the excesses in Britain by reading Dickens. We know of children of workers being forced into child labour under abominable conditions, and so on. Those things really happened under the laissez-faire free market system, where the state stood aside. So I always thought the role of the state, and my role as a politician, was to speak for those who had no voice. That's why when I saw this recent great infatuation with deregulation and strict reliance on the market as a purveyor of justice, I knew it was wrong. And I think the various hardships that were produced by deregulation – the savings-and-loan scandal in the United States, the abuse of junk bonds, the production of paper capital rather than effective goods and services, perhaps indeed the difficult economic times that we're experiencing – are certainly an indication that the market alone can't regulate the economy. As against the "invisible hand" of Adam Smith, there has to be a visible hand of politicians whose objective is to have the kind of society that is caring and humane.

I worked to put this view of social justice into effect throughout my years in office. Regional policy, including the creation of the Department of Regional Economic Expansion in 1968 with Jean Marchand as minister, aimed at equalizing opportunity in a territorial or geographic context; social policy tried to equalize opportunities for individual Canadians. Our first task had been to consolidate and fund the great social policy reforms introduced by Lester Pearson, so in a conscious shift of priorities in 1969 we froze defence spending for three years while the health and welfare budget went up. To maintain the effectiveness of the welfare state, we protected the social safety net and the real incomes of Canadians against inflation by indexing both benefits and tax brackets. Beyond funding and protecting the Pearson government's legacy, we also extended Canada's welfare state in three distinct areas: unemployment insurance, family policy, and easing poverty among the aged.

But social justice is much easier to achieve in a time of economic growth, and in the years after the 1974 election we were no longer in such a time. From 1947 to 1973, the world had experienced a golden age of almost uninterrupted economic expansion. Productivity galloped along at a three per cent annual rate of increase in the 1950s and 1960s – enough to double family incomes in just about thirty years. But in 1973, productivity slowed to an annual rate of one per cent. The OPEC oil price shocks of 1973 and 1979 destabilized the world economy, sent inflation through the roof, and increased social and political tensions. People are more optimistic, generous, and confident when incomes rise. When incomes stagnate, fear starts to take over. As faith in government declined, the pursuit of personal gain became the driving force not only in the economy but in society as a whole. The Love Generation of the sixties was moving towards the Me Generation of the eighties.

In the 1972–74 minority government, we managed to introduce a raft of progressive policies such as the indexation of tax brackets, family allowance increases, and the creation of Petro-Canada. We did this with the support of the NDP, led by David Lewis. I had admired David Lewis's intelligence and great gift of oratory long before entering politics. But after facing him for a while in the House of Commons, I realized he was no more immune to "politicking" than the rest of us!

In the period after the 1974 election, however, it was inflation that increasingly dominated the policy agenda. In 1973 and still at the time of the 1974 election, our inflation was externally caused, by the OPEC oil price shocks. But then it started being created internally in Canada, by our own expectations. People were saying: "Prices are going to go up because OPEC will increase oil prices again, so I should increase my prices before I sell my goods" or "I should demand higher wages before I sign my contract." Businesses were doing it, labour was doing it, and private savers were doing it: "Interest rates are going to go up, so I'll hold onto my money until I get higher interest rates." But when people expect higher interest rates, you get inflation; when people expect higher prices or higher wages, you get inflation. So in the year after the election, John Turner as finance minister, supported by myself and the whole Cabinet, tried to deal with this new situation. Ministers led by Turner met with scores of labour and business leaders to plead for voluntary restraint on both sides, but they didn't get very far.

By the fall of 1975, we had only three options. One was to continue our policy of exhorting business and labour to reduce their expectations voluntarily. But inflation had leaped to an annual rate of 10.8 per cent in 1975, and there was a danger that it would head completely out of control. The second option was to induce a recession by imposing draconian restraints and monetary measures. But by rejecting such a course, Canada had just successfully avoided the 1973–75 recession. And now, with unemployment already at seven per cent, we believed the cost of a policy-induced recession would be too high. The third alternative was wage and price controls. The Department of Finance had opposed controls when most of our recession was caused by external sources, but by the fall of 1975, with the voluntary restraint effort clearly failing, Finance officials were beginning to recommend a controls program as the only option. Turner and I were united in our belief that we should avoid if at all possible the imposition

Inflation was dominating our thoughts as Finance Minister John Turner and I planned the 1975 budget in June. (Canapress)

of wage and price controls, because we had been the two Liberal politicians most identified with criticizing Stanfield's policy.

In the midst of this dilemma, on September 10, John Turner came to me and resigned. Since he had given me no prior warning of his unhappiness, I was surprised and disappointed. We met in my office and he said, "I want to go." I said, "Why do you want to go? Stick around, we're just beginning this new mandate. What are your reasons?" He answered: "I've been here since 1962, a lot longer than you, and I've got my family to look after. It's that time in life. I've discussed it, and I have told a few of my friends and advisers that I was going to resign, and I'm coming to give you my resignation." Since I had always thought myself that I didn't want to stay in politics too long, especially now that I had children and wanted to watch them grow up, I understood. So I said, "Well, John, if that's your destiny as you see it, I'll accept your resignation. I'm sorry, but good luck and let me know if there is anything I can do."

You can tell me I handled it badly, tell me I should have got down on my knees and begged him to stay. But that's not the way I saw politics, then or now. Politics is a difficult game and you have to have your heart in it. And if his heart wasn't in it for one reason or another, either because of his family and his economic circumstances or because I was his leader, then perhaps it was right that he leave politics. Another type of leader might have handled it differently, but I have always believed that if an adult has thought carefully about his future, then he knows what is best for himself.

Years later, there were reports that he had left because he felt I had not supported him in his fight to limit inflation. I don't think John ever said that; whether he felt it, I doubt too. I remember that these puzzling reports inspired me to look up the Cabinet minutes from that time; the minutes throughout that whole period showed that I had constantly encouraged Turner to do what he was doing. Maybe if he had been me in that position, he would have invited the labour leaders and the business leaders to Ottawa to the prime minister's office and slapped their backs, or whatever, I don't know. But he knew me, he knew that I was not a back-slapper. And he certainly must have known, in his heart, that the facts – in the Cabinet discussions and in the work of his department that had my support – showed clearly that if there was anything I wanted, it was for his fight for voluntary restraint against inflation to succeed. Because I personally did not want controls. I was the leader who had opposed controls less than two years before in a hard-fought election campaign when controls were the main issue, and I knew that people would ignore the different economic circumstances. So it's just a mad hypothesis –

There was a crisis atmosphere after Turner's resignation in September 1975, and I faced a hostile press.
(NAC-TC/Duncan Cameron)

invented, I think, by the more imaginative elements of the press – that my heart wasn't in the fight against inflation and that I was not wholeheartedly behind the minister who was going to save my skin by fighting inflation without imposing controls.

Turner's resignation heightened the crisis atmosphere, particularly since our efforts to build a consensus for voluntary restraint had involved warning the public about the dangers of runaway inflation. When the finance minister – a long-serving and well-respected politician – suddenly left at this critical point, it created an impression that the situation was spinning out of control.

My choice of Donald Macdonald as Turner's successor was a last-ditch attempt to rescue the voluntary consensus effort and avoid controls. Macdonald had been one of the most vehement opponents of controls, and I knew that if there was any way to avoid them, Don would find it. He and I had got along very well from the very beginning, when we were both parliamentary secretaries delegated to the United Nations by Mike Pearson. Don was a good fighter, always very frank and outspoken. In fact, he was sometimes embarrassingly frank in the Cabinet: he would almost tell the prime minister – me – to go to hell, not much more gently than that. But I liked him because he had a strong character. He was very intelligent, very vigorous – he was known as "Thumper" and not just, as has been slanderously asserted, for the size of his feet. When I appointed him as minister of finance, I knew that his bureaucrats would not be able to stampede him into imposing wage and price controls. But to my great surprise, very shortly after he succeeded Turner, Macdonald came to the Cabinet and said: "There's no choice."

I had to swallow my doubts – and my words – and, ironically, on Thanksgiving Day, 1975, I went on national television and announced the creation of the Anti-Inflation Board, and the direct imposition of wage and price controls. This measure was augmented by freezing the salaries of members of Parliament and civil servants, and by expenditure cuts of $1.5 billion. The harsh medicine worked. From a rate of nearly 11 per cent in 1975, inflation declined to 7.5 per cent in 1976 and 7.9 per cent in 1977. In April 1978, the Anti-Inflation Board, which had been very ably chaired by Jean-Luc Pepin, was terminated, ahead of schedule. The AIB did not end Canada's inflation psychology. But it had quelled the crisis atmosphere of 1975 when events had threatened to get out of hand.

As I had feared, for imposing wage and price controls my government and I paid a heavy price in lost credibility. I know it cost me personally a great amount, because until

To Prime Minister Trudeau, on the occasion of our very welcome meeting at NATO Headquarters, May 30, 1975

Gerald R. Ford

President Gerald Ford and I became good friends. When I visited him at the end of 1975 we naturally discussed the economy. His memoirs, A Time to Heal, *record: "Other heads of state of the Western democracies faced problems very similar to mine. Canada's Pierre Elliott Trudeau, for example, visited me in Washington on December 4, [1975,] and when he described his country's economic plight, it sounded grimmer than our own." (NAC-TC)*

then I think I was respected as a straight-shooting guy who told the truth as he saw it and who wasn't just a devious politician who would say one thing and then go out and practise another. The extent of the damage became clear from the uproar that erupted over some rather innocuous remarks I made in December in a year-end television interview. I made the obvious point that "we haven't been able to make it work – the free market system." I suggested that a "new society" of the future might require more, not less, government intervention, including a resort to permanent controls if it proved impossible to achieve both consensus and reduced expectations voluntarily. I quoted John Kenneth Galbraith, the liberal Harvard economist (and the product of a long line of good Liberals in southwestern Ontario), on this point and the result was hysteria in many business and some labour circles. I found myself being accused of everything from communism to fascism.

I later told Ken Galbraith that I hoped my remarks had been good for his royalty statements. And in January I delivered a speech in which I gave explicit assurances that I had no plans to subvert the free enterprise system. That is the joy of being a politician: the champions of the business class would always say that we were too hard on them, and a labour leader would say exactly the opposite, that we were too much on the side of business and unfair to the ordinary workers. In our society, different groups contend, and it is the responsibility of the politicians to thread their way between the differing interests in order to determine the public interest.

In August of 1978, shortly after we had lifted the controls of the Anti-Inflation Board, I found myself embroiled in yet another economic controversy – this time about spending restraint. What the public and the media saw was me returning from the Bonn Economic Summit and going on national television to announce $2.5 billion in government spending cuts. Because I announced this package so soon after my return from Bonn, it quickly became conventional wisdom that Chancellor Helmut Schmidt had suddenly converted me to the cause of restraint and economic responsibility.

One of the pleasures of writing an autobiography is that

My old friend John Kenneth Galbraith towers above this Washington conversation. (NAC-TC)

one can take the opportunity to shoot down that kind of nonsense. The reality is that months before going to Bonn, I had met with the Cabinet and told every minister that we had to cut spending to keep inflation in check. We had even prepared precise targets for every department to attain. But on my return from Bonn, I discovered that the ministers had offered up only 10 per cent of what we had requested. So I told my office, "If nobody is volunteering cuts, let's do it by ourselves." We took the target of $2.5 billion that the Department of Finance and the Treasury Board thought appropriate, allocated it to the various ministries, and then went on television and announced it. Sometimes you just have to move.

The unfortunate aspect of moving so quickly – and one reason why I so strongly preferred an orderly Cabinet committee process – is that in the burst of activity to get the package assembled and announced, we did not involve Jean Chrétien, who was by this time the minister of finance. Chrétien should have been given the opportunity to be there, but it was mid-summer and he was in his constituency. I knew he was in agreement with the objective of deep cuts, and his officials were involved in working on the substance of the measures. But I only phoned him before announcing the package, rather than involving him in the initial decision-making phase, and he was justified in being upset. But Jean Chrétien is a good soldier and a happy warrior, and we quickly moved on to fight more battles side by side.

As for Schmidt, it certainly is true that he was among the people I regarded most highly in public life. He was someone that I respected highly and regarded as a friend. Though he was theoretically the leader of a social-democratic party, his views seemed very close to my middle-of-the-road liberalism. He used to say, in fact, that I was probably to his left rather than to his right. I particularly admired the way in which he had managed to keep the social contract alive in Germany. He would always travel with leaders of both business and labour accompanying him, and he made sure they had good communication with each other. On the occasion when Schmidt was wrongly thought to have sold me on fiscal restraint, I had gone sailing with him in the Baltic Sea, and when we got back to port, I enjoyed listening to him play the organ. The only business item we discussed was my attempt to persuade Germany to buy more Canadian-made aircraft. There had been no conversion on the economic road to Damascus.

Although the economic situation dominated much of our agenda during this period and rendered many of our carefully developed plans irrelevant, I don't want to give the impression that it was the only item on my plate. I was

Germany, 1978

1. Sailing on the Baltic with Helmut Schmidt, whose company I always enjoyed.

2. Exchanging ideas with Schmidt at an informal reception during the Bonn Economic Summit in July 1978.

3. By contrast, I have always been impatient with the set speeches that predominate at formal meetings of this type.

4. The inevitable formal photograph. From the left, Roy Jenkins, Takeo Fukuda, Giulio Andreotti, Jimmy Carter, Helmut Schmidt, Valéry Giscard d'Estaing, James Callaghan, and me.

5. The German and Canadian delegations (including Don Jamieson and Jean Chrétien) and their wives get together.

(NAC-TC)

devoting a great deal of attention, for instance, to Canada's place in the world.

It's fair to say that I had not entered politics in 1965 because of my interest in foreign policy. It was an area that, apart from the issue of nuclear weapons, really didn't interest me greatly at the time. I had occasionally written about foreign policy in *Cité libre*. And partly as a result of my travels abroad, I had developed strong feelings about the injustice suffered by the two-thirds of the world's population that lived in poverty. But I was neither fascinated by the study of foreign policy nor especially attracted by the practice of it, although I found my early work as an MP in France and at the United Nations to be interesting. When I became prime minister, I felt that Mike Pearson had been so good in this whole area that I wouldn't be able to add much to his insights and actions, except in some cases, such as recognizing Beijing, which we did during the first term. But as I gained more experience in office, I began to realize that a head of government had no choice but to be directly involved in foreign policy issues, if only because of the various summits, personal exchanges, and visits that inevitably occur. So I thought I should learn more about the field and tried to surround myself with some good advisers. Ivan Head, who had been an officer in the Department of External Affairs, became my most important personal foreign policy adviser through the 1970s. After Head left my office, my principal secretary, Tom Axworthy, and Robert Fowler from the Privy Council Office gave me advice in the late 1970s and early 1980s. Foreign policy came to take up a growing proportion of my time, particularly in the years after the 1974 election.

Prompted by the "Nixon shock" of 1971, when President

Richard Nixon arbitrarily imposed a 10 per cent sur-
charge on all goods entering the United States, in 1972
we had announced a new policy to enhance Canada's
autonomy and reduce our economic dependence on the
U.S. External Affairs Minister Sharp told Canadians they
had three options: first, maintenance of the status quo;
second, closer integration with the U.S. economy; and a
third option – "to develop and strengthen the Canadian
economy and other aspects of its national life and in the
process to reduce the present Canadian vulnerability." This
so-called "Third Option" approach to Canadian-American
relations had three main components: strengthening
Canadian ownership of the economy, protecting Canadian
culture, and diversifying Canada's trade abroad.

Enormous political will was needed to reverse the growing American ownership of the Canadian economy. Each
stage in the process led to disputes with the U.S. government, which I have always found to be vociferous in its support of any American-based corporation – and as these
disputes intensified, the Canadian business community
became more upset. But our measures worked. Canadians
were given generous tax incentives to save, through the
Registered Retirement Savings Plan (RRSP), and through
dividend tax credits and corporate and individual tax cuts.
Largely as a result of these policies, in 1983 the personal savings rate in Canada was 14 per cent, compared with four
per cent in the U.S. Starting in 1975, Canadians became net
exporters of equity capital, investing more in the United
States than Americans were investing here.

We also used regulation to control American ownership
of our economy. We created the Foreign Investment Review
Agency (FIRA) in 1973 to screen foreign investment and to

*When times
are tough
any leader
must feel
a bit like
a target.
(NAC-TC)*

bargain with foreign investors to ensure that the maximum possible benefits would accrue to Canada; I must confess that I fail to see why this should be regarded as a questionable policy. And we also used direct government ownership, by creating such instruments as the Canada Development Corporation, which bought foreign assets in mining and manufacturing, and Petro-Canada. Later, in 1980, the National Energy Program (NEP) called for 50 per cent Canadian ownership in the petroleum industry. The result of these policies was that by the mid-1980s, the tide had turned. Foreign control of the Canadian economy, as measured by Statistics Canada, fell from 37 per cent in 1971 to 23.6 per cent in 1986 – and American ownership fell from 28 per cent to 17 per cent.

In support of the Third Option strategy of diversifying our economic relationships, I devoted a lot of my time in the mid-1970s to expanding Canada's contacts with the world outside the United States. In 1974, I visited Brussels to discuss the idea of a contractual link with the European Economic Community. I returned to Europe again the following year to renew our case. Finally in 1976 we succeeded in winning an agreement that established a joint cooperation committee, gave most-favoured-nation status to both parties, and called for greater exchanges of scientists and other interested parties. In the fall of 1976, I followed this up by signing a similar agreement with Japan.

But sometimes, alas, even the soundest policies do not achieve their intended effects. The Third Option was forward-looking in recognizing the rising power of Japan and the growing importance of the European market – but our foreign policy successes did not succeed in changing Canada's ingrained export habits. I suppose that changing the individual decisions of thousands of exporters is likely to be beyond the power of any government.

In fact, after years in office, I eventually came to the conclusion that Canadian businesspeople have it so easy with the United States – where they already know the customers, the techniques, the language, and the geography – that they are a little lazier and less inclined towards initiatives in Asia or Africa or other parts of the world, even Europe. I think they are entrepreneurs with a difference. You see the Germans or the Americans or the French in the most faraway corners, but my successive ministers of international trade used to tell me that you have to kick Canadians in the pants to get them to go to a new market. And so our trade expanded, but it did not diversify.

My official travels did give me the opportunity to develop close personal links with a number of foreign leaders, however, and that served Canada's interests well on a number of occasions. The importance of personal chemistry between leaders is sometimes exaggerated by the media and others, because in the final analysis it is the national interest that most often determines policy. A responsible leader isn't likely to put his own country's interests second just because he happens to like you. But a good relationship enables you to pick up the phone, establish easy communications, and prevent any misunderstandings.

I recall, for instance, two meetings with Leonid Brezhnev of the Soviet Union. On my first official visit to Moscow in 1971, we met in the Kremlin in a medium-sized room with very plain furniture. Brezhnev was the boss of a big empire, and he behaved like one. He was gruff and loudspoken, but with an occasional twinkle in his eye. We were sitting at a long table and he was right opposite me, a very

In the Kremlin, accompanied by our ambassador to Moscow, R. A. D. Ford, I held formal talks with Leonid Brezhnev and his foreign secretary, Andrei Gromyko. In his memoirs Gromyko has an amusing description of me as "a man of great ability and tact ... although he always had a good supply of ammunition for use against his political opponents, he was careful never to insult anyone personally. It was a characteristic that everyone noted. People who know him well say he has no personal enemies." This is, I must confess, not strictly true. Gromyko also says of me, giving a view from the other side of the Iron Curtain: "Of course he is a bourgeois politician and his ideological views derive from his class. Nevertheless, in international affairs, he stood head and shoulders above statesmen of other NATO countries who are blinded by their hostility to socialism and either cannot or will not recognize the situation as it is." (NAC-TC)

short space away, peering at me with his powerful eyes from under very heavy eyebrows. As a character he was fascinating. Since in those days long hair was fashionable in the West, it's possible that he thought the same of my very un-Soviet look. In any case, he launched into a lengthy denunciation of capitalism. I didn't see any point in giving him an argument about Marxism or dialectical materialism, so I just let him go through his passionate exposé about how wrong the Americans were and how right the Soviets were. But then I did use the occasion to give him a list of nearly

300 family reunification cases, of Canadians who were attempting to get exit visas for relatives still living in the Soviet Union. Within a few months, most of these cases had been solved, and hundreds of Soviet citizens had been allowed to emigrate to Canada.

I met Brezhnev again in August 1975, at the Helsinki Conference on Security and Cooperation in Europe. This conference gave us the opportunity to press the Soviets on human rights and the free movement of peoples. The agreement reached in Helsinki was subsequently very important in establishing the legitimacy of dissident groups in Eastern Europe, such as the Charter 77 group in Czechoslovakia. But I was also able to use the occasion to settle an important bilateral dispute. The Soviet fishing fleet, with its huge factory ships, had refused to respect our rules on quotas for fishing, and already we could see a crisis looming as our fish stocks declined. Our only remaining recourse was to close our ports to Soviet vessels.

I decided to speak to Brezhnev if I had the chance while we were together at Helsinki. It came after we had all spoken on the accord and were sitting in this great amphitheatre. At one of the breaks, I went over to Brezhnev, who was a few aisles away surrounded by his coterie. Through an interpreter I asked him, "Can I bend your ear for a moment?" Once I had caught his attention I briefed him about the situation and said, "Tomorrow we are going to close our ports to your fishing fleet if we can't solve the problem." He picked up the phone at his desk, had some words with his officials, and a few days later we were no longer hearing the excuses from Soviet diplomats that it was impossible to tell captains on the high seas how many fish they could catch. After I talked to Brezhnev, somehow the captains on the seas near Canada got the message.

I have vivid memories, too, of my meeting with Mao Zedong in 1973. I had actually met him once before, in 1960, when I was head of a small Canadian delegation invited to see the October parades. They had invited the head of each delegation to meet Mao, and the audience took place on top of the portal at Tiananmen Square. I have vivid memories of meeting this former revolutionary, the son of a peasant, who now headed these vast armies of people. When I went back in 1973, I didn't ask to see Mao, but my delegation rather hoped – and, to be honest, so did I – that I would have the opportunity. It was known that he was sometimes incommunicado, that his health wasn't all that good; and the gossip among the foreign establishment was that, now that he was over eighty, he had lucid times and other times when his mind was less clear. Would the Great Helmsman be in good health while I was there, and would I be received? That was the big question, and every once in a while during our bilateral meetings with Chou Enlai someone would come in and whisper in somebody's ear, and we would pretend not to notice and go on with the agenda.

At one point, after one of these whispers, Chou Enlai said, "Well, we have to adjourn now. I have other business and so do you." There was no explanation. They just took me off with them. We drove to the Forbidden City and went to the area of the compound where Mao had his house.

We went into a very dark room with all the curtains drawn, and there was this venerable gentleman, with his round face and balding head, sitting, looking like a sort of Buddha. As I came in, he stood up to shake my hand, and the cameras were whirring away. I guess that's why they had closed the drapes, to get some artificial lighting for filming. We sat down and had a long talk. He did most of the talking. I was interested in his foreign policy views, and I remember that we had a long discussion about the Middle East. I felt that China was tilting a bit more towards the Arab side. He was saying that we in the West were tilting too much towards the Israeli side, and he explained to me his theory of counterweights, about which I knew something. All in all, it was a rather impressive occasion.

Chou Enlai was quite a fascinating personality in his own right. Although he was part of the Maoist revolutionary government and had himself been on the Long March, he had the style, the figure, the face, and the mannerisms of a mandarin. He was a man with a great deal of culture and a lot of knowledge, which was not flaunted but which was brought to bear on each question. As far as I could judge from our relatively brief meetings, he seemed a genuinely likeable and impressive individual.

Sometimes, of course, face-to-face discussions with foreign leaders produced good personal rapport but not a real meeting of minds. When I met with Fidel Castro on an official visit to Cuba in January 1976, for instance, I saw a very different side of the man from the fiery orator he is in public. Margaret and baby Michel were with me on this trip, and Castro invited us to spend a day and evening with him at a spartan cabin on a little island. We spent the day skin-diving. In spite of his cigar-smoking, he was a really good skin-diver. He could go down thirty or forty feet and hold his breath for a full minute while waiting for the fish to come. In private, in contrast to his public speeches, he was so quiet-spoken that you had to lean forward to understand him. He was very thoughtful and didn't overindulge in monologues; he would throw out questions and be prepared to have an exchange of views with you. This was a very different man from what the public sees, but both sides of his personality were quite magnetic – the powerful

1. *Meeting the Great Helmsman, Mao Zedong.*

2. *Chou Enlai – I found him to be a fascinating personality in his own right. A genuinely likeable and impressive individual.*

3. *Chou – a man with the style, the figure, and the face of a mandarin.*

4. *According to Henry Kissinger, Canada's recognition of China before U.S. recognition irritated Nixon. He recalls: "Giving vent to his dislike of Pierre Trudeau, [Nixon] remarked that future contacts or channels with the Chinese could take place any-where except Ottawa."*
(Canapress)

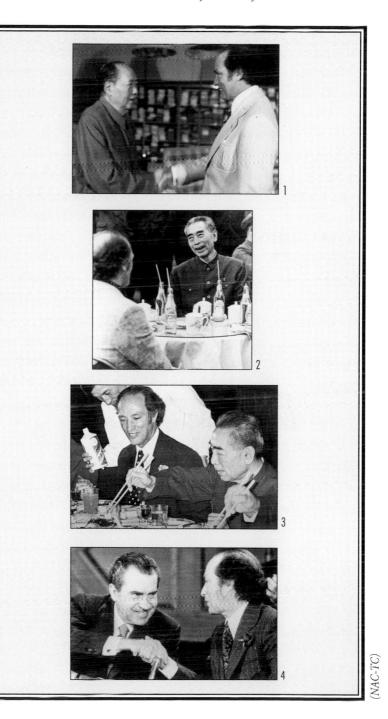

(NAC-TC)

orator and the soft-spoken, subdued revolutionary with only the beard as a reminder that he was a radical.

But this was the time of the Cuban involvement in Angola, and our government had taken a strong position in condemning Cuba's African military adventure. Castro and I had our discussion of that issue in a very friendly atmosphere, on that little island as the sun set and the moon came up. We in Canada didn't know too much about what was going on in Angola, but we already knew that some Cubans were there, engaged in the civil war. So I asked him, "Now, isn't this meddling in the internal affairs of a foreign country?" He explained that this was a different situation – very different from the Americans in Viet Nam – and that he was doing it only to assist the legitimate government of Angola, which was trying to protect itself against guerrillas backed by South Africa and some NATO powers. But the most important thing was that he minimized the number of troops he had there; he gave me a very low number, and said they would be there only very briefly, not for the long haul.

After I went home, it became obvious that the numbers were much higher and that the Cubans intended to stay in Angola. I said, "Now that we have the real numbers and it looks as though they're having more than just a quick incursion there, we'll stop foreign aid to them." Until then, we had traded with Cuba and given the country economic aid in spite of constant pressure on us from the United States to do the contrary. But because of the Angolan war, we cut off all aid to Cuba, except humanitarian aid. I did not meet Castro again until many years later, so I don't know what his reaction was to our tough policy. But I'm sure he didn't like it.

In the case of Indira Gandhi, there was both a lack of close personal rapport and disagreement on a very

isiting Fidel Castro

1. The official reception on arrival in Cuba at the José Martí International Airport in January 1976.

2. A less formal reception at the airport for the Trudeau family, including baby Michel.

3. Enjoying skin-diving in the waters off Cuba.

4. With Fidel Castro, who is a good skin-diver, a helper, and a very large fish.

5. Margaret and I found Castro to be friendly and informal, a very different man from what the public sees, and pleased to advertise Cuba's most famous national product.

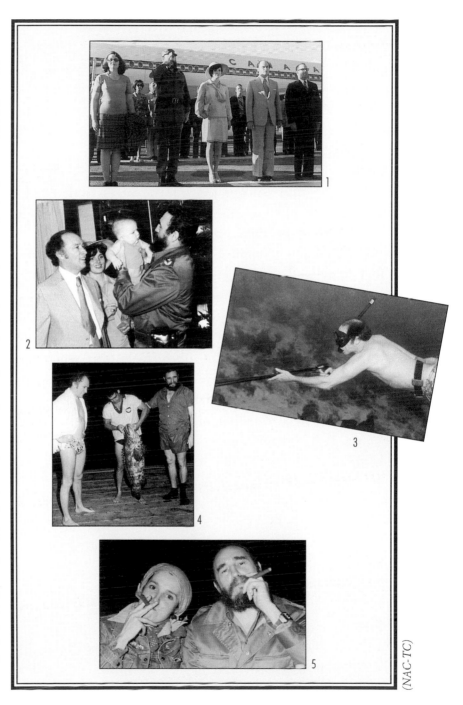

(NAC-TC)

important issue. I first met her in London at the 1969 Commonwealth Conference. I was new in office then – I think she was even newer – and it was a very strange meeting. I guess I expected more from her: she was if not sullen, at least very quiet and untalkative. Our first meeting was a series of silences between us; you could say that we didn't hit it off all that well. But, with my still-fresh memories of my travels in India, I had enormous respect for the magnitude of her job. As the years went by, we had an easier time communicating, but we were often in opposition to each other on various issues.

We had an especially bitter dispute over the Candu reactor and the issue of nuclear proliferation. Since 1956, as part of its aid program, Canada had sent nuclear technology to India. One main gift was a Candu nuclear reactor to provide electricity. As we began to suspect that the Indians were using some of the plutonium from this reactor to develop a "peaceful nuclear device," as she called it, I asked Mrs. Gandhi point-blank: "Are you working on a bomb?" She gave me her word that India was not doing anything like that. A short time later, in 1974, off went this thing that sounded an awful lot like a test of a nuclear bomb, but that the Indians called a "peaceful" nuclear explosion. I guess that was how she was able to play with words and give me her assurance that there was no bomb in the making.

At later meetings, Mrs. Gandhi expounded on her position by saying: "This is the kind of thing that we may need at some point to build a dam or move a mountain for development reasons." But I felt shocked and betrayed because I had talked with her at least twice about this matter, and we had had an exchange of letters in which I had made it very clear that in no way should our aid in nuclear technology for the generation of electricity be used to produce plutonium for an explosion. So there was no hesitation in my mind or the government's mind. Canada cut off all forms of nuclear technological assistance to India, and we imposed unilateral restraints on all uranium exports and announced stringent new safeguards on all exports of nuclear material.

My relations with Israel's prime minister Menachem Begin were also rather strained. When Begin visited Canada in 1978, I had several good exchanges with him, and I admired his willingness to negotiate peace with Egyptian president Anwar Sadat. But then he tried to pressure us to move our Canadian embassy from Tel Aviv to Jerusalem. This would have been a coup for his government, of course, since they were trying to have Jerusalem recognized internationally as an Israeli city. I explained that there was no way we could tilt our policy in this manner in what was defined by the United Nations as one of the occupied territories. Begin became rather nasty about it and said, "I'm going to tell your voters in Toronto that you're not supporting Israel on this." I told him: "They already know. You can tell them what you want, but I don't think

In November 1978 Menachem Begin, the prime minister of Israel, came to visit Ottawa. Here he is greeted by Barney Danson (right) and Don Jamieson. (NAC-TC)

it would be very courteous – and I don't think it would be very effective." I knew this because my own constituency in Mount Royal had a large Jewish population, and I often took the opportunity to exchange views with my constituents about Israel and the Palestinian issue.

We turned Begin down flat. But Joe Clark was not so wise, and he later got into a lot of difficulty when he followed the Begin line on moving our embassy to Jerusalem.

As I have indicated, our policies on behalf of Canada often caused friction with the American administration at the time, but my personal relations with the various American presidents I had to deal with were always good. I first met Richard Nixon and Henry Kissinger in March 1969, on my first visit to the White House. I didn't know much about Kissinger at the time, but I knew that Nixon had been a very successful politician who had overcome many reverses. He was an experienced, astute old pro and I was just a greenhorn, and I was trying to learn from somebody who knew more than I did about certain things. I never actually got around to taping conversations with my guests, but there are a lot of things you can learn from a man like Nixon.

In our dealings, I can't say there was any warmth of feeling on either side. We did business together. I felt I could have empathy for his problems in governing one of the world's superpowers, though I didn't feel warmly towards him as a person. In fact, my feelings about him were mixed. There was a huge contrast between the public and the private man. In public, he had a great facility with words, easily ad-libbing toasts or deflecting questions from the press and always maintaining a great dignity. Even after he had been badly damaged by the Watergate revelations, Nixon attracted people like a magnet. I remember, for instance,

*In official
meetings I
refused to
bow to the
considerable
pressure put
on me by
Begin to move
Canada's
embassy in
Israel to
Jerusalem.
(NAC-TC)*

that at a reception for dignitaries in Paris following the funeral of President Georges Pompidou – which was shortly before Nixon resigned – there were many heads of state and senior politicians, but it was only Nixon who attracted a crowd. People flocked around him, and I could see that even then, during the worst of Watergate, he was stoic in the face of his troubles and still held a great deal of fascination for other world leaders.

In contrast to this firm public presence, in private he was always stiff and perspiring, and occasionally had to ask Kissinger to explain certain things. He was obviously not at ease in his skin. Yet when it came to the official job, he was very able. A complex man.

During the whole Nixon era, Viet Nam dominated the foreign policy agenda. Our government was often criticized by Canadians for not condemning strongly enough the American presence in Viet Nam. We did condemn the 1970 American invasion of Cambodia and the resumption of bombing of the North in 1972, but on Viet Nam generally we did not make a great number of statements. I simply did not think they would have any effect on the American government. Clearly, there was no way the United States should have been there in the first place. But once they had made that original commitment, the Americans were stuck with guaranteeing the people of the South that they would be protected from the North. This dilemma worried me a lot; since I had no positive contribution to make to the solution, I didn't want to kibitz from the grandstand.

Nixon never raised Canada's condemnation of his invasion of Cambodia or our opposition to his bombing policy with me personally. But he was obviously distressed with our actions on the International Control Commission, where we were one of those countries that were supposed to supervise the "peace." Nixon repeatedly asked us to stay on, after the ceasefire broke down and Canadian lives were in danger. We informed the president that our job was not to supervise a war or be involved in fighting, but he asked us to stay on for a few more months until the Canadians could be replaced by somebody else. When this time had elapsed, we told Washington that the situation was intolerable and that Canada's peacekeepers were coming home. When Nixon's tapes later became public, it was obvious that Nixon was very angry with this decision and he had called me some nasty names. My only response was that I had been called worse things by better people.

Gerald Ford, who succeeded Nixon in unusual circumstances in 1974, was much more straightforward, much more at ease with himself. He didn't pretend to be a great geopolitician; he would turn to Kissinger for those things. But he was a very pleasant, honest man. And obviously he knew how to deal with Congress, which in the American system is a very important skill. I enjoyed his company. Even after retiring from politics, we would meet – and still do occasionally – at his Colorado retreat in Beaver Creek or before that in Vail. I would go down there for New Year's, and we would ski together. Of all the American presidents I had occasion to deal with, what set Ford apart was that he did nothing I can remember that rubbed Canada the wrong way.

It was Gerald Ford, in fact, who was responsible for one of the greatest achievements of Canadian foreign policy. In 1975, French president Valéry Giscard d'Estaing had initiated the first Economic Summit of the great economic powers. Canada was not invited to this first meeting. When I subsequently visited Washington, President Ford invited me for a boat ride on the Potomac, and he and I and Kissinger and Ivan Head had dinner together on board. In our discussion, Kissinger and Ford formed the idea that it might be a good idea if I was invited to the next Economic Summit, which was to be held in Puerto Rico with Ford as chairman. They felt that I could at least understand the point of view of the Americans, even though I didn't always share it. So I was invited, and in 1976 Canada was admitted to the Group of Seven leading industrialized nations. For a middle power like Canada, membership in this powerful group is important, so we owe much to Gerald Ford.

Jimmy Carter, the Democrat who succeeded Ford in 1977, was very cerebral, very well briefed, and highly principled. He was well known for promoting human rights and – even rarer for an American president – he had a genuine interest in the Third World. His real claim to greatness resides in the fact that he was a man of peace and was instrumental in bringing together Anwar Sadat and Menachem Begin at Camp David to negotiate the Israel-Egypt peace treaty. From my own dealings with Begin, I know how difficult this must have been.

But Carter had problems with the Congress. He lost a

lot of political credibility with the American people, for instance, after his bruising battle with the Senate over the Panama Canal Treaty, an issue where Carter proved himself very enlightened and where he was in the right.

Carter's weakness with Congress actually had an effect on Canada as well. He and I decided that it was time to resolve the longstanding dispute between our two countries over maritime boundaries and the management of fish stocks. Carter selected a very able Washington lawyer, Lloyd Cutler, as his negotiator, and I appointed Marcel Cadieux, one of Canada's most experienced diplomats. Cadieux negotiated well, and the talks produced an agreement to manage and share the resources of the Atlantic fishery. Carter accepted this agreement and sent it to the Senate for approval – but he was unable to persuade the Senate to approve it. The senators from New England thought we had gained too much in the negotiations, and that was the end of the agreement.

Later, in my final term, I even got along quite well with Ronald Reagan, even though we were about as far apart in outlook and personality as two people could be. I will recount more about my experiences with him further on, when I come to that period of my time in government.

I also had occasion, during my years in office, to deal with a whole succession of British prime ministers. The first was Harold Wilson, whom I knew in my earliest days as prime minister. I had known him by reputation as the boy wonder of the Labour Party. He seemed clever and skilful enough. But I didn't think, at the Commonwealth meetings and others that I attended with him, that he was really as outstanding as his reputation. His successor, Ted Heath, a Tory, was very intellectually and culturally gifted, and I respected him throughout for that. He was not only a

Washington, 1977

1. In 1977 I visited the new president, Jimmy Carter, at the White House, and presented him with a fine new Canadian book.

2. With President Carter and our wives outside the White House, giving the obligatory wave for the press corps.

3. Under the joint chairmanship of Vice-President Walter Mondale and House Speaker Tip O'Neill (right) I addressed the United States Congress.

4. At a reception we were pleased to meet Elizabeth Taylor and her husband, John Warner.
(Canapress)

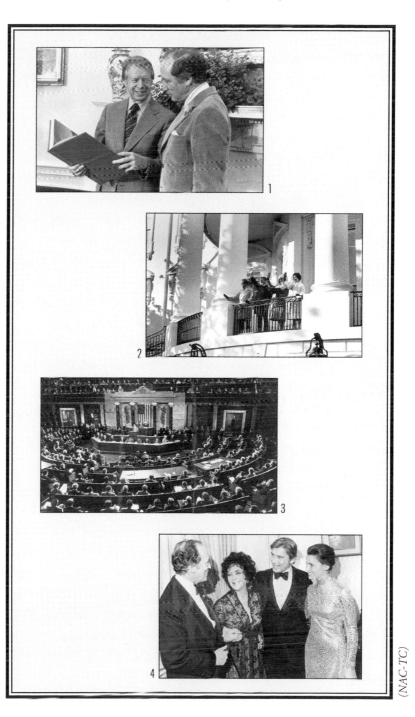

(NAC-TC)

good yachtsman, but also a good pianist and organist. As a politician, his time in office was short, but he was a leader who showed courage and foresight in attempting to bring Britain into the European Common Market.

Jim Callaghan, who followed him, is someone I like a lot. He's a man of real common sense and, I think, intellectual courage. Though a Labour prime minister, he was never wild-eyed; in fact, he sometimes struck me as overly prudent. He has a very warm personality, and at the various conferences where I saw him in action he was always a very responsible statesman. I see him nowadays at various international meetings, and I still admire his clarity of thinking and his sense of justice.

As for Margaret Thatcher, it's well known that we disagreed on many things, including East-West relations and North-South relations. At international summits, she often acted as President Reagan's spokesperson in articulating a very conservative viewpoint. But what's less well known is that though she'd be very critical of me, and I of her, we were not only civil with each other but friendly in an odd sort of way. After our tiffs, we'd make sure we had a walk in the garden together and have tea, and talk of other things. It was nice, because obviously what separated her and me were clear and wide ideological disputes, so wide that there was no point trying to convert each other. We would just talk over each other's heads to whatever audience we were appealing to. Often that audience was more inclined to be on her side than on mine anyway, particularly at the later summits. She and Reagan formed a very solid team, generally supported by Germany's Helmut Kohl and the Japanese prime minister of the day, whereas François Mitterrand of France and I were usually the odd men out.

Three British leaders

1. An informal shot of Ted Heath, in the course of his visit to Canada in 1973.
(Toronto Star/G.Bezant)

2. Jim Callaghan, another British prime minister whose intellect I admire. We still meet on occasion.
(Les Productions La Fête/Jean Demers)

3. Margaret Thatcher and I had such fierce debates that Ronald Reagan once noted in his diary: "I thought at one point Margaret Thatcher was going to order Pierre to go stand in a corner." Yet despite the fact that she regarded my opinions as hopelessly "wet" we were friendly in an odd sort of way.
(NAC-TC/Robert Cooper)

Overall, I think it's fair to say that my approach to international relations was really based on my approach to the Canadian community. The community of man should be treated in the same way you would treat your community of brothers or fellow citizens. It was an idealistic approach as opposed to a realpolitik approach. I felt it was the duty of a middle power like Canada, which could not sway the world with the force of its armies, to at least try to sway the world with the force of its ideals. I wanted to run Canada by applying the principles of justice and equality, and I wanted our foreign policy to reflect similar values.

That is why aid to Third World countries played an important part in my approach to foreign policy. In 1969–70, Canada was allocating $277 million, or 0.34 per cent of our GNP, to official development assistance. By 1975, we had increased this to $760 million, or 0.54 per cent of GNP. And in 1984–85, our foreign aid was over $2 billion, or 0.49 per cent of GNP. We also improved the content of our aid – from loans to grants – and changed its direction: in 1970, only 5 per cent of Canada's aid went to the least developed nations – the poorest of the poor – but by 1980 about 30 per cent was directed to these most destitute nations.

My interest in Third World issues also went beyond dollars and cents, to considerable personal involvement. I counted leaders like Michael Manley of Jamaica, Julius Nyerere of Tanzania, and Lee Kwan Yew of Singapore as personal friends, and whenever I could I tried to use Canada's membership in the Economic Summit, or meetings of the Commonwealth nations, La Francophonie, or other forums, to bring Third World concerns to the councils of the West.

I had seen enough of all those countries in the days

**Two views
of the
Third World:
Guyana,
1977**

*Arriving in
Guyana and
inspecting
the guard
of honour.*

*Guyanese
schoolchildren
in the country
form another
sort of guard
of honour.*

(NAC-TC)

Japan, October 1976

(from the official Japanese record)

In the course of our visit to Japan in October 1976, we were honoured by an audience at the Japanese Imperial Palace.

As a keen Judoka I was pleased to visit a judo centre with Japanese and foreign experts at Kodokan, Tokyo.

A formal and very traditional Japanese dinner with no chairs involved, and with a splendid print of Mount Fuji looming overhead.

(NAC-TC)

Official toasts beneath the flags of the two countries as Margaret and I are received at their official residence by Prime Minister and Mrs. Takeo Miki, October 22, 1976.

Signing a cultural agreement between Japan and Canada at Akasaka Palace, October 26, 1976.

(NAC-TC)

when I was travelling with a backpack that I had a feel, at least, for what it means to be the head of a Third World country and how limited they are in their choices. I was, I suppose, one of the most outspoken of the Northern heads of government when it came to advocating improvement of North-South relations, because I had lived and travelled in those countries of South America, Asia, and Africa and had seen what misery they suffered compared with what we call our own difficulties. When the Gallup polls would say, "Cut foreign aid, that should be the first thing because these are hard times and we have unemployment," I would be all too aware that our hard times were paradise compared with the hard times of many millions of people in the Third World who saw their children go to bed hungry every night and, all too often, die from starvation.

But while we were addressing the problems created by an inflation-ravaged economy and exploring new opportunities for Canada in foreign policy in the years immediately after the 1974 election, another issue was raising its head. This was the issue that had originally brought me into politics – national unity and the place of Quebec within Canada.

Things had been relatively quiet on this front from the failure of the Victoria Charter, in 1971, until 1974. The constitutional conference that met in Victoria on June 14–16, 1971, had been the seventh in a series of conferences that began with Prime Minister Lester Pearson's convening of a nationally televised federal-provincial meeting on the constitution in February 1968, when I was still justice minister. My own view from the outset had been that attempting constitutional reform would open a can of worms, and I had urged Pearson in 1967 to keep the constitutional file closed. When Pearson told me, "The provinces are pushing and we have to respond," I said, "Let them push." But once he had made the decision that the federal government should make constitutional reform a priority, I was determined that the government of Canada should not simply react to provincial demands but should have an agenda of its own.

At that 1968 meeting, Quebec premier Daniel Johnson had promoted his case for "equality or independence," and as minister of justice I had replied by making my case against special status for Quebec. Because we were arguing with each other in front of the Canadian people watching on television, perhaps Canadians began to understand better what was at stake in this sometimes arcane debate.

The 1971 Victoria constitutional conference that eventually resulted from all this came within a hair's breadth of success. It failed because Premier Robert Bourassa was not strong enough to keep his commitments. I don't believe in fretting too much about historical might-have-beens. But if we had succeeded in Victoria, Quebec would have achieved its dream of obtaining a constitutional veto, language rights would have been promoted across the country (perhaps avoiding the rancour that hurt Canada in the mid-1970s), and the country would have been spared a decade of constitutional wrangling. We all paid a heavy price for Bourassa's 1971 decision – or indecision – not least Robert Bourassa himself. Had he taken our offer of the veto in 1971, the constitution issue would have been off the table and he might have avoided his precipitate election call in 1976, which led to the election of the Parti Québécois. We certainly would have been spared the later agonies of Meech Lake and the Charlottetown Accord. In fact, much of Bourassa's subsequent career has been spent trying to regain what he was once so unwise as to refuse.

In April 1970, when Robert Bourassa defeated the Union Nationale to become premier of Quebec, I thought he was someone with whom we could make progress. He was a new man, a federalist, an economist with a clear mind, and a politician not particularly noted as a nationalist. Sensing a chance to break the constitutional impasse, I sent Gordon Robertson, the clerk of the Privy Council, and Marc Lalonde, my principal secretary, to Quebec City with the instructions: "Go to Quebec, talk to Mr. Bourassa and his officials, see what they want, and find out the bottom line. Then we'll know what this particular Quebec government wants and we'll see if we can accept it ourselves and sell it to the rest of the country."

Marc Lalonde, one of my most faithful political colleagues from the earliest days, was a bright lawyer whose family had farmed on Île Perrot for generations. From these roots Marc had gone on to a brilliant academic career at the Université de Montréal and then at Oxford. Robertson, my former boss in my early years in Ottawa, was the consummate civil servant. I had every confidence in both of them. This distinguished team duly met with Julien Chouinard, the secretary of the Quebec Cabinet, and every detail was approved by Bourassa himself. At one point Quebec proposed an amending formula that would give it a right of veto over any constitutional amendment, which was a big thing to ask of us, and a big thing to ask of the other premiers. But Bourassa said, "That's my bottom line." So we went to work, coming up with a package of proposals that

My old ally Marc Lalonde and I sit at the Cabinet table in Ottawa, recalling "battles long ago."
(Les Productions La Fête/Jean Demers)

met Quebec's demands at the time and yet went a long way towards meeting our federal objectives.

The Victoria Charter would have been good for all Canadians because it would have patriated the constitution with the elements of a charter of rights, provided a workable amending formula, and enshrined official languages in the legislative, judiciary, and executive functions of the government of Canada and several of the provinces. But while good for Canada, it was exceptional for Quebec: the government of Quebec would have obtained the veto; there would have been formal recognition that three judges of the Supreme Court would be members of the Quebec bar; provincial paramountcy would have been recognized over family, youth, and occupational training allowances; and the federal government would have given up the powers of reservation and disallowance. These were not minor concessions!

We went to work to sell this package to the other provinces. As you can imagine, selling the Quebec and Ontario veto to the other provinces was particularly difficult, but there was a lot of good will and we even persuaded several English-speaking provinces to deliver their services in French when they had a significant French-speaking population within their boundaries. Finally we hammered a deal together that allowed Marc Lalonde to go to Bourassa and his officials and say: "Okay, look at it, read every word and every line, and we'll go to the final conference at Victoria with that and we'll be on your side."

So we arrived in Victoria with a deal that Quebec had concocted with our assistance and support, and we had another tough debate at that conference. British Columbia was concerned that it would not receive a veto, and other provinces had doubts about the Supreme Court provision. But there was a real desire to show progress after the seven federal-provincial conferences we had endured together. Bit by bit, all the provinces agreed. Then Bourassa produced his shocker. He took me aside and said, "I'm going to ask Claude Castonguay, my minister of social affairs, to speak, because he has an extra request on social security."

It turned out Castonguay wanted more: rather than a shared jurisdiction, on which we had already agreed, he proposed that any provincial plan in social policy would automatically absorb any federal plan, with Ottawa paying the bill. In effect, Ottawa would be raising the money through taxes, but the provinces would receive it as a lump sum and distribute it as they wished.

This new demand at the last minute surprised me, to put it mildly. The Castonguay proposal meant that the federal government would become just an institution to raise taxes, but it would never have any direct relations with the citizens of Quebec. If we had agreed, I saw this as the beginning of a trend in which eventually other provinces would want to do the same thing and the government of Canada would end up being the tax collector for a confederation of shopping centres.

Marc Lalonde (half hidden) and I believed that we had received a commitment from the new Quebec premier, Robert Bourassa (right), to sign the Victoria constitutional accord in 1971. (Canapress)

So after Castonguay had made his pitch and we adjourned, I said privately to Bourassa, "It's obvious, Robert, that this is not going to fly. But I ask you to stick to your word and accept the document that you prepared and that you said you would sign." Bourassa replied: "Don't ask me to do that now. I want to go home to talk to my Cabinet, consult them – and especially I want to wait until the schools are out so there won't be any risk of student demonstrations." We agreed that the heads of the eleven governments would go home to reflect on the total package for twelve days, until June 28, 1971. I told Bourassa: "I'll be waiting for your phone call."

When he got back to Quebec, Bourassa encountered the predictable storm of opposition from the nationalists. On

June 23, just five days before the deadline, I received Bourassa's call. I was travelling in Ontario, staying in a motel, and I took the call after ten o'clock in the evening, which is late for me. Bourassa said: "I've been having a lot of consultations and I can't sell it to my ministers. Claude Morin is against it, and Claude Ryan is against it and he intends to write a lot of editorials in *Le Devoir* saying that we've given up our bargaining power, so my answer has to be no." I hung up the phone and said to myself, "Okay, we're going to put the worms back in the can and we're not going to open it again for a bloody long time."

In 1974, Bourassa's government inflamed language and unity tensions by passing Bill 22, making French the official language of Quebec. Bill 22 came hard on the heels of our Official Languages Act, just at the point when we were having a lot of trouble selling our concept of bilingualism to the rest of the country, where the phrase about having French "stuffed down our throats" was being repeated like a mantra. If Bourassa had talked about French as the principal language in Quebec, which it is, or the working language, which it was even under the Civil Code, we would have had no objection. But when the provincial government said there will be one official language in Quebec and it will be French – after we had been redoubling our efforts to sell the two official languages across the land, and after we had managed at Victoria to get the provinces to accept a measure of official bilingualism even at the provincial level – I thought the bill was politically stupid, and I said so in public.

Here was a premier who called himself a federalist, weakening our argument for bilingualism in the country. He was turning the clock back a hundred years. It was almost as if the bill had been deliberately designed to hurt our efforts to build a more tolerant Canada. Quebec laws that promote the use of French, or the excellence of French, or the teaching of the language to immigrants, or the ready access of immigrants to French-language schools – these are good laws. But when you begin to coerce people and take away free choice, that is using the law in an abusive way. I believe in promoting a language by promoting the excellence of the people who speak it. There is no question that French – here and abroad – is threatened because of the dynamism of English, especially in popular culture on television. But the question is, do you want to defend yourself by closing doors and coercing people, or do you want to defend your language by making it a source of excellence?

Yet, however much I philosophically disliked Bill 22 – and later the Parti Québécois's even more stringent Bill 101 – I had no intention of using the constitution to disallow the legislation. The way to change bad laws is to change the government, rather than using Ottawa to coerce a province. The best course was to hope that Quebec citizens would challenge the provincial legislation in the courts – which happened to several discriminatory provisions – and to hope as well that the people would become better informed and their politicians more open-minded.

Against this background, matters suddenly came to a head again in Quebec in the summer of 1976 with the Gens de l'air controversy over bilingual air traffic control – a political eruption so intense that it led to the resignation of one of my oldest friends and strongest ministers, Jean Marchand, and undoubtedly helped elect the Parti Québécois a few months later. All Marchand, as minister of transport, had been trying to do was implement the recommendation of a departmental task force that francophone pilots in Quebec be given the option of speaking French to air traffic controllers who spoke French, if both parties were more comfortable doing that, and if it made communications easier. This was consistent with the Official Languages Act we had passed in 1969; and, in fact, bilingual air traffic control services were already standard in Europe. But the Canadian Air Line Pilots Association and the Canadian Air Traffic Control Association opposed our bilingual policy in the strongest possible terms, invoking the issue of safety. And I think a lot of people who opposed the Official Languages Act for other reasons seized on this, because the cry of the pilots was, "We're endangering the lives of our passengers, and people are going to die if we start having French used in Quebec. We won't be able to understand each other from one plane to another, and it's going to cause great, great problems."

The whole debate took us by surprise. The introduction of French was such a reasonable proposition that it is still difficult to comprehend how it grew into such a crisis. But we know from history that emotional issues sometimes sweep away all reason. In any event, the rejection of bilingualism by the two national associations led to the formation of a breakaway Quebec group, the Association des gens de l'air, to represent Quebec pilots and controllers. Issues of job security, advancement, and competing unions now became enmeshed with the overriding concern about safety. In the midst of all this, in September 1975, while the issue was still comparatively low-key, there was a Cabinet shuffle in which Marchand went to the Department of the Environment and Otto Lang, a former law professor and a Westerner from Saskatchewan, came to Transport.

Saskatchewan's Otto Lang (left) – seen here with Marc Lalonde and me, and Eugene Whelan just behind Lang – was the man who handled the air traffic control strike in my absence. (NAC-TC)

Marchand's health was fragile and he was being exhausted by the demands of the huge transportation portfolio, so he had asked me to move him to a somewhat smaller department.

The language issue came to a head in June 1976 when the pilots and air controllers went on strike. It was a very nasty scene. I remember going west in those days and being jeered by the pilots and air controllers walking the picket lines at the airport. Air stewardesses would come over and buttonhole me in my seat and tell me that we were endangering the lives of passengers, painting gruesome pictures of planes banging together in mid-air, with maximum loss of life. Full-page ads were taken out in English-language newspapers denouncing bilingualism, and Quebec newspapers responded with editorials saying that Quebecers were being told to "speak white." We finally decided to set up a commission of inquiry headed by two judges to examine the whole issue, and I asked for prime time on national television on June 23 to address the public in an attempt to cool emotions and to assure everyone that safety came first.

But Otto Lang, meanwhile, still had a nasty strike to settle. Lang was one of my most intelligent ministers. What I particularly liked about Otto was that he would never beat a point into the ground. In Cabinet discussions, he'd make his rational argument, often with some heat and emphasis. But then he wouldn't go on and on. He'd assume that everybody at the table was intelligent enough to understand why he was right and why the other point of view was wrong. I valued that time-saving system, and thought it was a very effective approach.

After my televised speech, I delayed my departure for Puerto Rico for my first Economic Summit by a day to chair an emergency Cabinet meeting on the terms of a possible settlement. The next day, while I was away, Lang settled with the striking associations by making some very significant concessions: the terms of the commission of inquiry were broadened, any expansion of bilingual air services would only take place if the commission unanimously decided that safety was not affected, and a third commissioner approved by the Air Traffic Control Association would be added to the commission.

Perhaps not surprisingly, Jean Marchand was so upset with the concessions that he resigned. This was a big blow to me. His departure left an enormous hole. Gérard Pelletier had already left to become ambassador to France, but I had expected that, because he had told me he was only going to stay in politics for ten years, which proved to be 1965 to 1975. But in the case of Marchand, who was the leader of our group and the chief fighter for our cause, the departure was sudden, and it caused me a great deal of distress. My only consolation was that he told me, "Now that

I'm out of federal politics I'm going to go and fight the Parti Québécois in Quebec." In that sense, it wasn't a total loss to me. I was glad to see him fight on another front – one that had been envisaged in our earlier days when we were asking ourselves if Marchand at some point shouldn't become an active Quebec politician and perhaps eventually premier. Still, it was a big blow at the time. But the show must go on, and it did.

The Gens de l'air affair certainly affected our credibility in Quebec, because it was used by the separatists as proof that the "Trudeauites" had failed to sell bilingualism to the West and that Canadians had still not accepted the French fact. Fortunately, because of the things we had done up to that point, I was in a position to contain the damage somewhat by being able to respond: "The commissioner of the RCMP is a French Canadian; the Speaker of the Senate

Jean Marchand never did become premier of Quebec, but he became a senator and eventually attained the role (and the formal costume) of Speaker of the Senate, as this photograph attests. We have both come a long way from the Asbestos strike! (NAC-TC)

is a French Canadian; the Governor General is a French Canadian; the prime minister is a French Canadian; the chairman of the National Film Board is a French Canadian; the chief of the defence staff is a French Canadian...." That made it a little more difficult to argue that the French fact was being excluded from Canadian life! And, in time, of course, the inquiry reported that all over the world pilots speak languages other than English when they are in their home countries, and then English when they fly internationally. The whole issue petered out as quickly as it had blown up. Today you never hear anyone say that they are not going to fly over Quebec because some guy in a Piper Cub is speaking French to the air traffic controller, but that was the argument of the day. And in Quebec in the fall of 1976, many voters went to their polling stations on November 15 wearing buttons declaring, "Il y a du français dans l'air."

The election that day of a Parti Québécois government headed by René Lévesque neither surprised nor particularly alarmed me. I had welcomed the creation of the Parti Québécois in 1968 because it brought together the various groups and movements that had been fighting for separation on the political margin, and now the federalist forces in Quebec had a clear target to attack. It made it possible to have a fight out in the open in a democratic forum, instead of having to deal with all these malcontents mouthing off about independence and setting off bombs; since the late 1950s, they had been trying both mutterings and agitation behind the scenes, and violence.

My reaction to the election of a Parti Québécois government was a continuation of that same feeling. I said to myself, "Okay, now here's the adversary out in the open, and we'll be able to argue this thing to a decision. We'll see what kind of separatism they want – and what kind of support they have." And I always felt certain within myself that we would prevail. In May of that year, in fact, I had said that separatism was dead. Why? Because the Parti Québécois had only elected seven people and won 23 per cent of the vote in 1970, and got six people elected and 30 per cent of the vote in 1973, when they had tried both times to sell separatism. And now, in a curious way, the very victory of the Parti Québécois confirmed my analysis. Suddenly, in the 1976 campaign, there had been no more talk of immediate separation. Good government, not separation, was the theme. They told the voters, "We'll talk to you about separatism some day in a referendum, but right now it's just good government – you elect us for this." And people were fed up with Bourassa, so they voted for Lévesque and his party. In a way such an outcome had become virtually inevitable sooner or later, since the collapse of the Union Nationale had left the Parti Québécois as the only effective opposition if the voters ever wanted to get rid of the Liberals, which they did want to do in 1976.

I had known Lévesque a long time. He had a lot of appeal, a lot of personality, and was very dynamic and energetic. He was a bit of a prima donna, always wanting to be front and centre, but he had a lot of substance. If he had one weakness, it was that he was often disorganized and confused and always improvising. A good tactician, in other words, but not much of a strategist. But he was a worthy opponent. I like to think that he appealed to the emotions of the Quebec people, while I was trying to appeal to their reason. In any case, I knew it would be a good fight.

I went on national television to calm people's fears of

*Whether
I was with
Richard
Hatfield
of New
Brunswick
(in 1978)...*

what the election of a separatist government in Quebec might mean, and to make the point that Canada would survive only as a civil society and not by force of arms. Still, I made it clear that I felt it would be a sin against the spirit, a sin against humanity, if we were to be torn asunder. In a personal sense, I felt invigorated: it would be the fight of my life, and I like a good fight. Even if I had said, like Pelletier, "I'll get out in ten years," obviously the ten years were up and now I saw separatism being born as a government. I certainly wasn't about to leave. I was in for the duration.

The Parti Québécois had come to power on the promise of good government, but no sooner were they in office than they began talking about the referendum they were going to hold to have Quebecers decide between Canada and independence. And, of course, their line was that Canada was so

... or walking with Lévesque himself, the Quebec premier did not look on me with favour.
(Canapress)

far gone that it couldn't be fixed. Canada, they said, would never accommodate Quebec's legitimate aspirations, so it was no longer a matter of special status; Quebecers would be asked to vote for independence. Naturally, under the circumstances, I had no choice but to reopen the constitutional can of worms once again.

In point of fact, I had actually pried the lid ajar a little earlier, in 1975. Bourassa had won a significant election victory in 1973 and I had won a new majority in 1974, so with two strong, newly elected governments headed by Quebecers I thought the time was right to try again. On April 9, 1975, at a dinner with the provincial premiers, I raised the question whether it would be possible to take the results of Victoria in 1971 and simply patriate the constitution with the Victoria amending formula, leaving all other issues for future discussions. It was even suggested that we might be able to achieve patriation before the Olympic Games in Montreal in 1976. I quickly followed up that suggestion with a letter to the premiers, asking each of them to receive Gordon Robertson, the clerk of the Privy Council, who was by now an expert in this whole area, to discuss this possibility. In my letter, I suggested that we would have to complete this process by early 1976 so that the British Parliament could legislate by May or June of that year. I eventually discussed this possibility with British prime minister James Callaghan, who agreed to support any patriation proposal the Parliament of Canada chose to send him.

Quebec's opening position was that it would like most of what had been agreed at Victoria, plus "constitutional guarantees" for the French language and culture. Social security had been the cause célèbre in 1971; now it was cultural sovereignty. In November 1975, we sent a draft document to Bourassa that contained the essence of Victoria, plus a new section on the protection of the French language and culture. Quebec, I should add, was not alone in adding demands. Alberta and British Columbia, in particular, were now reconsidering their earlier support for the Victoria amending formula.

In March 1976, I met Bourassa in Quebec City to discuss the constitution, and this visit turned out to be the famous – or infamous, depending on your perspective – "hot dog eater" episode. The story was perhaps exaggerated by the press, but the meeting was a stormy encounter, all right. Here's how it all came about. On my way through the airport as I arrived at Quebec City, I had noticed a magazine with Bourassa on the cover eating a hot dog. I was in a great mood, and when the press asked me on the way in what we were going to have for lunch, I joked that everybody knows the premier likes to eat hot dogs. But by the time I came out, I was no longer in a joking mood or having a good time. Over lunch – and hot dogs were not on the menu – Bourassa told me, first, that he was no longer interested in the cultural guarantee we had secured for him and, second, that he was determined not to cooperate further unless there was a substantial transfer of federal powers to Quebec. It was the "powers for patriation" game all over again.

This did not come as a complete surprise to me, but at lunch Bourassa also annoyed me on another issue. In the preparations for the Montreal Olympics, which the Queen was to attend in the summer of 1976, Bourassa had begged us to make sure the Queen arrived in Quebec City so that he could get prestige and publicity out of her visit. But now he asked me to change the arrangements to make sure that the Queen was not seen in the provincial capital. I answered, "But she's coming by boat. Do you want the boat to fly to Montreal?" I was pretty impatient and said, "You know, your trouble is, you can't make up your mind." Still, when I went out to meet the press I was a perfect gentleman and said that no hot dogs were to be had and that we had eaten a very fine rare steak and had drunk a good bottle of Haut-Brion wine. Perhaps some of my irritation showed nevertheless.

But what was more important than any joke taken out of context, my irritation with Bourassa led me to say publicly what I had begun to think about privately: that the federal government might unilaterally patriate the constitution, because I had begun to despair of the possibility of negotiating a settlement without paying much too high a price in terms of federal power. This certainly caused a

The constant tension between Quebec separatists and Canada made it all the more delightful for me to receive at 24 Sussex Drive the Montreal Canadiens hockey team, a very successful example of biculturalism. Here I am talking with a group from the Stanley Cup winners including Serge Savard and Larry Robinson. (J.M. Carisse Photo)

controversy in Quebec and elsewhere. On a subsequent visit to Canada that September, Prime Minister Callaghan told Bourassa in a private meeting that in the patriation matter the British government would act on the advice of the Parliament of Canada. Whether this had a major impact on Bourassa or not, I don't know – but soon thereafter the premier saw fit to call an early election on a platform of stopping the so-called "unilateral Trudeau threat." The people, of course, couldn't have cared less about such niceties, and Bourassa lost that 1976 election to the Parti Québécois and their campaign on the theme of good government.

The election of the Parti Québécois in 1976 had a direct and immediate effect on the prospects for constitutional reform. It made negotiations both unavoidable and unlikely to succeed. When you look at the matter coldly, it's clear that there never was a realistic chance of persuading a

In the dining room at 24 Sussex Drive I and my colleague Francis Fox (right)
were political hosts to a number of Montreal Canadiens and their wives.
Keen hockey fans will be able to spot around the table Yvon Lambert,
Serge Savard, Jacques Lemaire, Guy Lafleur, and Réjean Houle.
(J.M. Carisse Photo)

separatist party to renew the constitution of Canada.
They were in politics to break up Canada, not to preserve it.
And so from 1976 on, whatever the tactics of the day-to-day
disputes and skirmishes we fought, my real battle was to
prepare Canadians – and especially Quebecers – for the day
when the federal government might have to break convention and make an appeal to London without having gained
unanimous provincial consent, and perhaps even unilaterally. From 1976 to 1979, our strategy was to be as reasonable
as possible, and to go more than halfway to meet the
provincial agenda – knowing all the while that any government headed by René Lévesque might never sign. Our real
task was to prepare public opinion for the dramatic moves
that would be necessary to cut the Gordian knot.

What made the negotiations seem all the more futile
was that the election of Lévesque was grist to the mill of the

other provincial premiers. They obviously didn't like separatism, but they were only too happy to use Lévesque as a
foil to try to get more for themselves. I recall Newfoundland premier Brian Peckford saying that his view of Canada
was closer to Lévesque's than it was to Trudeau's! The thinking of the premiers was, "Lévesque is going to reopen the
constitutional can of worms – and we'll make damn sure
that we get some good fishing bait for ourselves." So every
province added what it most wanted onto the negotiating
list: jurisdiction over cable television for one province,
indirect taxation for another, control over fisheries for a
third – so it went. And the more we met in federal-provincial conferences, the greater the provincial appetites grew.
Look at the results of the annual premiers' conferences of
1976, 1977, 1978, and you have a shopping list as long as
your arm of powers that have to go to the provinces in
exchange for their consent to patriation of the constitution.
This was a whole new dynamic, and unfortunately it was a
gambit accepted by the new leader of the federal Tory party.
Joe Clark was touring around saying, "Yes, we must decentralize much more," and he was talking of a "community of
communities" rather than of a strong Canadian people.

In response to this mania for decentralization, and
always keeping in mind that public opinion was the ultimate court of appeal, I considered it essential to be seen as
flexible rather than obstinate. When Peter Lougheed, in his
role as chairman of the 1976 Edmonton meeting of premiers, sent me a letter in January 1977, insisting that recon-
sideration of the division of powers must be part of any
package to patriate the constitution, I refused to go along
with the demand. But in October 1978, on the second day
of the federal-provincial conference, I produced a surprise

Constitutional conference with the first ministers in November 1978 – before the official photographer called us to order. From left to right, back row, are W. Bennett Campbell, P.E.I.; Bill Bennett, B.C.; Peter Lougheed, Alberta; me; Frank Moores, Newfoundland; Bill Davis, Ontario; Sterling Lyon, Manitoba. Seated: Richard Hatfield, N.B.; René Lévesque, Quebec; Allan Blakeney, Saskatchewan; John Buchanan, N.S. (NAC-TC)

by presenting a list of seven items that the federal government would be prepared to hand over to the provinces. "I've almost given away the store," I told reporters, earnestly demonstrating my flexibility. But in reality it was not a very big gamble.

I knew by then, from looking at their cumulative lists of demands, that the premiers couldn't say yes at that conference. I knew that René Lévesque, for one, was unlikely ever to sign anything, because he had always taken the line that Canada was broken and couldn't be fixed. The other premiers might have been interested if it had been early in my mandate and they knew that they were still saddled with me for a long time. But by then I was into my fourth year in office, with an election coming up, and the premiers were all gambling that I would be defeated and they could do better with Clark. So I didn't think that they would do it, but I was genuinely willing to do my level best to negotiate as many powers as I thought prudent in exchange for patriation (the ugly formal term that was invented for bringing Canada its own constitution). I was determined to show that I could be as generous as the next guy, and perhaps even more. But the premiers still said no, and it became obvious to more and more Canadians that they would never get their constitution home unless their government submitted to blackmail from some very greedy premiers. There was a significant shift in public opinion. That's when I felt the stage had been set for me to go to the Canadian people in the election that followed, in 1979, and talk to them – perhaps ad nauseam, perhaps unwisely – mainly about the constitution: about bringing it home, by means of a national referendum if necessary, and worrying about the division of powers later.

Some of my best political advisers, including people like Keith Davey, had urged me to call an election much earlier, in the early months of 1977, shortly after the Parti Québécois had come to power. At that time, many people both in our caucus and outside caucus were urging me to call an election because we were high in the polls, probably because people were afraid of the rise of separatism and they wanted someone with my view of Canada to remain prime minister. It's possible that we would have won an election at that time, but for me that wasn't a good enough reason. We had a good majority and there was still quite a bit of time left in our mandate. I had seen, in fact, how René Lévesque had won the election in Quebec because Bourassa had gone for an early election without really being justified.

Since then, we have seen many other examples of provincial premiers going for early elections, only to be swept out of office. So I am not sure that an election at that time would have produced favourable results.

Going into the 1979 election, I knew that it was bound to be a difficult fight. It was clear that a lot of political experts, including the premiers, were expecting us to lose. And I knew that I would be facing a tough new opponent in Joe Clark. I had been surprised when the Tories chose Clark to replace Stanfield in 1976, because he had squeezed up the middle between Brian Mulroney and Claude Wagner. But I had no doubt from the outset that he would be a more dangerous opponent than Stanfield, because he had been a tough son of a gun sitting in the third or fourth row of the House of Commons opposite me, pointing his finger at me and shouting all kinds of questions to upset my balance, or interrupting my speeches. I knew he would be a feisty leader of the Opposition, and he was. Even after I had defeated Clark in 1980 and he had lost the leadership to Brian Mulroney in 1983, I told my friends: "They chose the wrong guy." I thought that Joe Clark would be a far stronger opponent than Brian Mulroney.

In the 1979 election campaign, I travelled energetically and talked everywhere I went about the constitution. The Parti Québécois was in power and I wanted the Canadian people to understand that there were some tough decisions we would have to take if we did not want the separatists to succeed. I admit that I was preoccupied with this priority above all else in the campaign. I told the people precisely what I was going to do on the constitution, but on several other issues – especially the economy – I ran on our record. I told Canadians that this is a tough country to govern and we had not done so badly. I used a lot of facts and figures in my speeches in an exercise we called the "Economic Olympics" to show that, compared with the rest of the world, Canada was the first in job creation, and so on. But as one of my ministers, George McIlraith, used to tell me: "You never win an election on what you have done. People always ask: 'Never mind what you did yesterday, what are you going to do for me tomorrow?'" In 1979, I made the mistake of telling them especially what I was going to do on the constitution. It might have been clear to others during the campaign that we were heading for defeat – and all sorts of wise men and women emerged afterwards to say that they had known it all along – but I only accepted that when all the votes were counted and all the recounts completed. An election campaign is such an energy-draining business that until you've lost, you always think you're going to win – or you hope you're going to win, and make yourself think that you will. Otherwise, you wouldn't keep fighting.

In the prime minister's office, receiving Opposition leader Joe Clark – a far stronger opponent, in my opinion, than Brian Mulroney, who succeeded in deposing his leader in 1983.
(NAC-TC)

But the results of the May 22, 1979, election were that the Conservatives won 136 to the Liberal Party's 114, with 26 for the NDP and 6 for the Créditistes. The Tories were in, and we were out. After being prime minister for eleven uninterrupted years, I was out of office.

My first reaction, as always, was combative. I was not going to accept the defeat and I would lead the fight, as leader of the Opposition, to come back. I took the summer off to rest and reflect. I had no more official papers to read or big boxes of letters to sign. So I took a canoe trip in the Northwest Territories, indulging once again the love of canoeing I have had all my life.

I think a lot of people want to go back to the basics sometimes, to find their bearings. For me a good way to do that is to get into nature by canoe – to take myself as far away as possible from everyday life, from its complications and from the artificial wants created by civilization. Canoeing forces you to make a distinction between your needs and your wants. When you are canoeing, you have to deal with your needs: survival, food, sleep, protection from the weather. These are all things that you tend to take for granted when you are living in so-called civilization, with its constant pressures on you to do this or that for social reasons created by others, or to satisfy artificial wants created by advertising. Canoeing gets you back close to nature, using a method of travel that does not even call for roads or paths. You are following nature's roads; you are choosing the road less travelled by, as Robert Frost once wrote in another context, and that makes all the difference. You discover a sort of simplifying of your values, a distinction between values artificially created and those that are necessary to your spiritual and human development. That's why, from my youthful expeditions right up to the present day, canoeing has always been such an important activity in my life.

I've been fortunate, too, in the canoeing companions I have known, whether on the rivers and lakes close to home or in the wilds of the Nahanni. I'm sure that they will not mind my singling out perhaps the greatest canoeist of our time, the legendary Bill Mason, who knew how to make a canoe dance – and how to spread that knowledge, through his marvellous films and books, while also spreading his love for canoeing, and for life. I must also single out two other companions: Eric and Pam Morse, the ultimate *voyageurs* of the Canadian fur trade routes.

That summer after my election defeat, I also went out west to the Rockies by train to visit our national parks with my three boys. And in September I took a trip to Tibet. The summer of 1979 was really the first time since 1968 that I was free to do what I wanted, and I found that I was enjoying my freedom.

During this period, I was torn in two directions. One

Canoeing

Canoeing has always been important to me. Here I am shown canoeing late in the season of 1992.

(Les Productions La Fête/Jean Demers)

In August 1979, I attended the funeral of John Diefenbaker.
(Canapress)

part of me said, "The people have chosen, you are out of power, you have had a go at it, why not stay out?" I had young children, I loved them, and I naturally wanted to spend more time with them. I remember telling Gérard Pelletier that I could imagine someone else being prime minister, but I couldn't imagine anyone else being the father of my children. So my personal life weighed heavily on my mind during this period. But another part of me was just as engaged as ever. After our defeat, several Liberals who had been elected on my coat-tails and some senators who had been put in the Senate by my fiat began to say that Trudeau must go. That type of behaviour produced the contrary effect on me, provoking me to feel, "Dammit, I'm not going to go if they want to throw me out." So I vacillated between going and staying.

Waving my last farewell as I leave Parliament Hill after announcing my resignation. My driver Jack Deschambault prepares to take me away, apparently out of public life. (J.M. Carisse Photo)

When I came back from my Tibetan trip with a very full beard, my principal secretary, Jim Coutts, came to me with some very serious advice. Coutts, an Albertan who looked deceptively like a choirboy, was a very shrewd old political hand and he often felt obliged to give me harsh advice. On this occasion, the advice was highly personal. "Look," he said, "if you want to give the signal that you are out for good, keep the beard. But if you think you might like to stay on, you damn well better shave it off." Which I did. But even clean-shaven I was not overly combative or effective as Opposition leader.

For one thing, I don't think I was really mad at Clark for winning. I remember even saying, "We've got to give him a chance to govern." Ironically, I wasn't a very good leader of the Opposition in those days because I knew too much; I realized only too well that governing was a pretty difficult job. I hoped that once Canadians had a chance to compare my strong-Canada philosophy with Joe Clark's strong-provinces philosophy, the electorate would come back to the Liberal Party. But I was not thirsting to get back into power, and as the fall progressed I found that I was leaning more and more towards retiring. My thinking finally crystallized at a Liberal Party convention in Toronto in November 1979. I had visited a friend in the Beaches area of Toronto, and I decided to walk all the way back to my downtown hotel. As I walked – at first along the boardwalk beside the chilly deserted beach – I reviewed all the arguments in my mind. I knew that I had to decide soon whether I was going to leave or not. I remember thinking that walking on the beach as a free man is pretty desirable.

Finally, on November 21, 1979, my mind was made up. I announced my resignation as leader of the Liberal Party. I was retiring from politics. But the fates had more in store for me.

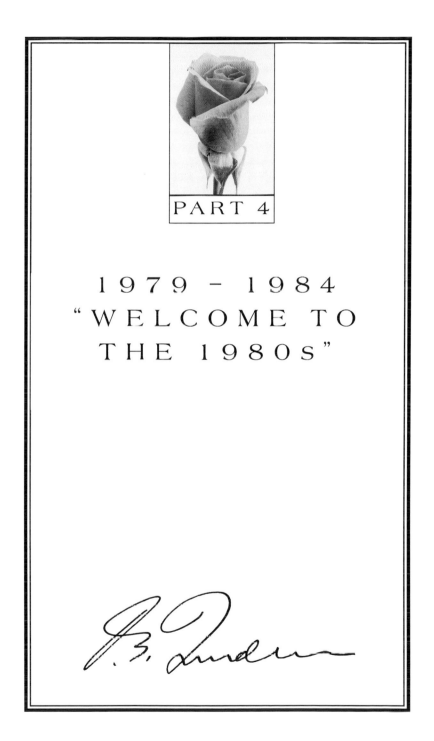

PART 4

1979 - 1984
"WELCOME TO
THE 1980s"

As early as September of 1979, we began hearing through our channels that Clark was having difficulties getting himself organized to govern. We knew that he was taking a long, long time before meeting Parliament. In fact, although he won the election in May, it took him until October to call Parliament into session. Clearly, he was having some trouble getting his policies or his Cabinet together. Clearly, too, he was also already failing to solve one of the problems for which he had been elected, namely to get Alberta premier Peter Lougheed to agree to a new formula for energy prices; the theory that these two guys from Alberta would soon be able to work things out was proving to be no more than a nice theory. Many of us, including myself, had a feeling that Clark wouldn't last six months in Parliament. In fact, one reason why I resigned in November was that I thought Clark's government would be defeated in Parliament by the spring, and I wanted the Liberal Party to have sufficient time to hold a leadership convention and choose my successor before that took place.

Even after my decision to resign had been announced, I continued, as leader of the Opposition, to be keenly involved in the daily affairs of Parliament. So I and my colleagues knew that the vote on the Clark government's first budget, on December 13, would be very, very close. John Crosbie's budget, with its 18-cent gasoline tax, had alienated all the Opposition parties, and a number of Tory MPs would not be in Ottawa in time to vote. Allan MacEachen, who was the House leader at the time, gave us a pep talk in caucus, saying, "You better all be there." We all were there (one brave soul coming by ambulance from an Ottawa hospital to cast his vote), though some participated reluctantly because they thought it would be a terrible mistake and the wrong kind of gamesmanship to upset the Clark government so early. But we won the vote, and the government was out.

Looking back on that extraordinary chain of events, I think that Clark was perhaps hoping to repeat John Diefenbaker's performance after the 1957 victory against the Liberals under Louis St. Laurent, when he went on to sweep the country in 1958. That was Clark's gamble, and I believe a lot of people in our caucus thought he would indeed sweep the country and they would lose their seats in the process. I always wondered why Clark didn't either postpone the vote or make some small modifications to his budget to win the support of the Créditistes, which would have enabled him to win the vote and remain prime minister. Perhaps he didn't think we – now officially a

I spy a Tory! Young Catherine Clark and I exchange pleasantries while her father, Joe Clark, watches with amusement. The setting is a children's Christmas party where the Trudeau boys also seem to be having a good time.
(J.M. Carisse Photo)

leaderless party, since I had announced my intention to resign – would have the nerve to defeat him and risk being wiped out in an election, or perhaps he was sure that if he lost in the House he would win the popular vote with ease. Certainly the feeling in my party about the wisdom of bringing down the government was by no means unanimous. But my own feeling was, "Well, I didn't think it would happen so soon, but I knew it was going to happen and it has. Hurray."

Immediately after he suffered his defeat in the House, Clark announced that a federal election would be held on February 18, 1980. Some people believe that I somehow manipulated this whole series of events and that my resignation three weeks earlier was a ploy to induce false confidence in Joe Clark. Had I had that kind of cunning, I would probably still be in politics today! But it certainly wasn't a ploy. As a matter of fact, until the morning of the day I came back, on December 17, I didn't know if I wanted to come back or not. As soon as Clark was defeated, many supporters asked me to return. I conjured up the true tale of a former prime minister of Yunan province in China who had been asked by the Emperor to come back to be prime minister again but replied, "I have had enough of it: I will come back only if the Emperor asks three times on bended knees." I told this story to my staff and they understood that I would need a lot of persuasion.

The first to ask me to return had to be the caucus itself. The caucus was reasonably loyal. They were fighters and they had been through a lot with me, but after our election loss some of them thought it would be better for their party and their future if we had a new leader. So I said, "Caucus is made up of the people I am with all the time in the House of Commons. If they're not enthusiastic about me, I'm not coming back." The caucus also included a certain number of senators who would have been, I think, quite happy to cut my throat. So I said, "Look, I left this party partly because I didn't appreciate some people plotting behind my back to get rid of me, so let's check with the caucus." The caucus debated the issue and Allan MacEachen informed me that in the end they had voted unanimously that I should return.

The second request had to be from the non-parliamentary party, because there were people in the executive of the party and at other senior levels who felt that the Liberals could win more readily with somebody other than Trudeau. After our defeat in the election, some of them had tried to rush through arrangements for an early party convention to give me a low vote of confidence that would have forced me to leave, and only Jean Marchand's intervention had dissuaded them. The race to succeed me had not really begun before we defeated the Conservatives in the House. John Turner had announced on December 10, three days before the Tories were ousted, that he would not be a candidate, but no one had formally come forward to seek to replace me. I was in favour of Donald Macdonald becoming leader, but by the time he had made up his mind to run I had already decided to return. The party executive met, and after what I gather was a long debate they too asked me to return.

And finally, if I was to stay on, the third effort of persuasion would have to come from my friends and close colleagues. I wanted to make sure they were prepared to stay on as well, because if I was not surrounded by friends and associates who were prepared to fight their way back with me, I was not going to return. I gathered several friends and advisers at Stornoway and found that not everyone was of the same view. Marc Lalonde didn't think we would win, and therefore out of friendship said, "Don't come back, you're going to be slaughtered." Jean Marchand had the same opinion: "You had a good go at it, you're going to be defeated, and therefore why go through it again? You've done your bit, we've done some things we wanted, so don't come back." I remember that I also phoned Gérard Pelletier in Paris because he had the distant observer's viewpoint, and he said, "Sure, you've got to go back because you're going to win. I can see that from talking to people who come through Paris, or by reading the media and so on, and I have a feeling you're going to be re-elected. That's going to be your chance, and we need you for the coming referendum." He was an ambassador and a civil servant, but he was also my friend and I think he was being very frank. René Lévesque had already announced that the Quebec referendum on independence would be held in the spring of 1980, and in the same week I was internally debating my return, Lévesque's Cabinet was debating the exact wording of the referendum question. Jim Coutts also especially emphasized the referendum in his arguments to me. And besides emphasizing the impact I could have on the referendum fight if I were prime minister again, he said: "What are you risking anyway? Just a couple of months of your life. You run and win. Or you run and lose and you're in the same place." There was obviously a division, but by and large the group of people closest to me also in effect said, "We're humbly asking you to come back, Prime Minister." Even those who had doubts about the outcome were willing to support me wholeheartedly.

The looming Quebec referendum was a very big factor in my decision to return. As far back as early 1977, I had given a speech to the Quebec City Chamber of Commerce at the Château Frontenac in which I had said: "As far as the constitution is concerned, the French have had seventeen of them in 170 years, so we can certainly give ourselves another one – but which one? Let's find out first whether Quebecers are Canadians or whether they are separatists." And I had called on the Parti Québécois government to put a clear question to the people of Quebec, to put it to them quickly, and to put it to them in a definitive way, so that the issue would not be reopened every five years if the separatists lost.

I was to learn much later that Lévesque and his strategists had made a calculation: they were elected in 1976 and I was re-elected in 1974, so I would have to hold an election by 1979 and, given the unfavourable polls, was likely to be out of office before their term expired. Their whole game

A somewhat irreverent photograph of Liberal Party insiders Senator Keith Davey (left) and Gordon Ashworth apparently "praying" for my return to politics after my resignation. (J.M. Carisse Photo)

plan was to delay the referendum until Trudeau was no longer there. In fact, it's rather amusing to recall that as soon as I resigned at the end of November, they said: "Good, now that Trudeau is gone, we'll set the date." Up until the moment I announced my departure, the matter of a referendum had been pushed off into some vague distant point in the future. Obviously, I beat them at their own game when I decided to come back, and that's largely why

Had they seen this photograph they might have been even more impressed by my apparent abilities. (J.M. Carisse Photo)

I did so. The strategy of the Péquistes ultimately blew up in their own faces. That was one of the main arguments my friends used in persuading me to return. They said, "Look, you can be there at the time of the referendum. You can fight a hell of a lot more effectively if you're the prime minister."

But even so, it was a difficult decision. After my friends had left Stornoway that evening, I walked for long hours through the surrounding neighbourhood of Rockcliffe Park trying to decide my destiny. And by the time I came home and went to bed, I had pretty much decided against a comeback. But I woke up abruptly the next morning – Tuesday, December 18 – and said to myself, "My God, I made the wrong decision last night. I'm going to reverse it." And that was when I called Jim Coutts, who had prepared the texts of two statements for me – what I would say if I was coming back, and what I would say if I wasn't – and told him: "Okay, we're doing it."

A lot of people have said that my 1980 campaign was more tightly controlled than my previous election campaigns. I suppose that's true. I had learned some lessons by then, and I certainly didn't intend to make a mistake. As had been the case after the 1972 election, political advisers such as Keith Davey and Jim Coutts now impressed on me that I had fought the 1979 campaign my way, and I had lost it. The mistake I had made was being too concerned with my own priorities, talking essentially about the constitution rather than about things that were more on people's minds. In 1980, it was a whole new world. We kept the campaign issues more simple, more appealing to the voters.

Joe Clark had made a certain number of enemies. Under pressure that I knew only too well, he had decided to move the Canadian embassy in Israel from Tel Aviv to Jerusalem, and then had to backtrack when the Arab world reacted with predictable anger. He had tried to succeed where we had failed in getting a new oil price agreement with Alberta. But even by being kind to Premier Lougheed and asking less of Alberta than we had, he wasn't able to get an agreement. So I campaigned essentially on the issue of leadership. I said, "It's not enough to be a leader. You have to be a *good* leader. You have to know what you're doing." I attacked Clark – I think, in retrospect, rather unkindly – for acting like the headwaiter of the provinces, because he was trying to do everything that would please the provinces, and I noted that he wasn't even able to produce results by doing this. I attacked him for his view of Canada as a "community of communities," when I chose to see it as a nation. I promised that we would bring in an energy policy that was vigorous, that was good for Canada, that wouldn't kowtow to any particular province, but that wouldn't be unfair to any province either. We were going to be the government of all of Canada.

The whole theme of the campaign was, "If you're the government, you've got to govern, and that means making decisions, and we can do it." As I travelled on the campaign trail from coast to coast, my advisers helped me to stay focused on this main thrust, without getting into too many little details. The polls soon showed that we were well in the lead. I didn't engage in a leaders' debate this time, because I had been pretty disappointed with the debate we had had in 1979, when I felt that it was being run by the journalists rather than by the participants in the election. I was also kept away from being in too many situations where there would be hecklers, because hecklers always aroused the fighting spirit in me and sometimes I would say things that were not all that politically wise. But I fought the campaign with enthusiasm, and on February 18, 1980, the Liberal Party received 148 seats to 103 for the Conservatives and 32 for Ed Broadbent's NDP.

"Welcome to the 1980s," I said on election night to a cheering crowd of Liberals at the Château Laurier. For me, it was a whole new beginning. Before the 1979 election, everything had seemed bogged down because of the economy and because the premiers had sensed that they could hold out until our government was defeated. At that point nothing had seemed to be moving, and it was hard to get anything done. So when we were given a second chance, it was exciting. Like Seneca, who wrote, "Live every day as though it is your last," I was resolved that I would govern in this next term as though it was going to be my last. This time I took quite a different approach to government. I told my staff to cut down on the amount of paperwork I had to handle, to give me fewer letters to sign, and to make their memos and briefing notes to me a little bit shorter. I decided to focus on just a few crucial issues – particularly the Quebec referendum, the energy issue, the economy, and the constitution. Above all I decided to take gambles that perhaps we would not have taken several years earlier, to achieve the results we wanted.

We had been in office a fairly long time. We had tried federal-provincial cooperation. We had tried to cooperate with business and labour. We had tried to cooperate with

When it was clear on election night that we had won a majority, I began my speech to the Liberal faithful gathered in the Château Laurier with the words "Welcome to the 1980s."
(J.M. Carisse Photo)

the energy-producing provinces. But for all our coopera-tion we were finding it hard to get anything done. I decided that enough was enough. I said: "I'm convinced, and I hope the people of Canada are convinced, that there are some things you have to do decisively, without cooperative feder-alism. You've got to do it alone, otherwise it will never be done." Take patriation of the constitution, for example.

Receiving NDP leader Ed Broadbent. He was very surprised when I offered him a coalition arrangement that would have brought some NDP MPs into the Cabinet. (NAC-TC)

Every prime minister since 1927, since Mackenzie King, had tried to patriate with the consent of the provinces, and no one had ever succeeded. I said, "It's obvious we'll never have a constitution of our own if we don't do it alone." And it was the same thing with energy, and the same thing with the economy. That was the spirit after 1980: we had demonstrated that a ponderous, careful pace doesn't get you more cooperation; perhaps it will get you less. So we just set out to get some things done.

One of my first actions after the election was to meet with NDP leader Ed Broadbent. He and I were never especially close, but we had some mutual respect; I knew him as an intelligent, well-educated man, a good debater, and an effective party leader in the House. Now I had a surprise for him. In an attempt to negotiate some sort of alliance with his party, I offered him and his colleagues some senior positions in our Cabinet. Even though we had a majority government, my reasoning was that strengthening the government's geographic representation would be very helpful in dealing with crucial national issues like energy and the constitution. We had a lot of members of Parliament from Newfoundland, Nova Scotia, New Brunswick, Prince Edward Island, Quebec, and Ontario, but only a handful of MPs from west of Ontario. The NDP, on the other hand, had a lot of members from everywhere in the West but Alberta. I felt that the unity effort would be strengthened if we could consolidate our forces. There had been talks with the NDP along these lines on and off since Pearson's day, of varying degrees of seriousness. This offer was very serious. But Broadbent declined my offer, because he feared that his party would lose its power and credibility. As it turned out, the NDP did generally support us on the constitution anyway.

As I've said, I am not someone who spends much time pondering historical might-have-beens. But others may find it interesting to speculate how the experience of the last decade might have been different if in that secret meeting Ed Broadbent and I had achieved a common front of progressive forces in our country.

❧

My first big challenge after the election was the Quebec referendum campaign. Canada's fate was at stake, and along with it the fate of our government. There is very little doubt in my mind that I would have resigned as prime minister if the separatists had won the referendum I would have said, "I've lost the confidence of the Quebec people. They have voted to separate from Canada. I have no mandate to negotiate that separation or the formation of an association with a sovereign Quebec." As a matter of fact,

I have always thought that René Lévesque should have taken the same position and resigned when the central element of his government's reason for existing was repudiated by the voters. But he and I never did see eye to eye on a number of things.

Directing the campaign for a No vote – that is, a vote in favour of Canada – was at the beginning exclusively in the hands of Claude Ryan, who had succeeded Robert Bourassa as leader of the Quebec Liberal Party. I have known Ryan for a long time, and it's fair to say that he and I come from different directions in our thinking. I think he made a very bad mistake as editor of *Le Devoir* during the 1970 FLQ Crisis when he signed the manifesto saying that we should release the so-called "political prisoners" in order to save the lives of Pierre Laporte and James Cross. But when he entered politics, joining the Quebec Liberal Party, I was pleased. I remember that when he was chosen as leader in place of Bourassa, I said, "Well, here's a man who's got clean hands, a man who knows how to think clearly, and he's going to bring new vigour and new people to the provincial party." I think that was a general feeling among a lot of Quebecers who felt that Bourassa's government had been defeated in 1976 because of what you might call a loosening of the leadership or even of the political morality of the Quebec Liberal Party. There was an expectation that Ryan was going to do a good job as leader. I wouldn't have supported him, but I remember feeling that it was not a bad choice.

But he soon showed his true colours – or perhaps showed himself to be what he had always been, a Quebec nationalist and a believer in distinct societies or "special status," as he had begun calling it in his *Le Devoir* days. As Liberal leader, he was still trying to solve the constitutional debate by calling for special powers for Quebec, and I felt

Family album

(NAC-TC)

strongly that this wasn't what he had been elected leader to do. He had been elected in order to help the Liberals defeat the separatist party, which surely meant keeping Canada strong and keeping a strong French-Canadian presence in Ottawa.

From the outset, we federal Liberals had extensive discussions in the Quebec caucus in Ottawa as to how we should participate in the referendum. I said, "First of all, we are all Quebecers. So a question about the separation of Quebec concerns us politicians at the federal level as much as it does those who are in Quebec. We are Quebecers; we will express ourselves. But we mustn't behave like the big brother who is coming in to run things, because that could work against us." We all felt that the No committee headed by Claude Ryan should run the campaign, and we would help them in whatever way they wanted. As for me, I remember telling everyone involved from the outset not to count on me to go from village to village talking to everyone. What would I have been explaining? People knew my views. It would have bored me, and therefore it would have bored them, too, to have me constantly repeating the same thing. I said, "I'll only make a few appearances in Quebec – but the rest of you go ahead and give the No forces a hand, and work as hard as possible."

The first round was won by the Parti Québécois. On December 20, 1979, René Lévesque had released the referendum question – which in my view was a trick question, for reasons I'll explain in a moment – and from March 4 to 20, 1980, the Quebec National Assembly debated the issue. This debate was televised, and the Parti Québécois organized itself in a very masterful way, with different speakers allocated to support the Yes side for a variety of reasons, to avoid repetition. The Quebec Liberals, on the other hand, got all bogged down in complicated alternative proposals for some kind of special status for Quebec. They were trying to explain their rather complex white paper – or yellow paper or paper of some other colour – which argued that Quebec should stay in Canada and be federalist, but that it should try to obtain a whole series of new powers. The Liberal Party was drowning in a swamp of its own verbiage, while the Parti Québécois was speaking out with pride and firmness.

As a result, the reports we were getting from Quebec were just devastating. My ministers and members of caucus were unanimous in the view that the debate had been won hands down by the Parti Québécois. After that, Claude Ryan as leader of the No forces began travelling around the province, almost from village to village, talking to little groups. He was working hard, but he wasn't hitting the headlines or having much impact on public opinion. It was at this point that I said, "Okay, we've got to give them a hand." I had already put Jean Chrétien in charge of our federalist troops in the Quebec caucus, but now I turned him loose, telling him, "Get in there a bit more vigorously. Play whatever role you want, because we're behind in the polls." Ryan soon realized that he was falling behind and he agreed that Chrétien should become co-chairman of the No forces. The arrival of Chrétien and his hard-working team began to turn things around.

As for me, I stuck to my plan of restricting myself to a few well-timed interventions. As the date of the vote drew closer, it became clear that people wanted to hear what this French Canadian who was prime minister in Ottawa had to say. I spoke a total of four times: on April 15 to the House of Commons, on May 7 to the Montreal Chamber of Commerce, on May 9 to a rally in Quebec City, and on May 14

After the 1980 election I decided to focus on just a few crucial issues – particularly the Quebec referendum, the energy issue, the economy, and the constitution. (NAC-TC)

at the Paul Sauvé Arena in Montreal. I gave each of these speeches without any formal text, using just a few notes to remind myself of key points I wanted to make.

My message to Quebecers was essentially that the Parti Québécois was trying to fool them with a trick question. It was a long, convoluted question that tried to get people to agree to separatism by degrees. I said, "If it had been a black-and-white question, 'Do you Quebecers want to separate, yes or no?' that would have been fair." But instead, they had created this intricate question in which people were to vote for sovereignty-association, after which there would be more negotiations and more referendums – and, of course, Quebec would supposedly still have the Canadian dollar, Canadian passports, and other Canadian advantages after all that. So I said to Quebecers, "They are asking you to say yes to a question that you can't honestly answer. They are asking you whether you want an association with the other provinces, but how can your vote in Quebec force the other provinces to want to associate with

Initially the fight against the Parti Québécois in the referendum was led by Claude Ryan (left), leader of the provincial Quebec Liberals. When the campaign began to falter, I appointed Jean Chrétien (right) to move in with all the federal forces at his command and offered to inject myself into the campaign at appropriate points. (NAC-TC)

you if you separate?" And, of course, I made sure that I talked to the premier of Ontario and a few of the others and said, "Look, they're telling you that you are going to have to associate with them. What do you think?" So Quebecers heard the answer from English Canada – which, of course, was a resounding no to association with an independent Quebec.

The counter-attack from the separatists was to say, "How can Trudeau claim that the rest of Canada won't agree to association if a great majority of Quebecers vote in favour of it? Doesn't Trudeau believe in democracy, and isn't that democracy in action?"

My answer was, "Yes, democracy, but a democratic people cannot bind another people. What if Cubans asked us by an overwhelming majority vote to let them join

Canada? Because we believe in democracy, does that mean we would have to accept Cuba becoming part of Canada? It's the same with Quebec if you decide to separate. If you vote Yes to this question, you are losing all your bargaining power, because you are really putting your fate in the hands of the other provinces – and they could tell you that you can have independence, but not association with them."

As the campaign neared its climax, the momentum had shifted, and the separatists had begun to make serious mistakes. One such mistake was the so-called "Yvette" incident that began when a prominent female minister in Lévesque's Cabinet made the terrible blunder of mocking women who weren't out there fighting for separatism and instead were staying at home minding the kids. And she made it even worse with a throwaway line about Claude Ryan's wife being one of those women – which was very unfair because Madeleine Ryan had always been very active in social affairs, particularly the Catholic Action movement. So, in effect, the PQ was saying to her and to other activist women, "If you're voting No, it means that you're just a patsy." And by also hitting those who weren't activists but who were at home taking care of the children and cooking the meals, the separatists inflicted a double whammy on themselves. Women in general, and particularly those who were already inclined towards the No vote, were incensed, and the incident gave rise to a vigorous women's campaign for the No.

The speech that people seem to recall most was the last one, at the Paul Sauvé Arena in Montreal. Unlike a lot of people, I don't remember it as one of my best speeches. I myself much preferred the one I gave in Quebec City early in 1977, because it was a far more logical analysis of the

Quebec issue. But I do recall that night in Montreal as being very exciting. There had been all those rallies jammed with separatists and Quebec flags. Now, on this night, we had jammed the arena with Canadian flags and with enthusiastic federalists. At that moment, I felt that we were going to win. I had always hoped we would. I always knew we would. But this time I *felt* it.

I felt, too, that I had been given a chance to respond to a foolish personal attack. Lévesque himself made the mistake of remarking about me: "His name is Pierre Elliott Trudeau and this is the Elliott side taking over, and that's the English side, so we French Canadians in Quebec can't expect any sympathy from him."

It was an absurd insult and a relatively trivial one in itself, when you consider that the separatists had long been calling me and my francophone ministers traitors for the great crime of defending Canada. But I took Lévesque up on it in my speech at the Paul Sauvé Arena, because it was a slip that demonstrated the intolerant side of separatism. Long before I entered politics, I had already been arguing that a state must govern for the good of all its people, not just for one religious or linguistic group. Yet here we had Lévesque implying that someone with an English name could not be a true Quebecer.

In my speech that evening, I reminded the crowd that Lévesque had said that part of my name was Elliott and since that's an "English" name (and a Scot would be quick to point out it was a Scottish one), somehow I was not as much of a Quebecer as those who were going to vote Yes. Yet, I pointed out, in the Parti Québécois itself there was a minister named Louis O'Neill, another named Pierre-Marc Johnson, and a former minister called Robert Burns. And

Claude Ryan was a good Quebecer with an "English" name and so was the late premier Daniel Johnson. Then I said: "Of course my name is Pierre Elliott Trudeau. Elliott was my mother's name. It was the name borne by the Elliotts who came to Canada more than two hundred years ago. It is the name of the Elliotts who, more than one hundred years ago, settled in Saint-Gabriel-de-Brandon, where you can still see their names on the tombstone in the cemetery. That is who the Elliotts are. My name is a Quebec name. But my name is a Canadian name also. And that's my name." It gave a spark to my speech, and I think it helped to show the Quebec people the kind of intolerance they were being asked by the separatists to endorse with their votes.

I also used this rally, which was the culmination of the referendum campaign, to make a statement that reverberated beyond the referendum itself and would influence the constitutional battle just ahead. "A 'No' means change," I told the crowd. "Following a No vote, we will immediately take action to renew the constitution and we will not stop until we have done that. And I make a solemn declaration to all Canadians in the other provinces: we, the Quebec MPs, are laying ourselves on the line, because we are telling Quebecers to vote No and telling you in the other provinces that we will not agree to your interpreting a No vote as an indication that everything is fine and can remain as it was before."

What I had in mind was the reaction of those premiers from across Canada who in 1978 and 1979 had told me, "What's the hurry, Prime Minister?" I was afraid that they would try to drag their feet again. I wanted them to know that right after the referendum we were going to start to work, and we were not going to stop until we finished, right through to the bitter end. And the changes I was promising were, of course, those we subsequently accomplished: bringing home our constitution, with a charter of rights and an amending formula.

Yet some people, usually separatists, have the gall to say that when I spoke of change, I meant that we would change the constitution in the same way that the Yes side would have tried to do it, if they had won. They say I led Quebecers to believe that I would transfer all sorts of powers to Quebec and give it special status. I don't know how these people can make these claims with a straight face. All my life, even in my writings long before I entered politics, I always fought against special status for Quebec. I always fought against excessive decentralization in a country that is already among the most decentralized in the world. So it is evident nonsense – I might use even stronger language – to suggest that I set out to win the referendum by undertaking to do exactly what those who lost it had wanted to do. I was fighting to have my ideas triumph, not those of my adversaries. Otherwise I would have voted for the Yes. And, of course, the separatists themselves knew that at the time. Only days before I made that promise, Lévesque himself was saying, in effect, "We know what Trudeau means when he talks of change. He's going to have more centralization." I doubt that any of them believed that if I won the referendum, I would make changes in the way they wanted. They knew they had lost in a fair fight. It was only much later that they began to raise the whining argument, "Well, he did promise us change." I promised Quebec change, and I gave Quebec change. I gave Quebec, and all the rest of Canada, a new made-in-Canada constitution, with a new amending formula and a new charter of rights.

On May 20, 1980, Quebecers voted resoundingly in

favour of Canada. The No vote was 59.6 per cent, and the Yes was 40.4 per cent. I told Canadians that evening, "Never have I felt so proud to be a Quebecer and a Canadian." I felt it important not to proclaim a great victory. It has never been my style, in any event, to go around raising my own fists and saying, "I won." I prefer to let people judge for themselves whether I have won or lost. But this, in particular, was not a night for gloating. I remember making the point, on the contrary, that we had all lost a little because we had fought among ourselves. Families were divided and friendships broken up over it. My ministers and members of the Quebec caucus who went back every weekend during the referendum to fight for Canada would return to Ottawa a little dispirited because they had met friends or family, parents or children, brothers or sisters who were divided. It was a very emotional time.

In my heart that evening, I was very happy that even on a trick question the people of Quebec had voted against any form of separation. We had won, fair and square. But, putting aside the emotion of the moment, I knew that we had to move fast to use the moral imperative of the referendum victory to settle the constitutional question. The very next day, I told Jean Chrétien, "Get on a plane and go and sell our package to the provinces."

Even while we proceeded with our pursuit of constitutional reform after the referendum, our next urgent priority was to address the need for a new energy agreement with Alberta. In 1973, the OPEC cartel of oil-producing countries had raised the world price of a barrel of oil from $2.59 U.S.

*July 1980.
I was
honoured
to have the
opportunity
to meet
Terry Fox
when he
passed
through
Ottawa in
the course
of his
Marathon
of Hope.
(NAC-TC)*

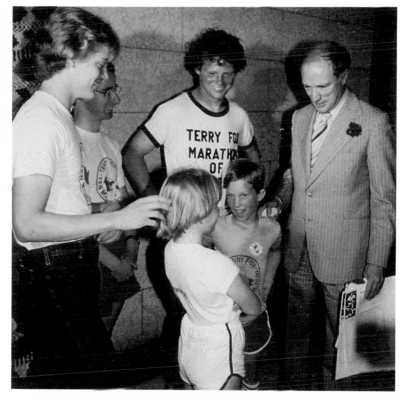

to $11.65 U.S. in less than a year, a change that had jolted every national economy around the globe. In response, I had announced a series of measures to increase Canada's energy self-reliance and reduce our exposure to world events. We had established a Canada-wide, one-price policy that set our price below the world price. The Interprovincial oil pipeline was extended from Sarnia, Ontario, to Montreal. An oil export tax prevented the United States from draining Canada's reserves. And we established Petro-Canada as a publicly owned company, to provide a window on the oil industry – then dominated by American-based companies that did not necessarily have Canada's best

Later, I was pleased to receive in my office the young Canadian skiers Steve Podborski, Ken Read, and Gerry Sorenson.
(J.M. Carisse Photo)

interests at heart – and to explore for new supplies. The government of Alberta, by far our largest oil-producing province, was bitterly unhappy at first with our 1973 policy. But by 1978, Canadian oil prices had gradually been raised to world levels, we had reached agreements with Alberta on resource sharing, and the federal, Alberta, and Ontario governments had even worked together to save the development of the Syncrude tarsands oil project. Stability seemed to have returned to the energy field. But then, in 1979, we suddenly had the second OPEC oil crisis, sparked by the Iranian revolution.

When the Shah was driven out and the Ayatollah Khomeini brought to power by the revolution, the Iranians stopped producing oil. As a result the price more than doubled virtually overnight, from $14 U.S. to $34 U.S. a barrel. And this time all the experts – not only in the industry, but in consumer organizations as well – were predicting that the price would keep soaring until it reached $90 or $100 a barrel. It was a whole new situation, one that Canada

Summer 1981.
Keith Davey
(right) brought
along his
friend
Gary Lautens,
the popular
Toronto Star
columnist,
and his family.
(NAC-TC)

couldn't possibly handle under the existing agreements that were giving the federal government only a 9 per cent share of oil and gas revenues, while the producing provinces got 50.5 per cent and the industry 40.5 per cent.

I was convinced that the central government needed a greater share for at least two reasons. First, we wanted a made-in-Canada oil price that would trend towards world prices but wouldn't go there overnight. That meant we needed money to be able to subsidize part of the price consumers would have to pay for the oil we imported. And second, if the price of oil had continued to rise under the existing revenue-sharing arrangement, so much money would have flowed out of the rest of the country to Alberta and to the oil companies that Canada wouldn't even have been able to continue its equalization program. Even Ontario would have become a have-not province under that previous formula.

I had spoken about all this during the 1980 election campaign. In a speech in Halifax, I had set out the broad

*Investigating the oil
situation in Canada's
North, aboard an
offshore drill ship in
the Beaufort Sea, near
Tuktoyaktuk in the
Northwest Territories.*
(Canapress)

framework of our energy policy. I promised a made-
in-Canada oil price because we have a lot of oil, it's a natural
advantage, and therefore we should use it against our competitors, just as they use their own natural advantages. I
promised a fair sharing of energy revenues between the
federal government, the producing provinces, and the
industry. And I promised to increase Canadian ownership
of the oil industry to 50 per cent, to improve our independence and self-sufficiency – an aim that every other country in the world would have regarded as a modest one.

Predictably enough, however, these policies were opposed
by the multinational oil companies and even more by the
premier of Alberta, Peter Lougheed. Lougheed was a tough
and distinguished premier who fought hard for the good of

The boys always enjoyed their Northern visits.
(NAC-TC)

I greatly enjoyed my travels in the North, too.
(NAC-TC)

his province. I never faulted him for that. When Joe Clark as prime minister failed to reach agreement with Alberta on a new pricing formula, the federal minister of finance, John Crosbie (an able man a little too fond of shooting from the quip), publicly referred to Lougheed as "Bokassa II," recalling the infamous emperor of the Central African Republic.

Others called the premier "the blue-eyed sheik of the North." But in my view he was just doing his job. It wasn't his job as premier to take the broad view of what is good for Canada. His focus was on what is good for Alberta, and I think that as a Westerner – particularly as an Albertan – he had good historical cause to be suspicious of the influence Toronto's Bay Street and Montreal's St. James Street have had on the government in Ottawa. Every provincial premier must fight for his own province. It is nice to hope that premiers would be thinking of Canada and the provinces at the same time, but it is their job to think of the provinces first – and it was my job to think of the whole country first.

The government of Canada and its ministers are elected to seek the good of the whole of the country, so sometimes that means saying no to one region and yes to another in order to redistribute equality of opportunity. The federal government is the balance wheel of the federal system, and the federal system means using counterweights. If one province is very rich and another very poor, my view is that there should be some redistribution of resources, with the federal government in charge of making sure that the distribution is done fairly.

I used to have this discussion with a lot of my own members of Parliament, who would come to me and insist, for instance, that it was absolutely essential that a given company be encouraged to locate in, say, Quebec rather than Newfoundland. I would tell them, "Look, it's true that you're here to argue for your own province, but you have to look at the broad common good. If you want to take care exclusively of Quebec's interests, go get elected provincially in Quebec. And I will respect that. But if you're here in Ottawa, you have to try to understand that Newfoundland is even poorer than Quebec and that perhaps it is reasonable to encourage a certain industrial development to go there." That is why, given the difference in our respective roles, throughout Confederation there has always been a tension between the provincial premiers and the federal government – ideally a creative tension, but a tension nonetheless.

In 1980, faced with soaring energy prices, we were a new government with a strong mandate to get things done. So I said, "Okay, this is a big item. Clark lost an election on it. We're going to accomplish what we believe needs to be done. And I'm not going to make the mistake that perhaps I made previously, the mistake of being too gentle with the premiers. I'm going to say, 'This is good for Canada, and we've got a mandate from the Canadian people.'" I gave Marc Lalonde – a tough, fair-minded, and clear-thinking minister who had done a good job in a number of other departments – the task as energy minister of reaching a new agreement with Alberta within the framework we had announced. In October 1980, we introduced our National Energy Program as part of the federal budget. New taxes were introduced at the wellhead to increase federal revenues. Exploration and development expenditure deductions were eliminated and replaced by a grants program that would increase the Canadianization of the petroleum industry, and special incentives were put in place to encourage exploration in the frontier lands. At the same time, to attack the problem at the other end, and in recognition of an important change in our attitudes towards non-renewable resources, a host of energy conservation measures were announced.

The Alberta government reacted with outrage. Lougheed in effect turned off some of the oil spigots and reduced the flow to other provinces. He went on television

Peter Lougheed, premier of Alberta, was always a tough bargainer. (NAC-TC/Robert Cooper)

to announce that Alberta would reduce its shipments to the rest of Canada by 180,000 barrels a day. We had to compensate for this by buying more expensive foreign oil. The fight lasted a little over a year, and it was a politically difficult time. They had bumper stickers in Alberta saying, "Let the Eastern bastards freeze in the dark." This did little for the cause of national unity.

The American-owned multinational oil companies, meanwhile, were so unhappy with our policy of Canadianization that even Ronald Reagan raised it with me at a lunch. I told him, "Look, I won an election on this platform. I don't tell you how to set the figures for your military budget, you can't tell me that I can't have my own energy policy in Canada." It ended there. I guess he saw that on this issue we wouldn't bend. Having won an election with this as one of our specific plans, it would have been a terrible abdication of Canadian pride and power to say as soon as we did anything the Americans didn't like, "Well, we'll try to adjust."

I tried to counter the anger in Alberta by explaining that what we were doing was the same as the National Oil Policy of the Diefenbaker government, only in reverse. In 1960, the Borden Royal Commission on Energy had recommended that in order to encourage the development of oil resources in the West, all oil sold east of the so-called Borden Line – which was roughly the Ottawa River – would be imported at the world price. But west of this line all consumers – largely in Ontario – would use Alberta and other Western oil at $1 to $1.50 a barrel *above the world price.* In effect, for most of the period from 1961 to 1973, the producers in Alberta had been subsidized by consumers in other provinces, and this had enabled the oil industry to establish itself in a way that led to Alberta's later prosperity. So my argument was that now that prices were going sky-high, the shoe should be on the other foot and we would share in the opposite direction. Alberta would send a greater percentage of its enormous increase in price to the rest of Canada, so that we could afford our equalization payments and so that we could subsidize those consumers who had to buy overseas oil. That seemed fair enough to me, but Albertans were not eager to remember the days when their industry was subsidized, finding it easier to see the money they were paying out today, and it was a difficult political battle.

Finally, after some tough bargaining, we negotiated a compromise deal with Alberta in September 1981. The federal share of oil revenues would increase from about 10 per cent to 26 per cent, while Alberta's share and the industry's share would each decline to 37 per cent. The Alberta government won its point on natural gas taxation and we withdrew our tax at the wellhead. But we had extended the Canadianization measures, which constituted a great breakthrough for a truly Canadian energy policy. I regarded the agreement as a triumph of the Canadian way, not of one particular government over the other. The 1981 agreement balanced competing interests, as Diefenbaker had done with the Borden Line in the 1960s, and as we had done with energy prices in the 1970s. It was a fair compromise. Lougheed and I toasted the agreement with champagne and publicly agreed that it was good for Alberta and good for Canada.

But the flaw of the National Energy Program, of course, was that, like almost everyone else, we had assumed that oil prices would rise. Our policy would have been a great success if oil had gone to $60 or more a barrel, as virtually the whole world was predicting at the time. But almost as soon as we had signed the agreement, oil prices began to stabilize and then to drop. So all our planning went for naught, because we were underwriting subsidies to the Canadian oil companies and lower prices to the Canadian consumers with money that we didn't get.

At the level of principle, however, I have no regrets about the National Energy Program. It distressed me that Albertans were so vehement about the policy and that it quickly became a scapegoat for all the subsequent ills of the oil industry, so that Liberals in Calgary almost became an endangered species for a while. But I still hold that we were right to use Canada's energy self-sufficiency to our country's advantage, by setting our own prices rather than allowing the companies to have a windfall that was

A fair compromise – good for Alberta, good for Canada, and good for a celebratory glass of champagne. (NAC-TC/Robert Cooper)

determined by the OPEC countries. It was natural for a federal government concerned about the development of the whole country and not just of one province to develop a policy that would give advantage not only to our oil producers but to our manufacturers as well. The role of the federal government is to distribute wealth from the affluent to the disadvantaged. That was our policy for individuals, for regional equalization, and for energy. We were consistent in our devotion to sharing, and I take pride in that.

The OPEC oil crisis that was touched off by the Iranian revolution also had economic implications for us that went far beyond the energy field. As world oil prices doubled, inflation again soared. The Federal Reserve Board of the United States, led by its chairman, Paul Volcker, decided on a dramatic remedy that would involve not fine-tuning but the use of a sledgehammer. Throughout the spring and summer of 1981, he allowed U.S. interest rates to rise to record levels, and the world economy was compelled to follow in lock-step. I remember that at the Economic Summit in Montebello, Quebec, in 1981, West German chancellor Helmut Schmidt told President Reagan that he was causing the highest interest rates since the time of Christ. Reagan did not have a convincing response to offer. But it was all to no avail. By August of 1981, the Bank of Canada had been forced to raise its rate from 7.5 per cent to an incredible 21 per cent. Predictably enough, as borrowers went broke trying to meet their interest payments, our unemployment shot up from 7.5 per cent in 1981 to 11 per cent in 1982, and Canada's gross domestic product underwent its only decline in my whole period in office.

It was in the midst of these new economic stresses that we had our ill-fated brush with tax reform in 1981. In preparing that budget, Finance Minister Allan MacEachen came to me and said that there were tax loopholes his public servants had been wanting to close since the 1970s. These loopholes allowed businesspeople and private entrepreneurs, lawyers, and other individual operators to pay less in taxes. It was all perfectly legal – the accountants and lawyers these people could afford to employ saw to that – but it meant that the ordinary working men and women of Canada were paying more than their share, whereas the privileged classes were paying less. MacEachen told me quite frankly what was going to be in the budget and said, "Look, we're going to close these loopholes." The reasoning was that since we seemed to be acting decisively on other fronts, it was time to get tough on the budgetary front too. There were some reservations about that in the Cabinet, with several ministers saying, "We've already got the provinces against us. We're fighting most of the premiers on the

constitution. We've got the western provinces against us on energy. How can we afford to make more enemies at the same time?" But by and large MacEachen's plan had the approval of the Cabinet, and he made it the centrepiece of his budget.

As soon as the budget was presented, all hell broke loose. We had raised tax reform as an issue in our 1980 election campaign but had not really emphasized it, so people seemed to be caught by surprise when it became the theme of the 1981 budget. The members of our caucus immediately started getting a terrible amount of flak from all those who had benefited from the loopholes and were suddenly being told that the days of easy write-offs were over, and they were going to pay more taxes. We very soon found that we didn't have the support of all of caucus for these measures. Quite frankly, neither I nor MacEachen nor anyone else in the Cabinet had realized the extent to which this budget would upset so many private interests in so many sectors of the population. The outcry was such that MacEachen was forced to withdraw many of his measures, and naturally that cost us a great deal of credibility, making us look like a government that couldn't even bring in a budget that was fair and that it could stand behind. Some people thought that I had not been paying attention because I was so busy with the constitution and other issues, but that was not the case. I think it's fair to say that I had spent as much time on that budget as I had spent on any other throughout my term in office. But, like MacEachen and others, I hadn't gauged the impact of it correctly.

What was much more successful was the "Six and Five" anti-inflation program in MacEachen's 1982 budget. It was, in fact, one of the most innovative economic experiments of our time in office. We found ourselves having to fight inflation again, but I saw that we couldn't afford politically to get into the kind of wrangle we had endured to impose wage and price controls in 1975. Had we tried to proceed by legislation, the bill would have been challenged in the Supreme Court and perhaps become as contentious as the Anti-Inflation Board had been. So I approached it by saying: "We're going to set an example for the country. Rather than impose controls on everybody, we're going to impose them on ourselves. It's going to be a six per cent limit on public service wage increases this year, and five per cent next year. We're going to do it by ourselves, and we're going to tell the provinces and hope that they will come along by doing the same thing in their own bailiwicks."

This approach was based on my belief in the sovereignty of the people. We were going to show the people how we – as a government – could give an example without forcing other institutions to follow. And the amazing thing is that eventually nearly everybody did follow. At first the unions were against it, and the public service, understandably

Flanked by two of my most trusted aides. On the left is Privy Council president Michael Pitfield and on the right is my principal secretary, the deceptively cherubic Jim Coutts.
(Canapress)

enough, said, "Why are we being made a victim of inflation? Nobody else is." Various premiers, for their part, said in media interviews that they doubted it would work. In fact, it is probably fair to say that almost nobody thought it would work. But we stuck with our approach and said, "We believe that this is right." We gave that leadership. And the provinces followed, one by one. And then we said to business: "The government can impose limits on wage increases. Why don't you show that you can do it too?" The result was that, with much less grief and confrontation, we were able to bring inflation down from 10.8 per cent in 1982 to 5.8 per cent in 1983 and 4.4 per cent in 1984. Our Six and Five program proved that sometimes you can catch more flies with honey than with vinegar.

Meanwhile, our efforts on the constitution had been proceeding. Immediately after the Quebec referendum in 1980, in accordance with my instructions to "get on a plane...," Jean Chrétien had flown across the country meeting with all the premiers – except Lévesque, who refused to receive him. He met and talked with all the other premiers within two and a half days, telling them that we should seize the moment to proceed quickly with renewing the constitution. In the atmosphere of relief at the referendum's result, the initial reaction was favourable. So throughout the summer, Chrétien, provincial ministers, and our officials had a series of meetings in which they worked hard on developing and refining an ambitious package. But it was clear from the beginning that getting actual agreement from the premiers wouldn't be easy.

On June 7, 1980, I invited the first ministers to 24 Sussex Drive for a day of private talks. The premiers – especially Peter Lougheed and Saskatchewan's Allan Blakeney – said they wanted to return to the agenda that had been on the table prior to our defeat in 1979. Of course they did, because that was the agenda with the jurisdictional concessions I had offered them in 1978 when I said I had almost "given away the store." But they had turned down those proposals, we were back with our big majority, and it was a whole different world. "That was then and this is now," I told them.

I had been in nearly continuous constitutional negotiations with many of these premiers since 1968. I had learned that the more I pressed for simple patriation of our constitution, the more the premiers demanded in provincial powers. And by now, I had concluded that the process of patriating our constitution from Great Britain, a process begun in 1927, would never be successful unless provincial

President Reagan visits Ottawa

1. Welcoming President Ronald Reagan in March 1981.

2. President Reagan addressing the House of Commons from his distinctive aide-mémoire cue cards.

3. Formal discussions between the Canadian team and, on the American side, President Reagan assisted by Alexander Haig and Lawrence Eagleburger.

4. In the Royal Box at the National Arts Centre with President and Mrs. Reagan.

5. At 24 Sussex Drive. President Reagan was not a man for thoughtful policy discussions, but he was pleasant and congenial and my children found him entertaining.

(NAC-TC)

blackmail attempts were broken. And I believed that any fair-minded observer of federal-provincial negotiations would agree that the Canadian people would never have a constitution of their own until the link between patriation and provincial powers was broken.

So I proposed that constitutional negotiations be approached in two stages. First, we wanted a "people's package" – consisting of patriation and a charter of rights – to be negotiated, and then we would get down to talking about the "politicians' package," the division of powers between the federal government and the provinces. We were willing to decentralize in some areas, but in exchange the federal government needed to strengthen the Canadian common market by removing provincial barriers to the free movement of goods and people. There would be no question of unconditional decentralization. It would have to be a matter of give and take, and we would no longer allow patriation and the charter to be held hostage to provincial demands for new powers. We would hold a formal constitutional conference in September to thrash it out.

The premiers, predictably enough, did not receive this proposal with great enthusiasm. But I was determined to keep up the pressure and saw to it that intense and constructive work at the ministerial level continued throughout the summer. We had no great illusions, however, as to the position the Lévesque government in particular would ultimately take. In fact, Chrétien reported to me that summer on a conversation he had had in Vancouver with Claude Charron, a senior Parti Québécois minister who was very close to Lévesque. The ministerial negotiations had been making good progress, and Chrétien told Charron he had the opportunity to sign a deal that would serve Quebec well. To this Charron had replied: "Listen, Jean, don't waste your time. We are separatists. So we are not really interested in renewing Canada. Independence is the first article of our party's program, and we will be faithful to it. We cannot sign. We will never sign."

By the time of the federal-provincial conference, Chrétien had made excellent progress with the provincial ministers on developing a package – but their bosses were refusing to come on-side. He told me: "The premiers are throwing away most of our work and they're going to start from scratch. Things don't look too good." So when I met the ten premiers on September 7 at a Sunday-night dinner hosted by Governor General Ed Schreyer to open the conference, the mood was already sour. And it got worse.

The first gambit of the premiers was to say, "Let's discuss form before substance. We think that you should share the chairmanship of the conference with one of us." I was just seething, and I said: "Okay, you propose that on television tomorrow and you'll see what my answer is. Who do you suppose the Canadian people would want to see co-chairing this conference with me – perhaps Mr. Lévesque, who has just gone through trying to bust up Canada? Or should it be Premier Peckford of Newfoundland, who has said that Lévesque is closer to his view of Canada than Trudeau is? The tradition since time immemorial has been that it is the prime minister of Canada who chairs federal-provincial conferences. Don't try to get me to change that now. I'm ready to do battle – on that too, if you want. So let's have that debate on television tomorrow." Needless to say, they dropped the idea right away. But the meal kept dragging on and we kept exchanging barbs, and finally that dinner seemed so endless that

A Cancún scrapbook

*Not just
an ordinary
day on the
beach (top of
facing page).
At the
Cancún
Conference
in Mexico
in 1981,
world heads
of state
gather for
a group photo
displaying
varying
degrees of
informality.*

*The other
photographs
show the
world's leaders
at work
and at play.*

(NAC-TC)

I asked the Governor General if we could hurry up with the dessert because I wanted to go home and do some work.

That night the Quebec officials were hard at work delivering to all of the other provincial delegations a leaked memo that described federal strategy in the discussions. Leaked by a federal official who was a PQ sympathizer, the memo served to reinforce the feeling of "us against them." The next provincial move was the so-called "Château consensus." The premiers had breakfast at the Château Laurier and examined a long paper drafted by Quebec that demanded ten powers in exchange for discussing patriation, and then another twelve before the deed was done. When the premiers presented this document to me, I hadn't read beyond two pages before I snorted and said: "Well, now we know there will never be an agreement. You guys are laughing at me – you're going back to square one. But I'm telling you gentlemen, I've been warning you since 1976 that we could introduce a resolution in the House of Commons patriating the constitution, and if necessary we'll do this unilaterally. So I'm telling you now, we're going to go it alone. We're going to introduce a resolution, and we'll go to London, and we won't even bother asking a premier to come with us."

Premier Sterling Lyon of Manitoba said: "If you do that, you're going to tear the country apart." My answer was: "If the country is going to be torn apart because we bring back from Britain our own constitution after 115 years of Confederation and after more than fifty years of fruitless discussions, and because we have asked for a Canadian charter of rights, when most of you already have provincial charters, then the country deserves to be torn up." I was quite categorical about it, and I still believe it to this day. If there was not the will in the country to

With the first ministers and Governor General Ed Schreyer, September 7, 1980. This photograph preceded the spectacularly unsuccessful dinner.
(NAC-TC/John Evans)

be constitutionally independent 115 years after Canada stopped being a colony, that would have meant there was no national will at all, and therefore no country worthy of the name.

I met my caucus on September 17, explained the Château consensus, and told them that all the work of the summer had come to nothing because the nine English-speaking premiers had accepted a completely new list of demands drafted by Quebec. The members of caucus shared my impatience. We were still riding pretty high after our election and referendum victories, and they were saying, "Of course, we'll go it alone. We can't just wait forever. We're a do-it government now, so let's do it." To make sure they understood clearly what we were getting into, I warned the caucus that unilateral patriation would be a gamble and a very tough fight. I had briefed the British prime minister, Margaret Thatcher, about our constitutional position in June 1980, and she had told me that if the Parliament of Canada asked for its constitution, there was nothing her Parliament could do but accede to that request. But I warned my caucus, as I had warned Margaret Thatcher, that a lot of provincial premiers and a lot of Native Canadians would show up in London on the doorstep of Number 10 Downing Street, protesting against what we were doing.

I explained to them as well that the more we expanded the charter of rights, the more troubles we would have with the premiers. Some of the premiers believed very strongly in the British view of the parliamentary system, which holds that the legislature must always have the last word on everything. A charter deviates from that, by setting out some basic rights that the courts can uphold and that no legislature can take away. My answer was always that the British system works for Britain, but we are not a unitary state like Great Britain and we have a lot of minorities. But the question now was whether a full charter was what we should unilaterally seek from Britain. We obviously had to have protection of the Official Languages Act and some other elements of a charter such as we had agreed to in Victoria, back in 1971. But the more rights we protected, the more we would be encroaching on parliamentary supremacy and therefore obliging the provinces as well as Parliament to modify some of their laws accordingly.

I was cautious about this, because I didn't want to risk going too far, leaving the caucus behind. But almost unanimously, the caucus wanted to go for a full charter. They were saying things like, "You care particularly about linguistic rights, but those of us from outside Quebec care more about civil liberties in general. So go for the full charter." One of our French-speaking members from the Gatineau stood up and said: "*Allons-y en Cadillac* – we haven't fought this long just to get parts of a charter, let's go first class." It would be the fight of our lives, but we all knew the stakes and the odds! I had warned them that if we lost, we might also lose power, perhaps for a long time. And the caucus had told me to go for the full package, to go Cadillac-style, to be liberal to the end, and not to temper our convictions with political expediency. I told them: "If that's the way you want it, I'm delighted."

When the Cabinet met the day after that gung-ho caucus meeting, the mood was equally ebullient. In fact, there were some ministers who wanted to go even farther and use patriation in order to grab the additional federal powers over the economy that we needed to have a proper common market within Canada. But I objected to that. I said, "No, I don't think we can use this to transfer powers to the federal government. We can take powers away from the provinces and the federal government alike by protecting the citizens in the charter, but we can't shift the balance between the federal and the provincial governments. There will be a second stage where we get a fair negotiating process over powers; that will be the politicians' package. But in the people's package, we shouldn't upset the balance."

The key issue in the Cabinet was whether to entrench the charter of rights. But like the caucus, almost without exception the Cabinet felt that minority-language education rights must be entrenched in a new constititution. And once we had made the decision to impose minority-language education rights, then logically our position had to be to impose the full charter. As a result, the charter that emerged from these Cabinet discussions was significantly expanded from the limited charter that had been accepted so long ago at the Victoria conference in 1971.

On October 2, 1980, I went on national television to announce the results of our deliberations. What I had first proposed in 1976 had come to pass. We would be going to Great Britain with regard to our constitution one last time, alone if necessary. Soon after my television address, the premiers of Ontario and New Brunswick announced that they would support this patriation package. Ontario's William Davis and New Brunswick's Richard Hatfield, although both Conservatives, were stout allies who stood with us through thick and thin. Davis was later to play an especially important role in persuading me to accept the final compromise position of November 1981. The federal NDP leader, Ed Broadbent, was also an important ally. I had briefed him before going on television, and Broadbent soon announced, "My party and I support unilateral action." To win the support of the NDP, I agreed to accept amendments to the constitution bill that increased some provincial powers over natural resources. These amendments were especially important to Saskatchewan, and Broadbent felt confident that they would enable him to persuade that province's NDP premier, Allan Blakeney, to accept our plan. He never did succeed in this. What my concession ultimately meant, however, was that the only change in the division of powers between the federal and provincial governments as a result of our entire patriation exercise was a strengthening of provincial powers over natural resources. So much for all the talk about a federal power grab! Quebec and the other provinces received a free jurisdictional gift for which the public thanks of their premiers has always been somewhat muted.

Richard Hatfield, the premier of New Brunswick, always took the federal side in our constitutional fight.
(NAC-TC)

The eight premiers who opposed our plan did not, of course, sit idly by. First, they lobbied hard in London to see if they could persuade the British Parliament to resort to its old colonial posture and second-guess the duly elected government of Canada. Quebec was particularly quick off the mark in this regard. Gilles Loiselle, Quebec's agent general in London, with the help of an expensive chef and a very fine cellar, wined and dined every British parliamentarian who wanted a free meal. But the efforts of the provinces in this lobbying war were countered very effectively on our behalf by the work of Jean Wadds, a Tory who had been appointed by Joe Clark as high commissioner to Great Britain and whom I had decided to retain in that post. I always say it was thanks to three women that we were eventually able to reform our constitution – the Queen, who was favourable, Margaret Thatcher, who undertook to do everything that our Parliament asked of her, and Jean Wadds, who represented the interests of Canada so well in London.

The second assault of the premiers was to take us to court. On October 14, 1980 – just twelve days after I had announced the patriation plan – the dissenting premiers met in Toronto and announced that they would fight the resolution in the courts. Challenges were launched in the courts of Manitoba, Newfoundland, and Quebec. The courts of Manitoba and Quebec ruled that our patriation bill was constitutional. But on March 31, 1981, the Supreme Court of Newfoundland declared that our resolution was illegal, setting the stage for an appeal to the Supreme Court of Canada.

As these court battles were unfolding, we were also battling the Conservatives in the House of Commons. A week before the Newfoundland court decision, the Tories had begun a filibuster in the House of Commons to keep us from passing the constitution bill; the Newfoundland court ruling against us gave them a great lift. Finally, on April 8, 1981, we struck a parliamentary deal to end the filibuster: we agreed to put off a final vote on our resolution until after the ruling by the Supreme Court. And so from April until September, we were forced to play a waiting game.

The third part of the premiers' offensive was to try to swing public opinion over to their side by developing their own alternative to our patriation plan. On April 16, 1981, the so-called "Gang of Eight" – the premiers of all the provinces except Ontario and New Brunswick – announced their position. Their proposal called for patriation, the Alberta amending formula (which provided fiscal compensation to any province that would "opt out" of a constitutional amendment), and a provision for the right to delegate legislative authority from Parliament to the legislatures. There wasn't even a mention of the

The Queen favoured my attempt to reform the constitution. I was always impressed not only by the grace she displayed in public at all times, but by the wisdom she showed in private conversation.
(NAC-TC)

charter of rights! But what was most astonishing was that René Lévesque had agreed to the Alberta amending formula, thereby dropping Quebec's traditional demand for the right of veto over constitutional change. Quebec was saying, in effect, that it was a province like the others! Obviously, maintaining his tactical political alliance with the English-speaking premiers seemed more important to Lévesque than the substance of Quebec's constitutional position. The eight premiers were so pleased with their plan that they bought large ads inscribed with their signatures in newspapers across the land. We at least had a good laugh at the sight of René Lévesque's signature scrawled across the ad under the banner of a large red maple leaf.

But the April 1981 proclamation of the Gang of Eight

The Commonwealth Conference in Melbourne, Australia, in October 1981 was a spectacular production, as the facing page demonstrates. (NAC-TC)

made it crystal clear that Lévesque was simply attempting to stop patriation, period. He had just won a provincial election against Claude Ryan a few days previously, and he must have been brimming over with confidence. By exchanging Quebec's demand for a veto – which he would later keep trying to regain – for the Alberta amending formula, he had accepted the principle of provincial equality. This was important. Ever since Jean Lesage, Quebec nationalists had favoured special status, *deux nations*, and sovereignty-association. Nationalists had always reacted with horror and indignation to the concept that Quebec was "a province like the others." Now Lévesque not only had accepted this, but had gone out of his way in his press statement to say that every province was equal. I knew then, for certain, that Lévesque would never negotiate a deal. His only purpose was to use the Gang of Eight to block us, and he must have felt very sure that he would succeed.

I was on the way to a Commonwealth Conference in Melbourne, Australia, in September 1981 when the decision of the Supreme Court was finally announced. By a

clear majority of seven judges to two, the court ruled that our unilateral patriation was legal. But it went on to say by a judgment of six to three (Justices Laskin, Estey, and McIntyre dissenting) that, though legal, it was not according to constitutional convention. Having said that our plan didn't conform with convention, the majority of the court had to state what the convention was. But their answer was only that there had to be a "substantial number" of provinces agreeing with the federal government. They never defined "substantial"; it was evidently some unstated number between two and ten.

This was, in my view, a faulty judgment. I believe the dissenting judges led by Chief Justice Bora Laskin were right when they said, in effect: "It's a legal question, and we can't talk about conventions, which are agreements among politicians." But all the time I was in office, I never criticized the Supreme Court judges. I just said, "Well, that's the judgment. We have to live with it." But, privately, I didn't have to like it, or agree with it.

We were on a stopover in Seoul, South Korea, when I learned of the Supreme Court's decision. I reacted to it on two different levels. As a lawyer, a teacher of constitutional law, and a former minister of justice, I felt that if the court said what we were doing was legal, we should go ahead and do it. But as a politician, I wondered whether the public would understand our decision, or whether they would think I was being reckless. It might seem that we were defying the judgment of the court by simply proceeding with what a majority had said was contrary to convention. Another question, of course, was how we would be received in London if we simply went ahead unilaterally after that judgment, which our enemies were publicizing far and wide in every political nook and cranny of Westminster. And, finally, I knew that the two premiers who were with us, Davis and Hatfield, weren't all that happy about the prospect of my going unilaterally at that point. They would have been forced either to come along reluctantly or to join the other provincial leaders in the Gang of Eight. So I decided to give it one last try. In November I would chair another meeting that would be one final attempt to make peace by reaching agreement with a "substantial" number of provinces.

I didn't really hold out much hope that we would ever be able to sign a deal as long as the Gang of Eight alliance held. Lévesque, I knew, would never agree. But it was important for us to be seen making the effort. And if we tried yet again and failed, I was determined that we would go to London and say: "We have exhausted all the alternatives. What we are doing is legal, and you must pass what the Canadian Parliament requests." If the British Parliament balked, we would have the option of a massive demonstration of national will, leading to a unilateral declaration of constitutional independence from Britain. The evening I returned from the Melbourne conference, I told my principal secretary, Tom Axworthy, to start making contingency plans for a referendum or an election in 1982. If it came to a showdown, we would need to have the people demonstrate their support for the people's package.

When that final constitutional conference began on Monday, November 2, I knew that the Eight were feeling very confident, perhaps even cocky, because of the Supreme Court's decision. I was aiming at one of two outcomes: I could either prove to the Canadian public that the Eight were being completely unreasonable and then go ahead alone, legally but perhaps unconventionally. Or I could break the solidarity among the Eight and go to London with the support of a substantial number of premiers, which I supposed would be anywhere between five and nine of them. Lévesque's goal was to keep the Gang of Eight intact to thwart me, and mine was to make a certain number of concessions that would split their ranks and bring some of the others on-side.

That was the spirit in which we began the negotiations, and on the first day of the conference we essentially restated our positions. Premier Lyon of Manitoba told me: "We

In these difficult days Canada was even losing at hockey! Here I am shown presenting the 1981 Canada Cup to the Soviet team, with an assist from Alan Eagleson of Hockey Canada. (NAC-TC)

already have an agreement. Sign our provincial package." I told the premiers that the federal government could be flexible on the timing and substance of a charter, but we would not yield on the principle of the charter itself. We spent the first two days of the conference going over this old and barren ground.

But then on Wednesday, November 4, we broke the Gang of Eight. Time was growing short. Lévesque had announced that he would leave the conference at noon that day, and it was obvious from the discussions up to that moment that neither side was prepared to bend. I decided it was a good time to try a fallback position that I had had in mind for quite a different purpose. I had been thinking that if it became necessary to go to London unilaterally and the British showed any reluctance to cooperate, I might say to them: "Just give us simple patriation of the constitution as it is. You can't refuse me that. And then we'll have up to two more years of negotiation in Canada on an amending formula and a charter of rights. If we still can't reach agreement within that time, we'll let the Canadian people decide on both those issues in a referendum." So now I decided to try out this idea on the premiers instead.

I turned to Lévesque after the coffee break, referred to his threat to leave the conference in an hour, and said: "Rather than break up in disarray and continue our fight on the doorstep of the British Parliament, why don't we get patriation first – nobody can object to that – then give ourselves two years to solve our problems over the amending formula and the charter, and, failing that, consult the people in a referendum? Surely a great democrat like yourself won't be against a referendum?"

Lévesque rose to the bait. I think he answered instinctively, without remembering that he was in the Gang of Eight, and said: "Well, I can buy that." I think he had in mind that this would be his chance to avenge his loss in the 1980 referendum, because I remember him saying, "I would like to fight the charter." I suppose he thought that he could win this one in Quebec. But I was confident, too, that I could win a fight over rights, including language rights. Lévesque was pleased enough with this new deal to announce that he would now delay his departure.

I seized the moment and said to the other premiers, particularly the rest of the Gang of Eight: "This is a triumph. There is suddenly a Quebec-Ottawa alliance. You are all surprised, gentlemen. Too bad for you." The cat was now among the pigeons! I adjourned for lunch. On the way out, I told the press about the new Quebec-Ottawa alliance as well, and went off to lunch rather happy.

The other seven premiers in the Gang of Eight were, of course, absolutely furious with Lévesque. He had constantly been making the others promise that they would never break the united front, insisting that it was the only way to stop Trudeau from getting his "substantial number" of premiers. And now Lévesque himself had been the first to break it. He soon became aware of his mistake; indeed, in his memoirs, he writes that my "manoeuvre served to drive a last nail in the coffin of the late common front." The other premiers were hopping mad, because my scheme meant that the only way for them to stop me would be to campaign with Lévesque against a charter of rights. Many of them had charters in their own provinces, and it also would have meant campaigning against Ottawa alongside a premier who believed in an independent Quebec. I don't think they relished the idea of such a referendum very much. Seeing the reaction of the other premiers and his own officials, Lévesque realized that he had fallen into a trap. After lunch, he began trying to extricate himself. He said he hadn't fully understood what was being proposed and was no longer in agreement with me on the referendum.

When Quebec backtracked after lunch, I thought the negotiating game was over. I expected that with Lévesque coming back into line, the eight premiers would present a solid front again, and we would never have a substantial number of provinces. What I didn't realize was that Lévesque (who, according to his memoirs, was already deeply suspicious of allies like Blakeney and Bill Bennett of British Columbia) had completely destroyed his credibility with his seven colleagues. It was already too late for him to undo the damage. The solidarity of the Gang of Eight was broken. The premiers finally sensed that here was a man who would never negotiate seriously because his only aim was to destroy the country – and who would later write critically of them that they were "still attached to the notion of 'national unity' which, in the last analysis, an

Anglo-Canadian puts before provincial autonomy." But not knowing their thinking at the time and seeing us back at square one at the negotiating table, I was ready to end the conference and announce that we were proceeding unilaterally. When Jean Chrétien whispered to me, "Can you give us some more time?" I replied, "Jean, you're asking a lot. I'm getting pretty impatient." But I agreed to adjourn until the next morning.

That afternoon, Jean Chrétien met with Roy Romanow and Roy McMurtry, the attorneys general of Saskatchewan and Ontario respectively. Romanow and Chrétien had jointly chaired the meetings of federal and provincial officials making up the Continuing Committee of Ministers on the Constitution in the summer of 1980, so they knew each other well and had a good working relationship. In a small kitchen off the federal delegation's meeting room, Chrétien, Romanow, and McMurtry began putting together the beginnings of a deal. It involved swapping provincial acceptance of a charter of rights, but with a notwithstanding legislative override clause, for federal acceptance of the Alberta amending formula, but without fiscal compensation for provinces that opted out.

I convened a meeting at 24 Sussex Drive with several ministers and advisers to hear the results of Chrétien's negotiations. Chrétien told us: "I think I can perhaps have a deal if we accept the premiers' amending formula rather than our Victoria one [which gave Quebec a veto], and if we water down the charter a little bit." My first reaction was to say, "Oh, no, no, the Alberta amending formula is terrible, and as far as the charter is concerned, there isn't going to be any watering down." But Chrétien argued strongly for his proposed agreement, and a very tough discussion ensued.

Several ministers opposed weakening the charter and preferred that we take our chances in a referendum or a federal election. Others were opposed to the Alberta amending formula because it took away the Quebec veto that had been part of our Victoria formula, and because it dropped our deadlock-breaking referendum provision, which was central to our belief in the sovereignty of the people.

I was definitely leaning on the side of the hardliners. The notwithstanding clause violated my sense of justice: it seemed wrong that any province could decide to suspend any part of the charter, even if the suspension was temporary and required various formal hurdles to be jumped by the provincial legislature. The charter had been enormously improved from our first draft in 1980. We had opened the door to the people to comment on it, and they had rushed through: 914 individuals and 294 groups had appeared before the Special Joint Committee on the Constitution, and as a result we had amended the charter to protect women (and mentally and physically disabled people), had affirmed aboriginal rights and recognized the Métis as an aboriginal people, and had strengthened the role of the courts. A national constituency had been created in favour of the charter, and that was as it should be.

I saw the charter as an expression of my long-held view that the subject of law must be the individual human being; the law must permit the individual to fulfil himself or herself to the utmost. Therefore the individual has certain basic rights that cannot be taken away by any government. So maintaining an unweakened charter was important to me in this basic philosophical sense. Besides, in another dimension, the charter was defining a system of values such as liberty, equality, and the rights of association that Canadians from coast to coast could share.

Ontario premier William Davis was always a stout ally in our constitutional negotiations, and his advice helped me to accept a compromise. (NAC-TC)

Writers and poets have always searched for the Canadian identity; my old friend Blair Fraser once wrote a book about Canada in the 1950s and 1960s with the title *The Search for Identity*. Almost instinctively, Canadians have tended to say that they are French Canadians or English Canadians or Ukrainian Canadians or whatever, or simply new Canadians. But what is Canada itself? With the charter in place, we can now say that Canada is a society where all people are equal and where they share some fundamental values based upon freedom. The search for this Canadian identity, as much as my philosophical views, had led me to insist on the charter. With these beliefs, I had little sympathy for provincial demands for an override by means of this mealy-mouthed "notwithstanding" clause. But just as I was saying that I didn't want to make these concessions, the phone rang; it was Ontario premier Bill Davis.

Bill Davis had a reputation for taking a while to talk around a subject, but he could be direct, too. Now he said, "I think that our people have worked out something pretty good. What do you think, Pierre?" I told him that I didn't like it, that we would be giving away too much. "Well," he said, "I've been talking this thing over with Hatfield, and he seems to feel that…" I interrupted to suggest that perhaps we should meet on it, but Davis said, "No, look, Pierre, I think we have to tell you that this is a good compromise from our point of view. Rather than fight this thing to the bitter end, we have to tell you that we wouldn't go to London supporting you as we have until now if you don't accept some sort of compromise of this nature. We can argue details tomorrow, but we like the outline of the compromise." I came back into the living room rather chastened, reported on the Davis conversation, and said, "I think we may have to go for the compromise solution even though I don't like it – because otherwise now we'd be going to London alone."

Some of my people still wanted to go to London on our own, which had a certain amount of panache. But I had been kept informed of the opposition that was beginning to develop in the House of Lords. What's more, Prime Minister Thatcher had sent me word that although she had promised to listen to my demand for patriation, it hadn't been clear to her at the time that there would be a charter. All this led me to believe there was a danger that if we went completely alone, the British might drag their feet and we would have a messy and potentially unpredictable situation. We might have won – but we also might have ended up with nothing. I was a sufficiently long-in-the-tooth politician by then to realize that sometimes you have to take second best, and Chrétien and the two provincial ministers had put together a framework that gave us the essentials of what we wanted. So I finally told my ministers, "Look, I'm authorizing Chrétien to work out a deal on this basis – but it better

In the closing session of the constitutional conference René Lévesque's bitterness is obvious.
(Canapress)

be good." And I told Chrétien on the way out, "Jean, if you can get seven provinces representing 50 per cent of the population, I might accept it." Then I went to bed.

I was wakened at seven o'clock the next morning by a telephone call from Chrétien saying, "Let's have breakfast. We've got every province except Quebec prepared to accept that deal." When the conference reconvened on that morning of November 5, 1981, I suggested out of a sense of irony – lost, I think, on the Newfoundland premier – that Brian Peckford should read out the terms of the agreement because he was the one who had said he was closest to Lévesque's view of Canada.

Then I turned to Lévesque, whose delegation had not been involved in the previous night's negotiations, and said, "Come on, surprise me. Make some kind of a gesture now that you've lost this inning. Come along and we'll all do this together." He became very emotional – later he described this as "the day of anger and shame... tricked by Trudeau, dropped by the others." In summary, he didn't think my last appeal was very interesting. At noon, nine of us signed the accord, toasts were drunk, and the conference was adjourned.

Immediately afterwards, I had to fly to Philadelphia for a speaking engagement that had been scheduled long before we knew there would be a federal-provincial conference. I reminded the American audience that in their city more than 200 years earlier the United States had declared its independence and written its constitution: "In Canada," I announced, "we did it this morning."

I remember it was quoted back to me later that Lévesque said, "Trudeau screwed me." But the reality was that René Lévesque was a gambler. He had taken a huge gamble, and he had lost. After the fact, the nationalists invented myths about how he had been left out during a night of the long knives. But it was quite obvious at the time that Lévesque left himself out, first when he broke the Gang of Eight, and then when he went back to his hotel in Hull for the night. I don't know whether he and his delegation were celebrating, just sleeping on it, or regretting that they had broken the solidarity. But they obviously were not prowling the corridors or working the phones, looking to negotiate a compromise as the others were; they decided they would rather sit it out than be part of a compromise. Lévesque wasn't trying to improve the constitution – he was a separatist. The other premiers finally realized what I had known all along, that it was a matter of two totally conflicting visions of Canada and Quebec fighting it out.

Lévesque had first tried to destroy our vision with his referendum; and he failed. Then he tried to block our vision in the negotiating process when Quebec drew up the Château consensus in September 1981; and he failed. Then he tried to stop our vision by going to the courts with the plea that our unilateral resolution was illegal; and he failed. So Lévesque next tried to shatter our vision by using the Gang of Eight. And when this failed because he broke up the Gang of Eight himself, his last recourse was to go home and have a vote in the National Assembly of Quebec against the agreement. That vote carried by seventy members to thirty-eight.

But even this final attempt to discredit the Canadian vision was really a failure, because when we brought the final constitution resolutions to a vote in the House of Commons, seventy-one out of seventy-five members from Quebec voted in favour. When you add up the National Assembly legislators in Quebec City and the members of Parliament from Quebec, a very clear majority of all elected members from Quebec voted for the patriation package. This arithmetic can be disputed only by those who think that only the Quebec government speaks for the Quebec people. But if you hold that view, you are by definition a separatist. If you believe in Canada, you say that *both* the Quebec National Assembly *and* the Parliament of Canada, including its Quebec members, speak for Quebec.

Patriation was done in conformity with the amending formula as provided by the Supreme Court. It was done with the support of almost 60 per cent of all elected members from Quebec. In so far as opinion polls have any value, it was done with the support of the Quebec people. In March 1982, according to a CROP poll, 48 per cent of Quebecers disagreed with the Lévesque government's refusal to sign the constitutional accord, with only 32 per cent supporting the Quebec government's position. And in June 1982, 49 per cent of Quebecers thought the 1982 Constitution Act "a good thing," compared with only 16

At St. Francis Xavier University in May 1982, I received an honorary Doctor of Laws and met some fellow Montrealers. (NAC-TC)

per cent who did not. The separatists lost every count in every fight, so it is pretty hard to argue that the whole thing was "fixed" against the will of the people of Quebec.

The Constitution Act of 1982 was proclaimed on April 17. It was not perfect. I would have much preferred not to have included the notwithstanding clause that limited the charter of rights. But I certainly prefer to have a charter with a notwithstanding clause than no charter at all. I regretted the dropping of the referendum provision, and I favoured the Victoria amending formula that would have given Quebec a veto. But it would have been hard to insist on a Quebec veto after the premier of Quebec himself had given it away in his April 1981 agreement with the Gang of Eight. On the whole, the Constitution Act largely enshrined the values I had been advocating since I wrote my first article in *Cité libre* in 1950. And most important, it meant that no longer would there be an easy way for provinces to blackmail the federal government by holding out for more and more new powers in exchange for allowing patriation.

I knew that there would be ongoing constitutional discussions over time, because in a federal state there is always debate about the division of powers. But after 1982, that debate could take place on a level playing field. The people's package of 1982 settled the issues of bringing home the constitution, with a charter of rights and an amending formula. Future statesmen could now concentrate on meeting people's practical needs. For the first time since the first patriation attempt in 1927, Canadians had the luxury of giving themselves constitutional peace by closing – for years to come, if need be – this particular can of worms. Who could have foretold that a new government would be so unwise as to reopen it, a couple of years later? But such thoughts were far from my mind on April 17, 1982, when the Queen came to Parliament Hill to sign the Constitution Act. The day began sunny and warm, but ended in a downpour – an omen, I suppose, of things to come.

The final major undertaking of my years in office was my so-called "peace initiative." Through the early 1980s, beginning with the Soviet invasion of Afghanistan in 1979 and the coming to power of the Reagan administration in 1981, the Cold War had been steadily going into its darkest days since the Cuban Missile Crisis of 1962. President Ronald Reagan was a great storyteller and a very sociable man. But his outlook was dominated by a deep faith in the free market system and by what I can only call an obsession with communism. His view of the world was largely anecdotal.

I remember, for instance, his first meeting with French president François Mitterrand at the Economic Summit

April 1982: Canada's constitution comes home

A proud moment for all Canadians as the Queen signs our new constitution, assisted by Michael Kirby (right) and Michael Pitfield, as Gerald Regan (left) watches approvingly.

In turn, I add my signature.

(NAC-TC/Robert Cooper)

A fitting conclusion to a royal visit – a performance at the National Arts Centre, with Her Majesty and the Duke of Edinburgh in attendance.

(NAC-TC)

that I chaired at Montebello in 1981. We were a fairly high-powered group, including Thatcher, Mitterrand, and Schmidt. We were debating East-West issues and Mitterrand was advocating some measures to improve relations with the Soviet Union. At that moment, Reagan launched into one of his anecdotes about his time as president of Actors Equity in Hollywood in the 1940s. His story concerned a priest who had allegedly been trained in Moscow as an agent of the KGB in order to spread discord among the actors in the union. After the meeting, Mitterrand came to me and said, "What planet is that man living on? Does he really believe that the Soviets would bring an American priest to Moscow in order to send him back to be a spokesman for Actors Equity?" I think it fair to say that Reagan could be pleasant company for social conversation but was not a man for thoughtful policy discussion.

By 1983, partly as a result of the rigidly anti-Soviet stance taken by Reagan and his ideological soulmate Margaret Thatcher in Great Britain, the Cold War had moved into one of its worst phases. Several ominous trends were coming to a head. The Soviets had withdrawn from all the arms control negotiations. No summit between Soviet and American leaders was in the works. As Britain's former foreign minister Lord Carrington put it, the superpower leaders were using megaphone diplomacy to shout past each other. The danger of tensions somehow slipping out of control and escalating into nuclear war seemed increasingly real.

Nuclear weapons have always horrified me. I had written about the mindless horror of nuclear war in *Cité libre* in the 1950s and 1960s. I had demonstrated against nuclear war as a student and as a teacher. Many years later, I would visit the devastation in Hiroshima. To me, it was always a self-evident proposition that a nuclear war cannot be won and therefore should never be fought. In fact, my aversion to nuclear weapons had delayed my entry into politics by two years, from 1963 to 1965, because the Liberal Party had switched course and begun to support arming various Canadian weapons systems with nuclear warheads. When I became prime minister in 1968, Canada had nuclear weapons under a dual-key arrangement with the United States on four weapons systems. One of my aims as prime minister was to get rid of these weapons. It took a while, but by the time I left office in 1984, Canada once again had an entirely nuclear-free military.

India's explosion of a nuclear device in 1974, using Canadian-supplied Candu reactor technology, had renewed my concern about the spread of nuclear weapons. I responded not only with specific measures to penalize India – to the great annoyance of Indira Gandhi – and restrict nuclear exports, but also with a detailed speech to the United Nations in 1978 on a strategy of "nuclear suffocation." My proposal was that new developments should be stopped in the laboratory while we went to work to reduce existing stockpiles. I told the United Nations that Canada was "not only the first country in the world with the capacity to produce nuclear weapons that chose not to do so, but we are also the first nuclear-armed country to have chosen to divest itself of nuclear weapons."

To cut off the "oxygen" on which any arms race feeds, I proposed: a comprehensive test ban, an agreement to stop the flight testing of all new strategic missiles, an agreement to prohibit all production of nuclear material for weapons purposes, and an agreement to limit and then progressively reduce military spending on new strategic nuclear weapons systems. This speech was well received by the United Nations, but the enthusiasm was more restrained when I delivered the same message to my allies at the NATO summit in Washington a few days later. NATO, at that point, was developing a "two-track strategy" that led to tremendous demonstrations both in Europe and in Canada. In essence, the two tracks were that the West would vigorously pursue peace overtures, but on the other hand we would meet any new Soviet weapons threat, arm for arm and gun for gun. In practical terms, this meant that the Europeans were prepared to allow the introduction of a new American missile to counter the powerful new Soviet SS-20s. As a result, Canada was asked to allow testing of the Cruise missile in our North, which resembles Soviet terrain.

I was very reluctant to agree. But Helmut Schmidt made a very convincing argument to me. He said, "Pierre, you're part of NATO and you're part of the club. You have reduced your troops and your budget, but if you are part of a club you must help the club. NATO has made a decision to deploy new missiles. I'm going to catch hell for that from my peace movement. You're being asked to test an un-armed Cruise missile over your North. That's the least you can do." I knew that testing the Cruise missile would cause us a lot of political problems, but I also knew that this missile was not a first-strike weapon. It takes two to three hours to reach its target, and you don't start a nuclear war by giving the enemy three hours notice. In a way, the Cruise missile went against my 1978 speech on suffocation, but it was obvious by now that neither superpower was practising suffocation: the Soviets in particular had begun to deploy their SS-20 missiles.

But I agonized over the decision. I asked the Cabinet

committee on foreign affairs and defence to study the American request for the tests, and they reported that we should agree. Then I did something that was very rare for me: I sent the issue back to the committee and asked them to review it a second time, looking at it especially from a political point of view. But their recommendation was still the same. So the issue went to the full Cabinet and we had some very heated discussions. Finally, in 1983, we agreed to let the Americans test the Cruise missile over Canadian soil. The effect of the Cruise missile argument, coupled with the general deterioration of East-West relations, was to focus my attention even more on the threat of nuclear war.

Throughout that summer of 1983, I spent a lot of time reflecting on the fact that I had done many of the things I wanted to do while I was in office, but I had not done anything about a long-lasting peace initiative. I had de-nuclearized Canada's military, but I had had precious little influence in de-nuclearizing anything else. I had my staff arrange several lunches and dinners with experts and activists such as Paul Warnke, the former U.S. national security adviser to Johnson and Carter; Robert McNamara, the U.S. secretary of defence in the 1960s; and Helen Caldicott, the Australian doctor who had become such an eloquent voice for peace. They all urged me to do something – anything – to try to move the world away from the crisis that seemed to be overtaking us.

But what probably influenced me most of all was thinking about all the retired generals, admirals, and politicians I had met over the years who had spoken out about peace only after they had left office. I said to myself, "Well, I'm not going to do that. I was for peace before I entered politics and I'm not going to wait until I'm out before speaking out and trying to get things changed." I had already reached this general conclusion when yet another frightening development added an even greater sense of urgency. On September 1, 1983, the Soviets shot down a Korean airliner that had strayed into Soviet airspace for a couple of hours; all 269 aboard, including ten Canadians, were killed. Amid the hysterical denunciations and mounting tensions that followed, I decided that Canada would do what it could to try to change the downward spiral of events. At a minimum, we had to get both sides talking again.

I put together a special task force of officials from my office, from External Affairs, and from National Defence and told them to develop a package of proposals. After a great deal of debate, we reduced the initial list of twenty-six ideas to five: a renewed dialogue between East and West, starting with the proposed Stockholm conference on disarmament; a strengthened non-proliferation treaty; a new emphasis on reducing the size of conventional army forces in Europe; a five-power nuclear disarmament conference; and a ban on high-altitude anti-satellite missiles.

Many senior officials in the external affairs department were highly sceptical, but I went ahead and announced my peace initiative and outlined these proposals in a speech at the University of Guelph on October 27. I told my audience – and, through the media, the world at large – that I intended to try to inject "a jolt of political energy" to reverse "the trend lines of crisis." I said I would visit as many capitals as would see me, starting with my allies in NATO. I then proceeded to visit the capitals of Western Europe in early November of 1983; India and China in late November; the United States in December; East Germany, Czechoslovakia, and Roumania in January of 1984; and the Soviet Union in February.

Informal times at home and abroad

1. Any politician will know the feeling! Celebrating Canada Day in Ottawa.

2. In 1981 on my official visit to Fiji I took a keen interest in the local dance traditions.

3. In Thailand, canoeing was a little different.

4. With the three boys and friends at Canada's Wonderland near Toronto.

5. At a party in Ottawa, I am framed by historians Bill Kilbourn (left) and Ramsay Cook (right), among other old friends.

(Gwen Whittall)

(NAC-TC)

My old ideological sparring partner Margaret Thatcher surprised me. When scheduling my European trip, I had not planned to visit Great Britain because I had had some long talks – and sharp exchanges – with the British prime minister on her September 1983 visit to Canada. I expected that further discussions with her on this subject would be futile. Ideologically we were miles apart – I believe that she thought my views hopelessly "wet," while I found her zeal for the miracles of the marketplace to be a little unrealistic – and her debating style, which I found hectoring, was not conducive to a fruitful exchange of views. But near the end of my European swing, I got an annoyed message from her, asking why I didn't intend to come to London. It was obvious that I was beginning to mobilize support, or at least attention, and world leaders like Mrs. Thatcher at least wanted to be seen discussing the Canadian peace initiative.

By the time I visited Reagan at the White House in December, I had already been to several countries, including China, and had attended the Commonwealth Conference in New Delhi. I think Reagan expected me to tackle him about his so-called "Star Wars" plan, but my tactic was to appeal to Reagan's good nature rather than criticize him. I told him, "You didn't create the Cold War, you inherited it. I'm not blaming you for anything, and I'm not about to ask you to change your direction radically. But you are a great communicator, and you keep telling me you believe in peace. Use your skills as a communicator to join me and other leaders who believe in peace." I was trying to get Reagan to understand that we had to demonstrate some political will. In all honesty, I can't say that he joined me – but he did wish me Godspeed as I left the White House. And although it may have been a matter of coincidence, very soon after my mission the Cold War rhetoric

Travels among world leaders

1. At the start of my world tour for peace I was received in Paris by François Mitterrand with due ceremony. On an earlier occasion in France I was congratulated by an interviewer on my fluency in French!

2. With Helmut Kohl and Justin.

3. I also visited the East German leader, Erich Honecker.

4. In the Philippines I visited President Ferdinand Marcos and his wife, Imelda, then at the height of their power.

5. Addressing the United Nations.

6. And at home we were visited by United States Vice-President George Bush, who seems to have been overwhelmed by Ottawa in the tulip season.

(NAC-TC)

of Western leaders generally, and of President Reagan in particular, became much more conciliatory.

I summed up the results of my peace initiative in a speech to the House of Commons on February 9, 1984. NATO did agree to send foreign ministers to the Stockholm conference on disarmament. But India rejected the non-proliferation proposals and Britain rejected the idea of a five-nation conference. What was perhaps more important than any agreement or disagreement with my specific pro-posals, however, was that by visiting so many capitals on both sides of the Cold War divide, I was able to establish some key principles of a common bond between East and West. We had put the megaphones away and were talking rather than shouting.

A little more than a year later, Mikhail Gorbachev became the unchallenged leader of the Soviet Union and a page of history turned for the better. In 1985 at the Geneva Summit, Gorbachev and Reagan embarked on a new course, in part by accepting some of the principles that I had advocated in my initiative – including my fun-damental point that a nuclear war cannot be won, and therefore must never be fought.

There had been many sceptics about my peace mission. Some Canadians feared that we would be subjecting the country to ridicule by daring to address issues that were not traditionally in our domain. Unnamed American officials and diplomats in foreign capitals sneered about Canada's presumption in giving advice to the superpowers. Yet the fact remains that in the fall of 1983 no major Western power except Canada had any peace initiative under way, and by the fall of 1984 there were many new ideas in the air. We aimed far and high, but we did not miss the mark. In

Before I left office an interesting new Soviet politician named Mikhail Gorbachev came on the scene, and visited Ottawa. I was impressed but had no idea what an impact he was to have on the world. (NAC-TC)

that dreadful fall of 1983, the government of Canada was the first to realize the necessity for speaking out. The sceptics were wrong. Our ideas of hope for an end to the Cold War carried more weight than their fears. I believe that what I said in that February 9 speech to the House of Commons serves as a fitting epitaph not only to the peace mission but also more generally to the whole of our foreign policy from 1968 to 1984: "Let it be said of Canada and of Canadians that we saw the crisis; that we did act; that we took risks; that we were loyal to our friends and open with our adversaries; that we have lived up to our ideals; and that we have done what we could to lift the shadow of war."

By the winter of 1984, when I looked around me I could see that the Parti Québécois government in Quebec was falling apart; Lévesque had lost six or eight of his main ministers, and was no longer pushing outright separation. After the rough times of 1982, the Canadian economy had started growing again. The constitution had been brought home. And so-called "French power" had found its niche in the nation's capital. So during all those long hours I spent on airplanes during my peace mission, thoughts of retirement were not far from my mind.

On the evening of February 28, 1984, I took another long walk in the snow in Ottawa. Sixteen years earlier, on a similar winter's walk, I had agonized over whether to stand for the leadership of the Liberal Party. My 1984 decision was easier to make. My three boys were entering their teens and I felt the need to spend more time with them. For all their lives until then, from the moment each of them was born, they had been the prime minister's children, set apart from others by that fact, accompanied by bodyguards and so on. I wanted them to spend at least their teenage years as ordinary youngsters in Montreal, entirely away from public life. I also didn't know whether I had the energy left to fight another gruelling election campaign.

But most important of all, I had done what I had come into politics to do. I had come to Ottawa to fight for a just society both at home and abroad. I had done my best. There wasn't much more to give. I thought it would be time for somebody else to take over. The philosopher George Santayana defines happiness as taking "the measure of your powers." That night I took the measure of mine. It was time to go home.

PART 5

LIFE AFTER POLITICS

My retirement from politics hasn't left me with any with-drawal symptoms. I have only good memories of my time in public life, yet certainly no regrets about having left it. I lead a very happy life. I work, I travel, I enjoy the company of my sons, I meet interesting people, I indulge my love of the outdoors and nature. I still ski every weekend I can during the winter, I still set off in my canoe, and I still scuba-dive at least once or twice a year.

I've already said that I left politics because my sons were entering their teens and I wanted to spend more time with them. That's exactly what I have done. We've spent many summers travelling together. We spent one marvellous summer in France, visiting all over and absorbing the culture. Another summer, we visited England and Ireland in a rented car. We drove in every direction, eventually arriving in Scotland where we sought out the territory of our

Elliott ancestors. They had been an especially tough bunch of "Borderers" – Scots who lived on the border with England in a state of almost constant warfare, with much freelance cattle-raiding on all sides. In the heart of ancient Elliott territory we visited the Chief's estate, then went on to historic Hermitage Castle; there, looking at the barren hills running to the horizon and listening to the lonely cries of the moorland birds, it was easy to understand why this harsh landscape bred hardy men and women who prospered when they emigrated.

Yet another summer, we toured China from north to south, partly on foot, partly on bicycles, partly by train; we climbed two of their three holiest mountains, which gave us a chance to see both the religious fervour of the pilgrims and some tremendous sights, because it's well known that the monks always build their monasteries in places from which there is a literally breathtaking view of the country. Another summer we were in Southeast Asia, and yet another in Siberia and Japan.

I've also done some very interesting travelling on my own, free from the constraints and formalities involved in travelling as prime minister. I particularly recall, for instance, a visit to South Africa in February 1992. One night I allowed myself to be spirited away out of Johannesburg and into the nearby black township of Soweto. Because its six and a half million inhabitants happen to be black, you won't find it on any official map of South Africa – yet. But with the aid of a car and driver supplied by the somewhat nervous embassy, Jonathan Manthorpe, a Canadian journalist who knew his way around Africa, took me and a couple of friends into the heart of Soweto, where we visited a very popular "shebeen" – an unofficial drinking place – called the Blue Fountain.

Three Ottawa encounters

At our Ottawa judo club in 1984, Michel succeeded, not for the first time, in throwing his father to the mat.
(Canapress)

In 1985, I was honoured to receive the Order of Canada from the Governor General, Jeanne Sauvé, at a ceremony in Rideau Hall.
(J.M. Carisse Photo)

In 1986, I broke my usual rule and returned to Ottawa on a political visit. I went to show support for Jacques Hébert, who was staging a hunger strike in defence of the youth program Katimavik.
(J.M. Carisse Photo)

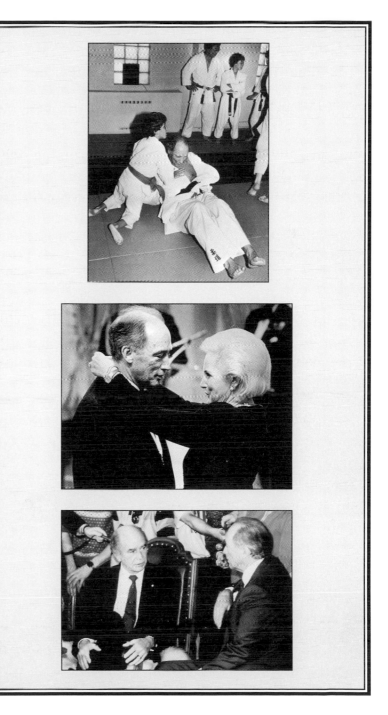

There we enjoyed a mixture of cold beer, warm hospitality, and hot Johannesburg jazz.

At home in Montreal, my sons and I live in the Art Deco house built by the great French-Canadian architect Ernest Cormier that I bought in 1979, complete with his furniture. I restored both as they had been when Cormier built the house in 1930. It's in downtown Montreal, on the side of the mountain, within a few minutes of McGill University – so close that my kids can run to the university for their courses if they're late leaving home. Justin is in his final year at McGill, Sacha has started this fall, and Michel is in his final year of high school at Brébeuf.

I have also built myself a little house in the country, on a lake in the Laurentians. It's much more modest than the prime ministerial retreat at Harrington Lake, but it permits me and the boys to continue living close to nature every weekend and also for longer periods in the summer. I still drive my Mercedes 300SL when snow and slush are off the ground. For more mundane purposes, I have a larger car, which makes it easy for us to take off with our skis or our tent and sleeping bags when ski trails or canoe routes beckon.

While my children are in school, I work as senior counsel at Heenan Blaikie, which is a growing and vigorous law firm in downtown Montreal. They don't overwork me, but they give me a fine office with a beautiful view looking towards the St. Lawrence River and the Eastern Townships. I have a first-class secretary and fax machines at my disposal, so I can operate very efficiently when I want to. The way I practise law is ideal from my point of view. I don't take clients of my own. I don't have to prepare witnesses or do the research for the cases. Instead, I'm

*In my office
at Heenan
Blaikie,
in 1991.
(I.M. Carisse
Photo)*

available to the senior lawyers of the firm who want to discuss an issue with me.

I do, however, also get involved in some overseas activities. For instance, when President Vaclav Havel came to power in Czechoslovakia (as it then was), even before he came to Canada and we had the chance to talk together, he contacted me to ask if I would advise him on the constitutional evolution of his country. As a result I attended meetings, first in Salzburg and then in Prague, along with some very senior constitutional lawyers from other federal countries – the U.S. and the Federal Republic of Germany – as well as with some distinguished British and French jurists. In addition, ambassadors from other countries come fairly frequently to my office for discussions.

The international situation has changed enormously in the years since I left office. It has been a time of great opportunities but also, I think, of many missed opportunities. Mikhail Gorbachev came to power in Moscow just after I left office, and I watched with admiration as almost singlehandedly he began to defuse tensions and put an end to the Cold War. It took a lot of courage, and rendering that service to humanity caused a lot of pain to his country, pain that the West in general was slow to recognize.

Following up on my peace initiatives, I had proposed to my fellow leaders meeting at the Economic Summit of industrialized nations, gathered in London in June 1984, that we attempt to reduce the ever-growing tensions between Moscow and Washington by writing to the Soviet leadership (which was then formed around Konstantin Chernenko), suggesting that both sides should publicly and jointly agree on a certain number of objectives and mutually beneficial aims, such as that a nuclear war can never be won and therefore should never be fought. I failed to get agreement, and therefore we lost a few years in putting an end to the Cold War. I gave the same advice to Gorbachev when I saw him in early July 1985, as he prepared for the first summit between the two superpowers since President Jimmy Carter's day. So naturally I was pleased to note that at the first meeting between Gorbachev and Ronald Reagan in Geneva late in 1985, they used the approach that I had been urging both East and West to adopt in order to change the trend line towards increasing tensions; in particular they stated jointly that a nuclear war cannot be won and therefore should never be fought.

Sadly, once Gorbachev began his radical reforms, we in the West seemed bent on ensuring not only that the Cold War was ended but that the Soviet Union came out of it as weak as possible. When Gorbachev was trying to hold the union together by transforming it into a truly federal state, we in the West made sure it would break up by rushing to recognize every Tom, Dick, and Harry republic that decided to proclaim its independence. By doing that, we helped create the chaos in that part of the world, which I think we will eventually regret. I'm not saying that some of those republics – the Baltics, to take one obvious example – had no right to consider the option of full sovereignty; I'm just saying that it would have been wiser to consider it in the context of an evolutionary process, rather than as an immediate break-up with the consequent domino effect on other parts of the Soviet Union.

I remember arguing this with Henry Kissinger at an international meeting. He was saying, "Well, we have to recognize the independence of a certain number of states as soon as they proclaim it." And I said, "Where do you stop? Wouldn't it be much better to wait until we make sure that each of those republics is prepared to respect and protect its minorities? And wouldn't it also be better to encourage them to keep the economic advantages of their common market, at least during the transition period, rather than throw them away in a whirlwind of break-ups?"

Henry Kissinger and I have met in many places over the years, but we still do not necessarily see eye to eye about world events since the Gorbachev revolution changed the world order. (NAC-TC)

In the matter of economic reforms, I kept pointing out in my discussions that when the Western countries including Canada came out of the Second World War, we slackened the tight wartime controls on our national economies only very slowly. We kept exchange controls, for example, and we kept rationing. I was in Britain and France in the 1950s, and even then they still maintained some controls. So we capitalist nations realized in our own cases that you could only decontrol a tightly managed economy very slowly. And yet here we were sending all kinds of zealous Thatcherite and Reaganite advisers to tell the Soviet Union that there was no option but converting instantly to a free market system: they must take a cold bath and decontrol overnight. And of course that created economic as well as political chaos.

When I say we may come to regret this, it's because the peace of the world is based on stability. If countries begin to feel threatened by others, they frequently resort to ethnic nationalism in self-defence, or they look for alliances that will upset the particular balance of power that they find threatening. It's obvious that we already have cause to regret deeply what has happened in Yugoslavia, Somalia, and too many other places. We are seeing such atrocities and horrors being committed that public opinion is forcing governments to intervene and to risk the lives of our own people in order to bring some measure of security to these ravaged countries. But they are ravaged partly as a result of our own politics and actions. In the case of Somalia, the superpowers used that luckless part of Africa as a cockpit (as they had before in Ethiopia and Central America) where they could fight their wars by proxy.

In the case of Yugoslavia, the European Community had wisely decided as a minimum not to recognize any independent breakaway state until it had given sufficient reassurances on the treatment of the minority ethnic groups within its boundaries. But then suddenly Germany was anxious to gain some political advantages, and various private interests wanted to gain new clients. So the rush began to recognize Slovenia, then Croatia, then Bosnia, and so it went: Canada and the United States and everyone else rushed in and destabilized the whole country by hastening to recognize every new republic that decided to proclaim its independence, without preconditions and without allowing for any period of transition. Naturally, the Serbs, who controlled the central government and the army, concluded that if they were unable to keep the former Yugoslavia together, they should at least preserve as much of it as possible under their rule. And so a civil war was on.

What is sad is that places like Bosnia and Czecho-slovakia, which were created after the First World War as multi-ethnic, pluralistic societies, are breaking up into little ethnic territories partly because Western nations blindly played footsie with the independentists in these countries. And now we have lived to witness the obscenity of "ethnic cleansing."

As for what has been happening within Canada, it hasn't caused me to feel any nostalgia for politics. I must confess that I don't follow the news very closely, particularly Canadian political news. I systematically refuse – with very few exceptions, maybe one or two in almost ten years – to speak in public for the record. I do agree to go on university campuses from time to time, to give a seminar now and then, and to talk with the students without the press being present. This helps me to keep abreast of the thinking of younger Canadians – or younger Americans when I visit American campuses. But I don't, as a rule, involve myself in politics. I feel you can't be half in and half out of politics. I didn't want to get back in, so mainly I have stayed out.

The unacceptable face of journalism? My relations with the media were not always friendly, but I enjoyed my encounters with some. (NAC-TC)

People often ask me what I think of the years of Mulroney government that followed my time in office. I'm not impartial on the subject, and therefore I'd rather not comment on it. Being a former prime minister myself, I've always taught my children to be respectful of the prime minister and his office, if not necessarily of his ideas. It's in my interest not to set a bad example for the Canadian people by demonstrating any lack of respect for a former prime minister.

I know, of course, that the record of my government is still attacked rather vigorously and almost obsessively by our Conservative successors. But rather than respond in kind, I prefer to let the facts speak for themselves and leave it to the people to form their own judgments.

In the case of the economy, for instance, for which we are still being blamed after nine years of Conservative rule, Canada was as healthy when I left office as any of our major competitors and was probably ahead in many respects. Comparing our record over the period from 1968 to 1984 with the performance of the top industrial nations in the same sixteen years, Canada was first in job creation, second in growth, and fourth in price stability. It's interesting, too, to compare the record of our sixteen years with that of the eight Mulroney years for which statistics exist. In the 1968–84 period, annual average growth in real gross domestic product was 4.1 per cent; for 1985–92, it was 2.6 per cent. Employment growth in our years was 2.4 per cent on average, compared with 1.7 per cent in the Mulroney years. Our average adjusted unemployment rates were 7.3 per cent; theirs were 9.1 per cent. With the exception of inflation – 7.5 per cent on average in our years, 4.6 per cent in theirs – the Mulroney government's economic performance was

I still enjoy dancing, whether at a ball in Montreal (right) or at a less formal Western celebration during the Calgary Liberal convention in 1990.

inferior to ours by every indicator. That's true even on the issue of the national debt, which the Tories have made their main priority: in sixteen years we added $180 billion to Canada's debt, and the Tories raised the national debt by a further $218 billion in only eight years.

There is no doubt that the national debt – not only the federal but the provincial debt as well – was very high during our years in office. But it's useful to note that it was much lower in our time than at the beginning of our longest period of prosperity, right after the Second World War. So the size of the debt is not what should be the main objective measurement of economic policy; it should be the health of the economy in general. From the point of view of economic growth, job growth, unemployment, and so on, we had a healthy record. And indeed the economic growth that began after the 1982 recession kept on right until 1989, so obviously the basis for continued growth was there.

I look back on such accomplishments without shame. But what gives me some of the greatest pleasure when I reflect on my years in office is the human dimension, what we were able to do for people. For example, during my time in office the percentage of Canadians living in poverty dropped from 23 percent (1969) to 12.8 percent (1984). Our concern for the elderly was reflected in the poverty rate for families headed by a senior citizen, which went from 49 percent in 1969 to 14 percent in 1980. We were indeed moving towards a Just Society, looking after those who most needed help.

I am also proud of the changes I made affecting individuals from groups in our society that had not been properly recognized in the past. Before the appointments I made as prime minister, a woman had never sat in the Speaker's chair of the House of Commons. A woman had never occupied the post of lieutenant-governor or of governor general. A woman had never sat on the Supreme Court of Canada, never sat as a chief justice of a superior court in Canada. Before my day no one voted until the age of twenty-one. There had never been a Jew in the Canadian Cabinet, and there were none on the benches of the Supreme Court. No French Canadian had ever been minister of finance, or even minister of trade. There was no Inuit Canadian sitting in the Senate. No aboriginal Canadian had been a member of the federal Cabinet nor lieutenant-governor of a province; in fact, there had been no provision in the constitution stating that aboriginal rights were entrenched and did exist. We were able to make the Canadian ideal of a truly pluralistic society that much more real, and in the process to demonstrate our evolving maturity as a nation.

With the exception of constitutional matters, about which I will say more in a moment, I commented publicly on Brian Mulroney only once, shortly after my retirement – and that was in special circumstances. In the fall of 1984, I was in Ottawa, working in the National Archives on my papers, when Mulroney called and asked me to come to his office, which I did. He said, "Would you be willing from time to time to give me some advice on foreign affairs?" I said, "Yes, and the first piece of advice I give you is this: be friends with the United States – the Canadian people like the Americans – but don't be subservient to the American government, because Canadians are very proud people."

That proved to be the only advice I ever gave him, because right after I left his office he called the press and made a big production out of the announcement that Trudeau was going to advise him on international affairs. Of course this didn't make very pleasant hearing for John Turner, as leader of the Liberal Party in Opposition, and I saw that Mulroney was playing political games. From then on, I advised him only publicly and only on the constitution. But since Mulroney had played political games when I left his office, I reciprocated shortly afterwards when I was asked to say a few words at a banquet in Montreal at which he was present: I made public the advice I had given him in private, not to be too subservient to the United States. And I think, as it turned out, Mulroney did choose

Interesting Canadians

1. An exchange with Professor John Polanyi, the Nobel prize-winner, in his office at the University of Toronto.

2. On the same campus, an old acquaintance, Robertson Davies, showed me the dining hall of Massey College.

3. In Vancouver, I also met my old friend Arthur Erickson, the distinguished architect.

4. I dropped in on some earnest young British Columbians whose French is coming along well.

(Les Productions La Fête)

to move Canada-U.S. relations in directions that generally are too subservient to the will of the American government of the day.

As a Liberal, naturally I believe in free trade. But I believe that when you're negotiating with the United States, an economic superpower, you have to be a much harder bargainer than we were. In theory freer trade may be a good thing for a country, but there were a lot of things thrown into the Free Trade Agreement package that are not good; and I would make the same remark about NAFTA, the North American Free Trade Agreement involving Canada, the United States, and Mexico, which the Mulroney government rushed to sign even before all its side agreements were in place.

As is well known, the one exception I made to my rule not to intervene in politics involved the constitution. The Mulroney government started moving forward with options for the constitution that I felt were contrary to the views of Canada that I had tried to promote and defend all the time I was in office. I felt that these options weren't being adequately rebutted by the various Opposition parties or by the media. So I took it upon myself to remind Canadians that there is another view of Canada than the one that was being proposed in the Meech Lake Accord of 1987.

It shocked me – and it must have shocked old John Diefenbaker in his grave, not to mention all of his predecessors – to learn a few years ago that the Tory party now accepts the right of self-determination of a province as a constitutional right. I find that position incompatible with my view: I hold that Canada is more than the sum of its parts; it is not a nation merely because the provinces

At a Senate hearing in 1987, I explained why I was strongly opposed to the Meech Lake Accord. My intervention may have played some part in encouraging public resistance to the accord.

(J.M. Carisse Photo)

permit it to be, it is a nation because the Canadian people want it to be. If, on the contrary, you concede that Canada is no more than a compact between ten provinces and two territories coming together, then I suppose you can accept that they can also come apart. As I said before the Canadian Senate when I was opposing the Meech Lake Accord, no country is eternal; it's possible that Canada will break up one day, as it's possible that the United States will break up one day, or a European country could break up, or China. It's possible, but I think that people who are in government today must not in any way recognize in advance the legitimacy of that process: their ultimate duty is to ensure that the constitution is obeyed.

It doesn't mean that I ever contemplated the need, as Abraham Lincoln did in the United States, to maintain unity by force. But we should remember that even in Lincoln's day, as he himself made clear, the South went to war in order to destroy the Union, and only then did he go to war in order to preserve the Union. Fortunately, so far we haven't had the example of any province going to war to destroy the country, and therefore the question of whether the federal government would go to war to preserve national unity is a hypothetical one.

By bringing home the constitution at last, with a charter of rights, we left a level playing field in 1982. After that no province could say, "I'll only give my consent for you to patriate the constitution if you give me more powers." But it was always understood that in due course after the "people's package," there would be a second package – the "politicians' package" – to discuss and modify if necessary the distribution of powers between the provincial and the federal governments.

Indeed one can say that when Mulroney chose to reopen the constitution in 1984 by making certain political speeches, there was a good and a bad side to it. The good side was that it could be interpreted as wanting to put together the "politicians' package," now that the "people's package" had been delivered in 1982. But the bad side was that instead of proceeding that way, the government chose to question the legitimacy of the 1982 patriation, even though it had been done strictly according to the rules defined by the Supreme Court. The Mulroney government played right into the hands of the Quebec nationalists by saying that in 1982 Quebec had been unfairly treated, even insulted and humiliated: that tilted the playing field in favour of the provinces.

I was very glad that after the rolling of the dice the Meech Lake Accord failed to get the necessary approval, first in Manitoba, then in Newfoundland, largely as a result of its growing unpopularity among the general public. As the government tried its luck again with the process that

La Maison Egg Roll was the unusual name of the Chinese restaurant in Montreal where I spoke out against the Charlottetown Accord in 1992.
(J.M. Carisse Photo)

would lead to the Charlottetown Accord, I was equally glad that Jean Chrétien, John Turner's successor as leader of the Opposition, steadfastly insisted on the importance of having whatever came out of Charlottetown put to a referendum. That was something he never flinched on, and of course it came to pass. I could see that none of the governments of Canada, provincial or federal, all of which favoured the Charlottetown Accord, were prepared to put forward the other view of Canada – what I think of as the people's view of Canada. Charlottetown was proposing to give more power to the provincial politicians, and nothing to Canada as such. And so I believed that a referendum might save us from the weaknesses of Charlottetown.

To be honest, I was far from sure that the so-called accord would be rejected by a majority of the Canadian people in a referendum. Everyone seemed to be in favour of the deal – big business, the Tory government, both the Liberal and the New Democratic Opposition parties, and every single provincial government. And in a sense that's why I felt that I should speak out on the Charlottetown Accord in 1992: I was afraid that a lot of Canadians – after having perhaps lost to a Yes majority, given this massive one-sided political pressure plus a media consensus that was heavily in favour – would feel like orphans if nobody had spoken for them. So I said, "At least I will make the case for those who want to vote No, both in Quebec and in the rest of the country. I will establish that there are some die-hard federalists like myself in Quebec who are going to vote No, not because they want more powers for Quebec but because they want a strong Canada."

The results came as a very pleasant surprise to me. I don't know what the effects of my interventions were. It's safe to say that it was obvious that the Canadian people, particularly in the case of Charlottetown, were distrustful of the way in which the constitution was being managed. As a result, Canadians produced a moment unique in our history. They rejected all the political élites who said the Charlottetown Accord must be accepted. The Canadian people did exactly what I had hoped they would do: they established that the locus of the sovereignty of Canada is the people, and they were telling every practising politician in the land: "You guys think one thing, we think another – and what we think is what will prevail." What they did really amounted to a revolt of the people against the political class.

I'm very happy about that. In fact, in my constitutional negotiations when I was in office, I always tried to insert a

With Jean Chrétien in 1992. I believe that those Quebecers who denigrate the man and his style do so because they don't like what he is saying in defence of Canada.
(Les Productions La Fête/Jean Demers)

preamble to the constitution that would say that Canada was a sovereign nation based on the sovereignty of the people – but the provinces would never agree to it. And that is why I hope the idea of a referendum to decide major constitutional issues will eventually become entrenched in the constitution.

My faith in Canada is, indeed, based on my faith in the people. Throughout my years in office, that faith proved justified over and over again, whenever the going was tough and the reforms we were trying to introduce were being opposed by the multinational corporations, by the provincial premiers, or by a superpower. I invariably found that if our cause was right, all we had to do to win was talk over the heads of our adversaries directly to the people of this land. To me, therefore, the referendum result augurs very well for the future, if Canadians retain the determination and the confidence to insist that it must be the broad public will, not anyone's narrower political agenda, that shapes our future.

For that future to be successful and prosperous, I believe we will have to pursue two complementary objectives that are equally essential to our country's harmonious existence and development. First, we will have to maintain a central government strong enough and sensitive enough to Canada's diversity to reflect our desire to live as one people, to settle conflicts of interest between provinces and regions with unquestioned political authority, and to speak on behalf of all Canadians, both at home and abroad. And, second, we will have to develop the means for coordinating the efforts of our two levels of government and for ensuring that the involvement of provincial governments in the affairs of our nation is substantial enough to make them feel full-fledged members of the federation. This, I hope, will encourage them more and more to plan their development within a broadly Canadian perspective.

When all is said and done, the Canadian federation presupposes that, over and above our respective neighbourhoods, towns, cities, and provinces, Canada is considered to be the homeland of all Canadians. To avoid making a clear choice as Canadians (rather than as members of this or that province or city) by choosing to have feeble federal institutions would be to condemn ourselves to collective weakness in a world that will not be kind to nations divided against themselves.

A country, after all, is not something you build as the pharaohs built the pyramids, and then leave standing there to defy eternity. A country is something that is built every day out of certain basic shared values. And so it is in the hands of every Canadian to determine how well and wisely we shall build the country of the future.

At the unveiling of my official portrait in Parliament, May 1992.
(J.M. Carisse Photo)

As for me, I find myself thinking yet again of that beautiful verse from the Rimbaud poem "Ma Bohème" that I quoted in my farewell speech to the Liberal Party's leadership convention in June 1984:

> I went off with my fists in torn pockets;
> My coat was completely threadbare.
> I followed you, Muse, where you led me,
> Dreamed of loves – ah – so fine and so rare.

*A final visit
to the
deserted
House.
(Les Productions
La Fête/Jean Demers)*

I feel that the Canadian people and I did dream together
of such loves in challenging times – love for ourselves, love
for our country, love for more peace and justice in the
world. To some extent, we rebuilt, renewed, strengthened,
and completed this country we all carry within ourselves. I
look back on those days, and the people I met, with warm
memories. And now, as long as there are fascinating new
places to explore, new pathways to discover through the
forests, new stars to notice in the wilderness sky, new experiences to share, and books to read, I will – God willing –
remain a happy man.

The Photographs: A Publisher's Note

A prime minister is a much-photographed personage. Over his sixteen or so years in office Pierre Trudeau was snapped, posed, or ambushed literally hundreds of thousands of times. In the private Trudeau file in the National Archives of Canada, to which we had access for this book, there are so many photographs that one collection alone numbers 160,000. The public record contains countless others produced by enterprising newspaper photographers over the years, and many thousands of amateur snapshots were donated to the Prime Minister's Office. We were also fortunate to be able to see the Trudeau family photographs.

In summary, a glance through the book will reveal to even the most casual browser that the more than 250 photographs have come from a fascinating range of sources, which have revealed scores of rare photographs never before seen by the public.

Primary credit for the wide-ranging choice must go to Les Productions La Fête, the company responsible for the forthcoming documentary television series on Pierre Trudeau's life. The photo researcher engaged for the film, Holly Dressel, did a truly outstanding job. In turn, Monique Giroux, the production coordinator, organized the photographs collected with calm efficiency. Thanks to the generosity of Kevin Tierney and Rock Demers, the collection amassed by the film company, including the photographs specially taken by Jean Demers, was made available for inclusion in the book.

The photographs fall into several distinct groups. The first group came from Suzette (Trudeau) Rouleau, the keeper of the Trudeau family photographs, who graciously made them available for the film and the book. We are all in her debt.

The second group are those on the public record. For these, thanks must go to the people in the Canapress offices in Montreal and Toronto, where Steve McLean deserves special mention for his help. At the *Toronto Star*, John Honderich, the editor, personally intervened to smooth the way, and credit must go to the *Star*'s efficient photo service. Naturally our thanks go to all of the press photographers whose effort and skill is recorded on these pages (including Jean Marc Carisse, who has added to his collection by following the former prime minister's career beyond 1984), and to all those institutions who graciously granted us permission to use their work.

The photographs from the private Trudeau collection in the National Archives are well represented here, as the frequency of the credit (NAC-TC) demonstrates; thanks are due to official photographers such as Duncan Cameron,

Robert Cooper, and those others who contributed to that collection. The range of photographs contained in the archives posed a special opportunity and a special challenge. Thanks to the remarkable organizing skills of Sylvie Gervais and the able and enthusiastic assistance of Michèle Jackson, Helen De Roia, and Micheline Robert, who cheerfully worked overtime on the project, I was able to discover interesting photographs from many unlikely sources, such as the official books sent by host countries to commemorate Prime Minister Trudeau's visit to their land. In turn, Mr. Trudeau was able to enliven the photographs by contributing to the captions his own recollections of the scenes and the people portrayed there.

Inside McClelland & Stewart the task of organizing the photographs and fitting them into the text was undertaken by the usual suspects, who performed the usual heroics, and will undoubtedly be rewarded in another life.

The result of this team effort, stretching over many months, is a complex, varied collection of photographs that we hope serves to enrich the experience of reading these remarkable memoirs.

Douglas Gibson
Publisher
McClelland & Stewart
August 1993

Index

Académie Querbes, 4, 6, 13, 17-18
Afghanistan, 52, 329
Agnew, Spiro, 120
Agnew, Mrs. Spiro, 120
Ahidjo, Ahmadou, 79
Andreotti, Giulio, 201
Angola, 212
Anti-Inflation Board, 196, 198
Asbestos strike, 62-63
Ashworth, Gordon, 267
Australia, 314-15
Austria, 49
Axworthy, Tom, 160, 183, 185,
   202, 317

Barrette, Antonio, 68
Begin, Menachem, 215-16,
   217, 219
Bélanger, Michel, 123
Bélanger, Paul, 140
Bennett, Bill, 249, 320
Bernier, Robert, 25
Bevan, Aneurin (Nye), 46
Bill 101, 235

Bill 22, 234-35
Blakeney, Allan, 249, 300,
   310, 320
Boulanger, Jean-Baptiste, 23-24
Bourassa, Henri, 38
Bourassa, Robert, 123, 134,
   137-38, 141-42, 143, 151,
   229-30, 233-35, 241, 243,
   244-46, 250, 274
Bourguiba, Habib, 79
Braque, 15
Breecher brothers, 28
Brezhnev, Leonid, 156, 206-8
Britain, 39, 41, 45-47, 220,
   222-23, 244, 246, 308, 310,
   311, 317, 324, 338, 340,
   345, 352
Broadbent, Ed, 270, 272-73, 310
Brüning, Heinrich, 37
Buchanan, John, 249
Bulgaria, 49
Burma, 52
Bush, George, 339

Cabinet reforms, 107-14
Cadieux, Marcel, 220
Caldicott, Helen, 335
Callaghan, James, 201, 222, 223, 244, 246
Cameroon, 79
Camp, Dalton, 168
Campbell, W. Bennett, 249
Canada Development Corporation, 156, 205
Canadian Officers Training Corps, 34
Cancún Conference, 304-5
Carrington, Lord, 332
Carter, Jimmy, 201, 219-20, 221
Carter, Mrs. Jimmy, 221
Casgrain, Thérèse, 70
Castonguay, Claude, 232, 233
Castro, Fidel, 210, 212, 213
Ceylon, 155
Charbonneau, Yvon, 140
Charlottetown Accord, 230, 363-66
Charron, Claude, 302-3
Château consensus, 306-7, 326
Chernenko, Konstantin, 350
Chiang Kai-shek, 59, 60
China, 53, 58-60, 69, 164, 168-71, 202, 209-10, 211, 336, 346
Chou Enlai, 168, 170, 171, 209, 210, 211
Chouinard, Julien, 230
Chrétien, Jean, 85, 199-200, 201, 277, 279, 284, 300, 302-3, 321, 324-25, 363, 365
Cité libre, 45, 65, 202, 328, 332
Clark, Catherine, 263
Clark, Joe, 216, 248, 250, 251-52, 253, 258, 261-64, 269, 289, 291, 311
Collège Jean-de-Brébeuf, 17, 18-26, 135, 188

Commons reforms, 114-17
Commonwealth Conferences, 124, 154, 162-63, 214, 314-15, 338
Confédération des travailleurs catholiques du Canada, 66
Constitution Act of 1982, 327-29, 330
Cook, Ramsay, 337
Cormier, Ernest, 348
Corry, J.A., 64
Coutts, Jim, 160, 183, 185, 257-58, 266, 268, 299
Criminal Code amendments, 80-84
Crosbie, John, 262, 289
Cross, James, 130, 134, 135, 149
Cruise missiles, 334-35
Cuba, 210, 212, 213
Cutler, Lloyd, 220
Czechoslovakia, 49, 336, 349-50, 353-54

Danson, Barney, 215
Daoust, Fernand, 140
Davey, Jim, 160
Davey, Keith, 160, 183-84, 250, 267, 268, 287
Davies, Robertson, 359
Davis, William, 249, 310, 316, 323-24
Deng Xiaoping, 168, 171
Department of Regional Economic Expansion, 104, 190
Desaulniers, Guy, 64
Desautels, Andrée, 23
Deschambault, Jack, 257
Deslierres, Paul, 59
Desrosiers cousins, 27
Diefenbaker, John, 74, 113, 116, 119, 182-83, 256, 262, 293, 360
Douglas, Tommy, 143

Drapeau, Jean, 34, 105, 136, 138, 142, 153
Dubé, Rodolphe, 21-23
Dubuc, Carl, 27
Dumas, Pierre, 64
Dumont, Fernand, 140
Dunton, Davidson, 123, 128
Duplessis, Maurice, 12, 44-45, 61, 63-64, 68, 71

Eagleburger, Lawrence, 301
Eagleson, Alan, 318
East Germany, 336, 339
Eastern Europe, 48-49, 189, 208
École Bonsecours, 4
École libre des sciences politiques, 39, 40
Economic Summits, 198, 201, 219, 238, 296, 329, 332, 350
Edinburgh, Duke of, 162, 163, 331
Elections Act reforms, 117-18
Elizabeth II, 162, 163, 245, 311, 313, 329, 330-31
Elliott, Gordon, 14-15
Elliott ancestors, 282, 346
Elliott grandparents, 3-4, 5, 14, 15, 17
Erickson, Arthur, 359
Estey, Willard, 315

Favreau, Guy, 76, 77
Fiji, 337
Filion, Gaby, 27
FLQ (Front de libération du Québec), 130-52, 274
Ford, Gerald, 197, 218-19
Ford, R.A.D., 207
Foreign Investment Review Agency, 167-68, 203, 205
Forsey, Eugene, 70, 148
Fortier, D'Iberville, 64
Fowler, Robert, 202

Fox, Francis, 247
Fox, Terry, 285
France, 14-15, 23, 40-45, 79, 202, 339, 345, 352
Francoeur, Louis, 34
Fraser, Blair, 323
Free Trade Agreement, 360
Fukuda, Takeo, 201

Gagnon, Jean-Louis, 16, 70
Galbraith, John Kenneth, 198, 199
Gandhi, Indira, 166, 212, 214, 333
"Gang of Eight," 312-21, 326, 327
Gascon, Jean, 36, 45
Gélinas, Jean, 27, 35
Geneva Summit, 340, 351
Gens de l'air, 235-40
Geoffrion, Antoine, 68
Geoffroy, Jean-Paul, 65
Germany, 14, 16, 187, 200, 339, 353
Giscard d'Estaing, Valéry, 201, 219
Goldfarb, Martin, 183
Gorbachev, Mikhail, 340, 341, 350-51
Gordon, Walter, 74
Goulet, Robert, 120
Grafstein, Jerry, 183
Green, T.H., 47
Gromyko, Andrei, 207
Guyana, 187, 225

Haig, Alexander, 301
Harvard University, 37-39, 41, 47, 189
Hatfield, Richard, 242, 249, 310, 311, 316, 324
Havel, Vaclav, 349-50
Head, Ivan, 202, 219
Heath, Edward, 155, 162, 220, 222, 223
Hébert, Jacques, 69, 347
Helsinki Conference, 156, 208

Hertel, François. *See* Dubé, Rodolphe
Honecker, Erich, 339
Houde, Camillien, 12
Houle, Réjean, 247
Hungary, 49
Hurtubise, Claude, 16

Ignatieff, Michael, 41
India, 47-48, 55-58, 155, 166, 214-15, 333, 336, 340
Indochina, 52-53
Iran, 286
Iraq, 53-54
Ireland, 345
Israel, 49-51, 215-16, 219, 269
Italy, 14, 16

Jamaica, 166, 224
Jamieson, Don, 81, 121, 147, 201, 215
Japan, 60, 205, 226-27, 346
Jenkins, Roy, 201
Jerusalem, 50-51, 215-16, 269
Johnson, Daniel, 82, 105, 229
Just Society, 87, 104, 357

Kilbourn, Bill, 337
Kirby, Michael, 330
Kirouac, Jean-Marc, 140
Kissinger, Henry, 167, 211, 216, 217, 218, 219, 351, 352
Knowles, Stanley, 116
Kohl, Helmut, 222, 339

Laberge, Louis, 140
LaFlèche, Léo, 34
Lafleur, Guy, 247
Laird, Melvin, 120
Laliberté, Raymond, 140
Lalonde, Marc, 183, 230-33, 237, 265, 291

LaMarsh, Judy, 82
Lambert, Yvon, 247
Lamontagne, Maurice, 77
Lamoureux, Lucien, 109
Lang, Otto, 236, 237, 238
Lapalme, Georges-Émile, 69
Lapointe, Ernest, 32-33
Laporte, Françoise, 144
Laporte, Pierre, 130, 135-38, 142, 144
Laski, Harold, 46
Laskin, Bora, 315, 316
Laurendeau, André, 38, 71, 102-3, 119, 123, 128
Laurin, Camille, 140
Lautens, Gary, 287
Leblond cousins, 8
Lee Kwan Yew, 224
Léger, Jules, 64
Lemaire, Jacques, 247
Lennon, John, 122
Lesage, Jean, 71, 314
Levasseur, Pierre, 160
Lévesque, René, 71, 72, 107, 139, 148, 149, 152, 240-43, 247-50, 266, 274, 276, 281, 283, 300, 302-3, 313-14, 317-21, 325, 326-27, 342
Lewis, David, 116, 164, 191
Llewellyn, Robert, 28-29
Loiselle, Gilles, 311
London School of Economics, 39, 41, 45-47
Lougheed, Peter, 248, 249, 261, 269, 288-90, 291-92, 294, 295, 300
Lussier, Charles, 64
Lyon, Sterling, 249, 306, 317-18

Macdonald, Donald, 195-96, 265
MacEachen, Allan, 176, 177, 262, 264, 296-98

McIlraith, George, 252
McIntyre, William, 315
Mackasey, Bryce, 160
McMurtry, Roy, 321
McNamara, Robert, 335
Manley, Michael, 166, 224
Manthorpe, Jonathan, 346
Mao Zedong, 59, 60, 168, 171, 209-10, 211
Marchand, Jean, 64, 65, 66, 71, 72, 75-77, 78, 84, 91, 94, 102, 123, 183, 184, 190, 235-37, 238-39, 264-65
Marcos, Ferdinand, 339
Marcos, Imelda, 339
Marcotte, Gilles, 16
Maritain, Jacques, 40
Martin, Paul (Sr.), 87
Mason, Bill, 254
Maurault, Olivier, 28
Meech Lake Accord, 230, 360-62
Mercredi, Ovide, 73
Mexico, 28-29
Michener, Roland, 98
Miki, Takeo, 227
Miki, Mrs. Takeo, 227
Minville, Esdras, 38, 64
Miró, 15
Mitterrand, François, 222, 329, 332, 339
Mondale, Walter, 221
Montpetit, Édouard, 38, 63
Moores, Frank, 249
Morin, Claude, 234
Morse, Eric, 254
Morse, Pam, 254
Mounier, Emmanuel, 40
Mulroney, Brian, 189, 251, 252, 253, 328, 355-56, 358, 360, 362
Mulroney, Mrs. Brian, 328
Munro, John, 139

National Energy Program, 205, 291-95
Nixon, Richard, 120, 121, 156, 167, 203, 211, 216-18
Nixon, Mrs. Richard, 121
Noiseux, Denis, 20
Normand, Jacques, 61
North American Free Trade Agreement, 360
Nyerere, Julius, 224

O'Connor, Gerald, 6
October Crisis, 130-52, 274
Official Languages Act, 118-28, 234, 236, 308
O'Leary, Dostaler, 28
Oliver, Michael, 70
O'Neill, Tip, 221
Ono, Yoko, 122
OPEC, 179, 182, 191, 284-85, 286, 295

Pakistan, 52
Palestine, 49-51
Paris, 23, 40-45, 79
Parizeau, Jacques, 123, 140
Parti Québécois, 132, 133, 148-49, 151-52, 229, 235, 240-43, 246-47, 252, 266-68, 276-80, 342. *See also* Lévesque, René
Pearson, Lester, 74, 75, 76, 78, 79, 81, 82, 84, 85, 87, 92, 95, 97, 108, 113, 160, 190, 196, 202, 228-29, 273
Peckford, Brian, 248, 303, 325
Pelletier, Gérard, 16, 41, 45, 62, 64, 71, 75-77, 84, 94, 101, 102, 105, 123, 136, 238, 242, 256, 265
Pepin, Jean-Luc, 196
Pépin, Marcel, 139

Perrault, Jacques, 64, 70
Petro-Canada, 167, 191, 205, 285
Philippines, 339
Picard, Gérard, 66
Pitfield, Michael, 299, 330
Podborski, Steve, 286
Poland, 49
Polanyi, John, 359
Pompidou, Georges, 79, 217
Porteous, Timothy, 159
Pouliot, Gaston, 28
Privy Council Office, 64, 119

Quebec referendum, 107, 152,
    265-68, 273-74, 276-84, 326

Rassemblement, 70
Read, Ken, 286
Reagan, Ronald, 189, 220, 222,
    223, 292, 296, 301, 329, 332,
    338, 340, 351
Reagan, Mrs. Ronald, 301
Regan, Gerald, 330
Richard, Father, 19-20
Rimbaud, Arthur, 367
Rioux, Marcel, 140
Rioux, Mathias, 140
Robertson, Gordon, 64, 65, 66,
    230, 244
Robinson, Larry, 246
Rocher, Guy, 140
Rockefeller, Nelson, 121
Rolland, Roger, 23, 36, 42, 43,
    45, 64
Romanow, Roy, 321
Rose, Paul, 148
Rouleau, Alfred, 139
Roumania, 336
Roux, Jean-Louis, 36, 45
Roy, Léo "Kid," 7
Royal Commission on
    Bilingualism and
    Biculturalism, 102, 123, 128

Ryan, Claude, 140, 234, 274, 276,
    277, 279, 280, 314
Ryan, Madeleine, 280

Saint-Exupéry, Antoine de, 188
Saint-Jean-Baptiste Day (1968),
    104-6
St. Laurent, Louis, 119
Saint-Michel-de-Napierville, 3,
    5, 7-8
Santayana, George, 342
Saulnier, Lucien, 138
Sauvé, Jeanne, 347
Sauvé, Maurice, 77
Sauvé, Sarah, 4. *See also*
    Trudeau grandparents
Savard, Serge, 246, 247
Schmidt, Helmut, 198, 200, 201,
    296, 332, 334
Schreyer, Ed, 303, 306, 307
Scotland, 345-46
Scott, Frank, 70
Seneca, 270
Senegal, 79
Senghor, Léopold, 79
Sharp, Mitchell, 86, 134-35, 203
Sinclair, Margaret. *See* Trudeau,
    Margaret
Singapore, 154, 224
"Six and Five" program, 298-99
Somalia, 353
Sorenson, Gerry, 286
South Africa, 346, 348
Southeast Asia, 346
Soviet Union, 69, 154, 156, 206-8,
    332, 336, 340, 350-52
Sri Lanka, 155
Stanfield, Robert, 99, 109, 126,
    159, 179, 182-83, 251
Stockholm conference, 336, 340
Streisand, Barbra, 129

Tanzania, 224
Taschereau, Louis-Alexandre, 12
Taylor, Elizabeth, 221
Thailand, 337
Thatcher, Margaret, 96, 189,
   222, 223, 307-8, 311, 324, 332,
   338
"Third Option," 203, 205
Third World, 224-25, 228
"Three Wise Men," 75
Tibet, 254
Transjordan, 49-52
Tremblant, Lac, 8-11, 26
Trudeau, Charles (Tip, brother),
   9, 14-16, 24, 26, 64-65, 67, 180
Trudeau, Charles-Émile (father),
   3, 4, 6, 7, 8, 9, 10-18, 30
Trudeau, Grace Elliott (mother),
   4, 5, 8, 9, 10, 12, 14, 15, 17, 30,
   31, 67
Trudeau, Justin (son), 179, 180-
   81, 254, 275, 289, 301, 337,
   339, 342, 345-46, 348
Trudeau, Margaret (*née* Sinclair,
   wife), 153, 154, 156, 162, 166,
   168, 170, 178, 180-81, 184, 210,
   213, 221, 226-27
Trudeau, Michel (son), 179, 181,
   210, 213, 254, 275, 289, 337,
   342, 345-46, 347, 348
Trudeau, Sacha (son), 41, 179,
   180-81, 254, 275, 289, 301, 337,
   342, 345-46, 348
Trudeau, Suzette (sister), 5, 9,
   14-16, 28, 30, 67
Trudeau grandparents, 3, 5, 8,
   17, 18
Trudeaumania, 99-102, 157
Tunisia, 79
Turkey, 49
Turner, John, 85, 176, 192-95,
   265, 358, 363
24 Sussex Drive, 92-93

Union des forces démocratiques,
   70
United Kingdom. *See* Britain
United Nations, 79, 80, 202,
   333-34, 339
United States, 120, 164, 203, 205-6,
   211, 216-20, 221, 295-96, 326,
   336, 338, 353, 358, 360
Université de Montréal, 32, 37,
   63-64, 71
Ur, 53-54

Vadeboncoeur, Pierre, 18, 20,
   37, 64
Vallières, Pierre, 151
Viau, Guy, 20, 26-27, 35
Victoria Charter, 228, 229-34,
   243-44, 308, 310, 321, 322, 328
Viet Nam, 217-18
Vignaux, Paul, 165
Vigneau, Roger, 20
Volcker, Paul, 295

Wadds, Jean, 311
Wagner, Claude, 251
War Measures Act, 137-39,
   142-47, 149
Warner, John, 221
Warnke, Paul, 335
Washington, 120, 197, 219, 221,
   338. *See also* United States
Webster, Jack, 354
Western Europe, 205, 336
Whelan, Eugene, 237
Williams, Glanville, 46
Wilson, Harold, 124, 220
Writings of French Canada, 16

Yugoslavia, 49, 353-54

Fall 1992